Business Organizations
Law Review Manual

Business Organizations Law Review Manual

Denise A. Hill, J.D.

Virginia Koerselman, J.D.

In Cooperation with
The National Association of Legal Assistants, Inc.
Tulsa, Oklahoma

WEST LEGAL STUDIES
Thomson Learning™

Africa · Australia · Canada · Denmark · Japan · Mexico · New Zealand · Philippines
Puerto Rico · Singapore · Spain · United Kingdom · United States

NOTICE TO THE READER

West Legal Studies Staff:
Business Unit Director: Susan Simpfenderfer
Executive Editor: Marlene McHugh Pratt
Acquisitions Editor: Joan M. Gill
Editorial Assistant: Lisa H. Flatley
Executive Marketing Manager: Donna Lewis
Executive Production Manager: Wendy A. Troeger
Production Editor: Laurie A. Boyce

Printed in Canada
 2 3 4 5 6 7 8 9 10 XXX 05 04 03 02 01 00

For more information, contact Delmar, 3 Columbia Circle, PO Box 15015, Albany, NY 12212-0515; or find us on the World Wide Web at http://www.westlegalstudies.com

Library of Congress Cataloging-in-Publication Data

Hill, Denise.
    Business organizations law review manual / Denise Hill, Virginia
Koerselman.
       p. cm.
    "In cooperation with the National Association of Legal Assistants,
Inc., Tulsa, Oklahoma."
    ISBN 0-314-12688-0
    1. Business enterprises—Law and legislation—United States.
I. Koerselman, Virginia. II. National Association of Legal
Assistants. III. Title.
KF1355.Z9H55 1999   99-34538
346.73'065—dc21   CIP

Dedication

To my parents, Bruce and Lee Ann Hill.
Without their support, I would not be where I am today.

Contents

| 9 | Internal Organization of a Corporation | 69 |

| 10 | Other Corporate Forms | 77 |

| 11 | Extraordinary Corporate Matters | 85 |

| 12 | Financial Structure of a Corporation | 95 |

Preface

This book provides legal assistants with the information they need to know about the various types of business structures as well as how to create and to deal with each of them. It is a comprehensive overview for the NALA business organizations specialty examination; however, it is not intended to be the only source of study for the exam.

The text refers to the Model Business Corporation Act or the MBCA at various places. The most recent version of that Act is intended, technically called the Revised Model Business Corporation Act (see Appendix C).

Key terms and test questions are provided at the end of each chapter. Forms also are included, but they should not be copied for individual use. The forms are included as examples only.

Acknowledgments

Writing my first book definitely was a unique experience. I wish to thank my editor, Virginia Koerselman. Without her direction and help, I do not believe that I would have made it through the review and edit process. I also wish to thank the many friends and co-workers who gave me encouragement and support throughout this process, most particularly:

Karen Obermeier
  Omaha, Nebraska
Laura Simonson
  Omaha, Nebraska
Mary Jewell, J.D.
  Omaha, Nebraska
Ellie Fehrman, Legal Assistant
  Omaha, Nebraska

Special thanks to the reviewers who evaluated the manuscript on behalf of the publisher and provided clear and concise analysis. Their comments and suggestions were of great assistance.

Susan H. Brewer
  J. Sargeant Reynolds Community College
Barbara DeBerry
Partricia S. Callahan, CLAS
  Porter, Wright, Morris & Arthur
Deborah Chesi
  Pueblo Community College
Linda K. Van Dyke
  Ferguson Enterprises, Inc.

And to my many legal assistant students.

DENISE A. HILL
July 27, 1998

About the Author

Denise A. Hill was admitted to the practice of law in Nebraska in 1980. Ms. Hill attended the University of Nebraska at Omaha and received a bachelor's degree in criminal justice. She graduated from Creighton University School of Law, where she published in the law review's annual survey of the Eighth Circuit Court of Appeals decisions. Ms. Hill was an Assistant City Attorney for the City of Omaha from 1980 to 1987 and was in private practice until 1990. She then was a Deputy County Attorney for Douglas County, Nebraska, until 1993. Ms. Hill now is a Claims Attorney for Empire Fire & Marine Insurance Company in Omaha, Nebraska. She has taught paralegal classes since 1989 at various local colleges, including Metropolitan Community College and College of St. Mary. Ms. Hill is a member of the Omaha Bar Association, for which she is a past secretary and committee chair; and a member of the Nebraska State Bar Association, where she has served as chair of both the Litigation Section and of the Women & the Law Section.

1 Introduction to Business Organizations and Agency

There are many types of structures for business organizations. The form selected for a particular business depends on several factors, such as ease of formation, financial interests, taxation issues, and control and management, to name a few.

Business structures range from the sole proprietorship (single owner) to huge conglomerates of corporations. The basic structures of sole proprietorship, partnership (limited and general), limited liability company, and corporations are reviewed in this manual.

First, however, one must have a basic understanding of the law of agency to understand how businesses work.

Agency

An **agency** is a fiduciary relationship in which one party (the **principal**) has a second party (the **agent**) manage a business transaction on behalf of the first party. The principal controls the agent. Agency is created when one controls another. Agencies can exist other than in the business environment.

Joe asks Susan to go to the store to buy a loaf of bread for him.

An agency relationship may be created once Susan, in the example, agrees to perform the task. Another familiar example in business is the relationship of employer (principal) and employee (agent).

Agency is governed by contract law. There must be an offer and acceptance; consideration; capacity to contract; and legality of the contract's subject matter. In some instances, a writing is also required.

Agency is voluntary, so there must be mutual assent by both parties. Consideration is required if the agency is to be legally enforceable. In the example given earlier, if the agent decides not to go to the store, there is nothing the principal can do unless the principal has paid the agent. An employee's salary is one form of consideration for work performed for the employer.

Because the agent acts for the principal, the principal must have the capacity to enter into a contract. A written document is not needed unless the agency contract falls within the Statute of Frauds. The Statute of Frauds governs agency as it does other contracts. Contracts that fall within the Statute of Frauds include those involving real estate and those that cannot be performed within one year, for example.

An agent is different from a representative. An agent has the power to bring about or alter a business relationship between the principal and a third party.

An agency can be "express," as the result of an oral or written agreement. An agency also can be "implied," in which event its existence is proved by inferences from facts and circumstances, such as similar, prior dealings between the parties.

Principal

There are three types of principals. A **disclosed principal** is one whose existence is known to the third party. A primary example is an automobile dealership that hires a salesperson to act on its behalf. The purchaser of a vehicle (the third party) knows that the salesperson is acting on behalf of the dealership and knows that the vehicle is owned by the dealership.

The second type of principal is the **partially disclosed principal**. When a seller of a house deals with the buyer's real estate agent, the seller knows that someone other than the agent is the purchaser but does not know the identity of the buyer (principal).

The third type of principal is an **undisclosed principal**. This type of principal is involved when a third party does not know she is dealing with an agent. Both the identity and the existence of the principal are unknown to the third party.

> Fernando wants to buy a large tract of land; however, he does not want the property owner to know he is interested, for fear the price will go up. Fernando hires an agent to negotiate a deal with the property owner. The agent does not disclose that he is negotiating for Fernando and does not disclose Fernando's identity.

Many business transactions are handled this way.

Duties Owed to Agent   The principal has these duties related to the agent:

- Cooperate with the agent
- Comply with the agency contract
- Compensate the agent for her services

    In an employment situation the employer has a duty to pay the employee as agreed once the employee performs the work. An amount should be agreed before the agent performs the work. If no agreement was reached in advance, the agent must prove existence of the agency and the value of the work performed.

- Act in good faith (not interfere with the agency) by allowing the agent to do the work she was hired to do
- Take action to prevent harm to the agent

The principal is liable for acts of the agent that are performed within the scope of the authority given the agent. The following *Everett Monte Cristo Hotel* opinion illustrates this point.

United States v. Everett Monte Cristo Hotel, 524 F.2d 127 (9th Cir. 1975)

A corporation was formed to operate a historic hotel, Everett Monte Cristo Hotel Inc. (Hotel). The hotel plans were not successful and the corporation defaulted on its loans from the Small Business Administration. Management of the hotel changed and Jack Brown became a director. He decided that the corporation could make money on the hotel by changing it to an office building and leasing it to a state agency. This conversion necessitated extensive rewiring of the building. Brown testified that he had the oral approval of the other directors. There was no evidence that a formal meeting was ever had on the subject. Brown testified that he sought written authorization for the conversion and that he was told by other directors the authorization was forthcoming—but it never was. Brown then contacted Veca Electric Co. Inc. (Veca) to do the necessary rewiring. Brown secured a written guarantee for the work from another director, Griffin. Veca never received the written guarantee. Veca commenced the rewiring and expended approximately $6,000 on goods and services. Brown never told Veca of the existence of Hotel. Griffin received the bills and refused to pay them. Veca filed a lien against the hotel. Veca finally became an intervenor in this action.

The trial court found the lien invalid because Brown had not been authorized to make the contract on behalf of Hotel. Brown, Griffin, and other directors were assumed to be acting as agents for Hotel, but the presence of Hotel was undisclosed to Veca. Agents of an undisclosed principal are personally liable to third persons with whom they contract. The record showed that the other directors had authorized Brown to undertake the renovations. Thus, Brown became their subagent. Agents of subagents are liable as if they were principals. The other directors and Brown were liable to Veca for Brown's acts within the scope of his authority.

The hotel case also illustrates that an agent can be held liable for his own acts if he fails to disclose the existence of the agency. If a third party deals with an agent and does not know the agency exists, the agent is liable to the third party along with the principal. Under the law of agency, of course, if the agent acts within his authority, the principal has a duty to indemnify the agent.

Agent

Just as there are several types of principals, there are several types of agents. A **general agent** is one who performs tasks connected with the principal's business. The most common form of general agency is an employee in the typical employer-employee relationship. The employee's work is for the benefit of the principal.

A **special agent** performs one specific task or a series of tasks to accomplish one transaction for the principal. For example, a business entrepreneur might request a special agent to secure office space for her venture.

An **independent contractor** is one who is hired by another to do a specific task but is not controlled by the principal. A real estate agent is one example of this type of agent. The real estate agent is hired to sell a house, for instance, but goes about this task in his or her own way. Another example is a house painter. The painter is hired to do a specific task, but the property owner does not tell the painter how to do the job and has no control. An independent contractor is not an employee.

Finally, a **subagent** is an agent of the original agent. A subagent is hired by the agent to assist the agent in performing the agency contract. An agent is liable to his subagent as if the agent were a principal. This concept was discussed in *United States v. Everett Monte Cristo Hotel,* (see preceding case excerpt). Subagents are further categorized as general agents, special agents, or independent contractors.

If an agent is considered an employee, many duties and responsibilities are imposed on the principal through employment law. However, that subject is outside the scope of this manual.

Authority of Agent   The authority of an agent to act on behalf of a principal comes from the principal. An agent acts for the benefit of the principal.

An agent can have **actual authority** granted by the principal. When one hires a real estate agent to sell a house for a certain price, the real estate agent has actual authority to sell the house. This authority can be granted either by written agreement or by oral agreement; both are express authority. **Express authority** is actual authority that exists when the agency relationship has been discussed and agreed between the agent and the principal.

If a principal holds the agent out as having authority, the agent has **apparent authority**.

> Judy Smith (principal) tells Sara Jones, a commercial leasing agent, to negotiate with Denise Stone, who is Smith's employee, in finding office space for Smith.

In this example, Judy Smith holds Denise Stone out as having authority. Accordingly, Denise Stone can obligate Judy Smith to a lease for office space.

An agent also may have **implied authority** based upon business usage and custom. In addition, a principal can ratify the prior acts of an agent, thus creating an agency.

In some cases, an agency is created by the courts. This is common in family relationships. For example, a spouse may be liable for some acts done by the other spouse; parents may be responsible for what their children do in some situations.

Duties Owed to the Principal   The duties owed to the principal by an agent can be set out in an agreement or can be imposed by law. The duties are imposed because of the agency relationship, whether or not the principal is disclosed.

An agent has a duty to act only as authorized. The agent will use her skill and diligence in performing her work. There is an implied duty of loyalty, honesty, good faith, and obedience. This comes from the fiduciary relationship that is created by the agency. An agent is expected to disclose information to the principal and not to work for someone else at the same time on the same matter. The agent also is expected to follow instructions.

The agent has a duty to account for all property and money received from the principal or others and paid on behalf of the principal. The agent must make this accounting available to the principal. An agent must maintain accounts of the principal separate from accounts of the agent, in much the same way that a lawyer must keep a separate account for client funds.

There is also a duty not to act on behalf of third parties. The principal can expect the agent to perform work for the principal and not for anyone else. A dual agency may be created if an agent performs the same work for more than one principal. The *L. Byron Culver* case illustrates this point.

L. Byron Culver & Associates v. Jaoudi Industrial & Trading Corp., 1 Cal. Rptr. 2d 680 (Ct. App. 1991)

L. Byron Culver & Associates (Culver), appealed a judgment barring recovery of a commission from a land sale. The trial court held that there was an undisclosed dual agency. Culver was the agent for the seller and buyer. Culver contended that Jaoudi Industrial & Trading Corp. (Jaoudi) knew Culver was an agent for both Jaoudi and the buyer.

The buyer, Klein, hired Culver to find property for acquisition. Culver found 33.5 acres owned by Jaoudi. An employee of Culver contacted Jaoudi about the tract of land. The agent entered into a one-time listing agreement with a commission. Jaoudi specifically inquired of the agent if Culver and Klein were associated. The agent denied any association. Eventually a problem arose with the sale. The agent instructed Jaoudi how to correct the problem so the sale could be completed. The sale was finalized, but Jaoudi refused to pay the commission to Culver. Culver sued.

The appellate court affirmed the trial court decision. It held that Culver could not receive a commission from either party. The court stated:

> In the context of an agreement to sell real property on another's behalf, "[a] real estate agent must refrain from dual representation in a sale transaction unless he or she obtains the consent of both principals after full disclosure" [citations omitted]. Unless both principals know of the dual agency at the time of the transaction, the agent cannot recover a commission from either [citations omitted]. The reason for the rule is that he thereby puts himself in a position where his duty to one conflicts with his duty to the other, where his own interests tempt him to be unfaithful to both principals … . *Id.* at 682–83 [citations omitted].

Liability to Third Parties   Principals are liable to third parties for acts of their agents performed within the agency relationship. The doctrine of **respondeat superior** imposes liability upon the employer for harm caused by the employee within the scope of her employment. This doctrine imposes **vicarious liability** upon the employer. Vicarious liability is liability without regard to personal involvement of the employer. If an employee uses the company car and causes an accident, the injured party could sue the employer.

The principal also is liable to third parties for an agent's misrepresentations. This is true whether the agent fraudulently or innocently makes a misrepresentation to third parties, as long as the agent had actual or apparent authority and as long as the misrepresentations were made within the scope of the agency. If a bank employee requires a customer to provide collateral for a loan when collateral is not required and if the employee uses the collateral for his own benefit, the bank is liable to the customer for all losses. The legal theory is that if the agent appears to act within the scope of his authority, the person placing the agent in this position (the bank in this illustration) is liable.

Termination

An agency relationship can terminate for a variety of reasons. It can terminate at a specified time. A real estate contract with an agent is usually for a specified period of time, so the contract could terminate by sale of the house or by lapse of time.

The agency also will terminate if the purpose of the agency is accomplished.

> Judy Smith (principal) hires Sam Johns (agent) to acquire office space and to set up the office. Once that has been accomplished, the agency no longer exists.

The agency relationship may terminate by mutual agreement, or one party may terminate the agency contract. For example, an employer could fire an employee, even though the employer remains liable to pay for days worked, for out-of-pocket expenses, and the like. Similarly, the employee could quit her job.

Agency contracts sometimes are terminated by operation of law. The general rule is that death or insanity of either the principal or the agent terminates the relationship. Also, if the subject matter of the agency is lost or destroyed, the agency terminates. For example, if Pam Jones hires Susan Smith to sell her car and if the car later is destroyed in an accident, Susan Smith's authority to sell the car terminates.

Bankruptcy of either the principal or the agent generally terminates the agency relationship. If an agent's financial status is irrelevant, the agency may continue in some cases.

Notice is required to terminate an agency relationship. The agent's authority continues until notice of termination is given to the agent by the principal. The principal also has a duty to notify third parties who customarily deal with the agent of the termination. Fairness requires that third parties be told that the agent no longer has authority to act on behalf of the principal.

No particular form of notice is required. An agent can be told directly by the principal, or the agent can learn by some other means.

> Ezra, a construction contractor, is hired to construct a building only if a particular tract of land is purchased. The contractor finds out through associates that the tract of land was not purchased. Ezra no longer has a duty to construct the building.

However, if the agent's authority is written, the notice of termination must also be in writing. Otherwise, the principal may still be liable based upon the apparent authority of the agent.

The agency relationship is the cornerstone of all business transactions. Sole proprietors, partnerships, and corporations all enter into agency relationships. Anyone who hires employees or has someone perform a task for the business has entered into an agency relationship. In the following chapters, the different types of business organizations are discussed.

Key Terms

actual authority	independent contractor
agency	partially disclosed principal
agent	principal
apparent authority	respondeat superior
disclosed principal	special agent
express authority	subagent
general agent	undisclosed principal
implied authority	vicarious liability

Quiz

1. Explain briefly what an "agency" is.

2. Who are the parties to an agency?

3. List and define the three types of principals.

4. What duty does a principal owe to an agent? Explain briefly.

5. List and describe briefly the different types of agents.

6. List and describe briefly the three types of authority that an agent may have.

7. What duty does an agent owe a principal? Explain briefly.

8. Define the doctrine of respondeat superior and vicarious liability in agency.

9. Describe the ways in which an agency relationship may be terminated.

10. Agency is controlled by contract law. List the contractual elements that must be present to form an agency.

11. An agency can be express or implied. Explain how these two concepts apply in agency law.

2   Sole Proprietorship

The most basic and common form of business is the **sole proprietorship**. A sole proprietor can own and operate any type of business, but a sole proprietorship usually is a small business.

There is only one owner. However, a sole proprietor can have as many employees and agents as needed to operate the business.

The advantages of a sole proprietorship are the ease of formation and the degree of flexibility in management. It takes few legal forms, if any, to start a sole proprietorship. The sole proprietor makes all management and business decisions. She decides what business to enter into, how many employees to use, when to terminate the business, when to expand, and so forth. Another advantage is that the sole proprietor receives all the profits.

A major disadvantage is that the sole proprietor takes all the risks. Also, the business *is* the sole proprietor. If she does not have the necessary business knowledge, her business likely will fail. The size of the business may be limited by the financing the sole proprietor has or can procure. The availability of alternative sources of capital is another major disadvantage of the sole proprietorship. There is no continuity of the business; if the sole proprietor dies, the business ends.

Liability

Because the sole proprietor is the sole owner, she faces unlimited **liability**. In other words, the sole proprietor bears the legal responsibility for all losses or liabilities incurred by the business. If the business fails, the sole proprietor is personally liable for all debts to creditors.

In contrast, a corporate shareholder or a member of a limited liability company limits personal risk to the amount of the investment in the business. Liability is an issue to consider when deciding what type of business entity to form.

However, the flexibility of management and control of the business as a sole proprietor are great advantages. This form allows the sole proprietor to have full control over business liability, assets, and management of the business.

Formation

Although there are few, if any, legal formalities required to form a sole proprietorship, some restrictions may apply. If the sole proprietor hires employees, operates a regulated business, uses a trade name, or does business in other states, there may be laws that impose duties or responsibilities.

If a sole proprietor has employees, there are taxes to be paid at the federal and state levels and employment forms to be completed. (See Figure 2-1.) If the business is a restaurant, there usually are health regulations that apply. State and local licenses may be required. Professionals such as attorneys or physicians must be licensed to practice law or medicine.

A sole proprietor may conduct business under another name. This is known as a *trade name* or an *assumed name.* State statutes usually require that a trade name or assumed name be registered. As a general rule, the trade name cannot be the same or deceptively similar to one already in use. However, if the trade name uses the surname of the sole proprietor, it need not be registered. State and local laws vary on the requirements for a business name.

FIGURE 2-1 Application for Federal Employer Identification Number

Form **SS-4**
(Rev. November 1985)
Department of the Treasury
Internal Revenue Service

Application for Employer Identification Number
(For use by employers and others. Please read the separate instructions before completing this form.)
For Paperwork Reduction Act Notice, see separate instructions.

OMB No. 1545-0003
Expires 8-31-88

1 Name (True name. See instructions.)
2 Social security no., if sole proprietor
3 Ending month of accounting year
4 Trade name of business if different from item 1
5 General partner's name, if partnership; principal officer's name, if corporation; or grantor's name, if trust
6 Address of principal place of business (Number and street)
7 Mailing address, if different
8 City, state, and ZIP code
9 City, state, and ZIP code
10 Type of organization ☐ Individual ☐ Trust ☐ Partnership ☐ Plan administrator ☐ Governmental ☐ Nonprofit organization ☐ Corporation ☐ Other (specify)
11 County of principal business location
12 Reason for applying ☐ Started new business ☐ Purchased going business ☐ Other (specify)
13 Acquisition or starting date (Mo., day, year). See instructions.
14 Nature of principal activity (See instructions.)
15 First date wages or annuities were paid or will be paid (Mo., day, year).
16 Peak number of employees expected in the next 12 months (If none, enter "0") ▶ Nonagricultural | Agricultural | Household
17 Does the applicant operate more than one place of business? ☐ Yes ☐ No
18 Most of the products or services are sold to whom? ☐ Business establishments (wholesale) ☐ General public (retail) ☐ Other (specify) ☐ N/A
19 If nature of business is manufacturing, state principal product and raw material used.
20 Has the applicant ever applied for an identification number for this or any other business? ☐ Yes ☐ No
If "Yes," enter name and trade name. Also enter approx. date, city, and state where the application was filed and previous number if known. ▶

Under penalties of perjury, I declare that I have examined this application, and to the best of my knowledge and belief it is true, correct, and complete.
Telephone number (include area code)
Signature and Title ▶ Date ▶

Please leave blank ▶	Geo.	Ind.	Class	Size	Reas. for appl.	**Part I**

A sole proprietor can do business in other states. Licensing and assumed-name statutes must be followed and may be different from state to state as well as from county to county.

Formation and operation of a sole proprietorship is flexible. The only regulations are licensing requirements and reports that may be mandatory periodically (tax reports). The sole proprietor has the freedom to decide expansion, salaries, capital improvements, and other matters that affect the business.

Taxation

The law provides that income or loss for a sole proprietor is treated as individual income or loss, and it is taxed as such. The business income/loss and any business deductions are reported on a separate schedule attached to the individual tax return (Schedule C of Form 1040). Individual **tax rates** apply.

A tax professional should be consulted when determining what type of business entity to use. For many years, the federal individual income tax rates have been less than the corporate rate. However, tax planning is crucial, as tax regulations change constantly.

While the business is young, it may be advantageous to be a sole proprietor; however, incorporating may be better as the business grows.

Termination

The sole proprietorship **terminates** by law upon the death of the owner. It is possible to enter into an agreement to buy and continue the business after death, but this is very rare. The owner can will the business but without an agreement, the continuity of the business is not guaranteed. If it is continued, a new ownership entity must be created.

The business may be liquidated or sold if not continued by an employee or relative. Liquidation is accomplished by a representative of the deceased sole proprietor's estate. It cannot be done by an agent, because an agency terminates at death.

Of course, the sole proprietor can terminate the business at any time. The owner is liable to all creditors. The business also will terminate if the owner files for bankruptcy. If the owner becomes incapacitated and is no longer able to operate the business, it will be terminated.

A sole proprietorship has flexibility and ease of formation, but it also carries all of the liability. Many small businesses are set up as sole proprietorships.

Key Terms

liability   tax rates

sole proprietorship   terminate

Quiz

1. Define a sole proprietorship.

2. Describe briefly the advantages of a sole proprietorship.

3. Describe briefly the disadvantages of a sole proprietorship.

4. How is the income or loss of the sole proprietorship taxed? Explain briefly.

5. Describe the ways in which a sole proprietorship can be terminated.

6. What is a trade name?

7. How can a sole proprietor guarantee continuity of the business at death?

3 General Partnership

Chapter 2 reviewed an entity with just one owner. This chapter and the next (on limited partnerships) look at business entities requiring two or more owners.

A **partnership** is defined by the Uniform Partnership Act (UPA) as an association of two or more persons to carry on as co-owners a business for profit (UPA § 6). The UPA has been adopted in all states except Georgia and Louisiana. There are two types of partnerships: general and limited. Limited partnerships are discussed in Chapter 4. This chapter focuses on general partnerships.

The law of partnership is rooted in common law and is related to agency. Each partner is an agent for the other partners and for the partnership.

Most partnerships adopt a written agreement that sets out the rights and responsibilities of the parties. The agreement does not have to be written; however, a written agreement may prevent future problems and misunderstandings. A partnership may be formed by a simple, oral agreement between two or more parties.

Partnerships have many of the same legal characteristics as a sole proprietorship:

- Each partner is personally responsible for all debts and obligations of the partnership
- Management vests equally in all partners unless the agreement states otherwise
- A partnership dissolves upon death or retirement of a partner
- Profits and losses are taxed to each partner individually.

Modern commercial law treats a partnership as a separate entity as well as existing through the partners, which has activities separate from the individual partners. Property is bought and owned in the partnership name instead of through individual partners; partners quite often are employees of the partnership and are paid salaries for their services; licensing requirements for a particular type of business are secured in the partnership name; and judgments can be enforced against partnership property.

Partnerships are different from corporations. Corporations are separate legal entities in all respects. Partnerships are governed by individual state statutes but also are controlled by the law of contracts.

Formation of a General Partnership

A partnership is an entity formed by two or more persons to carry on a business for profit. It usually is formed for general or continuing businesses. Small businesses as well as multinational businesses are formed as partnerships. Unlike a joint venture, which is formed for an isolated or single transaction, a general partnership can be formed for any legal purpose.

Who Can Be a Partner Under the UPA, partners do not have to be individuals. The partners can be other partnerships, corporations, natural persons, or associations. The Model Business Corporation Act (MBCA), which governs the law of corporations, allows a corporation to be a partner. Each partner must have the capacity to enter into a contract.

Name   A partnership name may include all partners' surnames. However, if fewer than all partners' names are used in the title, the name is fictitious and may have to be registered. If Diana Johnson, Susan Smith, and Amy Thompson formed Johnson, Smith & Thompson, this would not be a fictitious name. However, if they formed Johnson & Smith, or Johnson & Co., the name might have to be registered.

A partnership can choose any name as long as it is not deceptively similar to that of another business. A few years ago, for example, a group that formed to protest nuclear war named itself "Mutual of Omaha" as a takeoff on the name of a large insurance company, Mutual of Omaha. Mutual of Omaha took the protest group to court, alleging that the name was deceptively similar, and won. Most states require that a partnership register its name if it is fictitious.

Duration   The partnership begins when business is actually carried on. The partnership agreement can specify a particular term for the partnership's existence. If it does not, the partnership will exist as long as the partners wish or until it is dissolved by law. If the agreement specifies a particular term and if a partner dissolves the partnership without consent of all partners, the **dissolution** constitutes a breach of the agreement. The partner in breach is liable to the other partners for any losses resulting from the dissolution.

A partnership may be formed for a definite term. It may be subject to **termination** by mutual agreement or may terminate at will when one partner gives notice to the other partners. The partnership may be terminated upon completion of its purpose or upon the happening of a contingent event.

State Formalities   Partnerships can conduct any legal business. Some businesses require certain licenses. For example, if the partnership were formed to own a restaurant, it would have to comply with many local and state health regulations. If liquor were to be served, a liquor license usually would be required. Therefore, a check of state and local law is necessary to ensure that all licensing and regulatory requirements are met for the particular business.

Partnerships are required to file information tax returns with the Internal Revenue Service (IRS) and with state revenue departments. Therefore, tax identification numbers are necessary. The partnership itself must have a tax identification number. If employees are hired, the partnership also must obtain an employer's tax identification number to report tax withholding information. The partnership applies to the state and to the IRS for these numbers.

Agreement

The **partnership agreement** may be oral, written, or implied by conduct. The Statute of Frauds requires that any agreement dealing with real property must be in writing to be valid. If the partnership will be involved in buying and selling real estate, the partnership agreement must be in writing.

Regardless of statutory requirements, it is best to put the agreement in writing to avoid misunderstandings. Partners can contribute money, goods, or services to the partnership. The value of goods and services should be determined in the agreement.

> Silvia contributed her time for six months to get the business off the ground, while Joe contributed $10,000. When the business started making money, Joe felt he should get more than half of the profits. Without an agreement, however, Joe is entitled only to one-half of the profits under the UPA.

A written agreement could have solved this problem.

The agreement should detail the basic structure of the partnership, including the date it begins, names and addresses of the partners, name of the partnership, place of business, term, purpose, and recitals setting out the nature of the relationship. Figure 3-1 is an example of the basic structure.

FIGURE 3-1   General Partnership Agreement

PARTNERSHIP AGREEMENT

AGREEMENT made this 5th day of June, 1997, between Sally A. Smith, 123 Main Street, Morgan City, NE, and Joyce B. Jones, 456 Elm St., Morgan City, NE (hereinafter referred to collectively or individually as "partners").

Whereas Sally Smith has acquired certain expertise in computerized tax accounting; and

Whereas Joyce Jones has the financial ability to contribute certain sums of money for computerized tax accounting.

NOW, THEREFORE, it is agreed:

1. The partners hereby form a General Partnership pursuant to the laws of Nebraska.

2. The business of the Partnership shall be conducted under the name of Smith & Jones.

3. The principal place of business of the firm shall be located at 789 Morgan Street, Morgan City, NE, or such other place as shall be designated by the partners from time to time. (If there are branch offices, list them here.)

4. The partnership shall commence on June 5, 1997. Either partner may give 30 days' written notice to the other to dissolve the partnership.

5. The purpose for which the Partnership is organized is to provide computerized tax accounting and any such other lawful business as permitted by law and as may be agreed upon from time to time by the partners.

_____
Signature

_____
Signature

The agreement also should state the contribution made to the partnership by each partner. This contribution is known as **capital**. If the partner's contribution is goods or services, a value should be placed on the goods and services and stated in the agreement. The goods and services should be described in detail.

The agreement may include a paragraph on additional capital that must be contributed by the partners if additional capital is needed by the partnership. This will obligate all partners to contribute additional capital when the time comes. Also, if the capital will accumulate interest, that provision must be included. The agreement also may require profits to be accumulated as profits, while allowing withdrawal of capital.

If salaries and expenses will be paid to the partners, authority to do so must be set out in the agreement. How profits and losses are determined should be set out in the agreement as well. Profits and losses can be shared in a variety of ways:

- Equally
- According to proportion of capital contribution

- Allocating to a partner who provides financial backing until paid in full
- Losses caused by willful conduct or default of a partner to be borne by that partner
- Guaranteed profits to certain partners

Other items for consideration in the agreement are cash distributions. The distributions can be in the same proportions as profits and losses, but this is not mandatory. The partners can determine the allocation in the agreement. Also, a taxable year must be established. The taxable year should coincide with the tax year of the partners. If the partners are individuals, it is the calendar year. If it is different from the calendar year, the partnership must establish a legitimate business purpose to justify the variation. Furthermore, the method of accounting (accrual or cash) must be decided, as well as where the books will be located, bank accounts, who will be responsible for periodic reports and keeping the books, and when and where the partnership meetings will be held.

Management   Another important item to include in the agreement is management. Will the partners have equal voice in management? Will it be other than equal? Will there be a managing partner? If there is a managing partner, the partnership may want to limit her authority. One way is to use a noncompetition clause in the agreement. A partner bound by such a clause cannot compete directly against the partnership business during or after her tenure as a partner.

Sale of Partner's Interest   A partner usually cannot sell his interest in a partnership. Because the partnership ceases to exist if a partner terminates his association with it, allowing the sale of his interest will defeat the partnership structure. It can be allowed if there is unanimous consent among all partners. Of course, if a partner sells his interest, a new partnership is formed with a new partner or with the remaining partners.

Causes of Dissolution   Many things can cause a partnership to dissolve: retirement, withdrawal, expulsion, bankruptcy of a partner, death, or disability, to name a few. The agreement can allow continuation of the business if a partner leaves for any reason. There may be a provision for the partnership or for one partner to purchase the terminating partner's interest. Establish in the agreement how to value the interest. Typical alternatives include:

1. Stipulated value in agreement
2. Return of capital plus interest
3. Purchase life insurance in an agreed amount
4. Formula based on earnings
5. Formula based on value of assets (book value)
6. Appraisal by independent third party.

If the business does not continue at dissolution, the business must be liquidated and its affairs **wound up**. The agreement should provide whether, after debts are paid, assets are to be distributed or whether everything is to be sold and the proceeds distributed. If there is a loss, the agreement should specify who will bear it.

Of course, all partnerships are entered into to be successful and to continue for years. However, future problems can be avoided if everyone is practical from the beginning and thinks about the items discussed here. Resolve them at the beginning by drafting a complete, well-considered, written agreement.

The *DeSimoni* case illustrates problems that can arise in a partnership.

> ### *DeSimoni v. Brusco,* 236 Cal. 711 (Ct. App. 1987)
>
> The partnership agreement provided for employment of a managing partner by Class A partners. Defendant was appointed managing partner. After three years, a majority of Class A partners voted to remove defendant and to appoint plaintiff. Defendant refused to turn over the books and records to plaintiff. Defendant argued that his removal violated the partnership agreement. The court disagreed.
>
> The agreement provided:
>
> > Only the Class A partners shall participate in the control, management and direction of the business of the Partnership; Brusco is appointed Managing Partner for this purpose.
>
> *Id.* at 712.
>
> The court interpreted this to mean that control, management, and direction included the hiring and firing of the managing partner. The court affirmed the trial court.

Rights and Duties of Partners

UPA §§ 18, 19, 20, and 21 list the rights and duties of partners. Most were discussed earlier in this chapter as provisions in the partnership agreement. The rights of partners contained in the UPA include:

1. Share equally in profits
2. Receive repayment of contribution
3. Receive indemnification for payments made on behalf of partnership
4. Receive interest on advances and (in certain circumstances) on capital contributions
5. Share in management
6. Have access to partnership books
7. Receive formal accounting of partnership affairs.

Duties contained in the UPA include:

1. Contribute toward losses
2. Work for partnership without remuneration
3. Submit to a majority vote of partners when disputes arise
4. Disclose to other partners any information a partner has regarding partnership matters
5. Account to partnership for any profits derived by partnership transactions or use of partnership property
6. **Fiduciary duty** (duty to act in good faith).

Liabilities of Partners

Partners are liable to the partnership for whatever they do in regard to the partnership. Partners are agents of each other and of the partnership. They can obligate the partnership.

> Jones, Smith, and Doe form a partnership. Smith can enter into a lease for office space; if she does so, all partners are liable for the lease.

This is the same as a sole proprietorship. Each partner is 100 percent liable for all debts of the partnership. This is why it is a good idea to have an agreement that sets out what the partners can and cannot do to obligate the partnership.

Partners are protected by a rule called **marshalling of assets.** This rule requires creditors of the partnership to look to partnership assets first to satisfy the debt before seeking payment from the individual partners. Nevertheless, partners still have a potential for unlimited liability.

Taxation

Partners are taxed on their individual tax returns. The partnership files an informational tax return called a *1065 filing.* The partnership is a pass-through entity for tax purposes. Partners are taxed on profits whether they receive the profits or not. The partners attach Schedule K to their individual tax returns. If a partner has other income, it is to the partner's advantage if there are partnership losses. The losses can be offset against the partner's other, personal income.

Dissolution and Termination of a Partnership

The law requires that if a partner ceases to be associated with the partnership, that partnership dissolves. However, because a partnership is an association of two or more persons, dissolution of the partnership does not necessarily mean termination of the business. The remaining partner(s) may continue the business. A new partnership or a sole proprietorship can be formed by the remaining partner or partners.

One of several situations can cause dissolution of a partnership:

1. By agreement—a provision requiring dissolution on a certain date or upon the occurrence of a certain event, such as losses reaching a stated dollar amount
2. Partner withdraws voluntarily
3. Expulsion—involuntary termination of a partner's interest
4. Operation of law—death, bankruptcy, or engaging in an illegal business
5. Court order based on lack of mental capacity or disagreements among partners that result in lawsuits.

Review the *Branton* case regarding the dissolution of a partnership.

Branton v. Mendelsohn, 727 S.W.2d 513 (Tex. 1987)

Suit was brought on dissolution of the partnership to equalize distribution of partnership assets per the partnership written agreement. Plaintiff and defendant were partners in a law firm. They agreed to dissolve. Plaintiff remained in the offices and took a disproportionate share of personal property. The value of the personal property kept by plaintiff was stipulated at $42,466.72, and the value of the personal property kept by defendant was $13,773.64.

Plaintiff interpreted a provision in the agreement to mean that he was to pay, in cash, to defendant, one-half the difference between the personal property. Defendant argued that the provision in the agreement required that the total difference in value was to be paid to him in cash.

The court stated that to interpret the agreement pursuant to defendant's version would then just reverse the unequal division of the personal property. The court found for plaintiff and held that what he had paid into the court discharged his obligation to defendant.

Even with a written agreement, disputes can arise. Without an agreement, the type and number of possible disputes are limited only by the imaginations of disgruntled partners and their attorneys.

Key Terms

capital   partnership
dissolution   partnership agreement
fiduciary duty   termination
marshalling of assets   winding up

Quiz

1. How many owners must a general partnership have?

2. List the two types of partnerships.

3. Who can be a partner?

4. Discuss briefly the importance of a written partnership agreement.

5. On what grounds can a partnership be terminated? Describe briefly.

6. Describe the lawful contributions that a partner may make to a partnership.

7. Describe briefly the rights and duties of partners to the partnership.

8. Discuss briefly the liability exposure for partners.

9. Describe briefly how the income and losses of a partnership are taxed.

10. How is a partnership formed? Describe briefly.

11. Modern commercial law books view partnerships as separate entities. Briefly discuss the basis for this position.

12. Under what circumstances must a partnership name be registered? Discuss briefly.

13. Explain briefly how profits and losses may be shared in a partnership.

14. Explain what is meant by the term "marshalling of assets."

4 Limited Partnership

In Chapter 3 we looked at general partnerships. Now we will look at a different type of partnership, the limited partnership.

A **limited partnership** is a partnership formed by two or more persons, with one or more general partners and one or more **limited partners**. Parties to a limited partnership do not necessarily have to be natural persons. Some states allow corporations and general partnerships to be partners, either general or limited, in a limited partnership. The main purpose of a limited partnership is to allow one to invest without becoming liable for debts. Since it was first introduced in 1976, most states have adopted at least part of the Revised Uniform Limited Partnership Act (RULPA).

Limited partnerships were unknown at common law but have been authorized in New York since 1822. The early twentieth century saw many states adopting limited partnership statutes. In 1916, the first Uniform Limited Partnership Act was proposed by the American Law Institute.

The limited partner has **limited liability**. She is liable only for the amount invested —unlike the general partner, who has unlimited liability. In return, however, the limited partner has no say in management and no control of the business. This is advantageous mainly for an investor who wants the tax advantage but does not want an active role in management.

Limited partnerships have characteristics of both corporations and partnerships. A limited partnership consists of one or more general partners and one or more limited partners. The general partner actively manages the business while the limited partners, by law, may do little more than invest in it. General partners have the same powers and duties as partners in a general partnership (see Chapter 3). Limited partners are like shareholders in a corporation. They have a say in decisions that affect their interests, but not in day-to-day activities.

Limited partnerships tend to be formed to undertake a particular venture, such as developing an office park or a residential development. See Figure 4-1 for a sample limited partnership agreement. However, unless statutory requirements are met, a court could conclude that the partners formed a general partnership.

FIGURE 4-1 Limited Partnership Agreement

LIMITED PARTNERSHIP AGREEMENT

AGREEMENT OF LIMITED PARTNERSHIP made this _____ day of _____, 19____, between _____ and _____, both of Nebraska (herein referred to as general partners), and _____ of Nebraska and _____ of Nebraska (herein referred to as limited partners).

1. **Formation.** The parties hereby form a limited partnership pursuant to sections 67-344 *et seq.* of the Revised Statutes of the State of Nebraska, known as the Uniform Limited Partnership Act.

2. **Certificate.** The parties shall sign and swear to a certificate prepared in accordance with the provisions of the Uniform Limited Partnership Act cited above and shall cause the same to be filed for record in the office of the Secretary of State, Lincoln, Nebraska.

3. **Name.** The name of the limited partnership is _____, L.L.P.

4. **Business.** The purpose of the limited partnership shall be to engage in the business of the day care for dogs, day spa (grooming), and supplies, and in any other business necessary and related to it.

5. **Place of Business.** The principal place of business of the limited partnership shall be at _____, but additional places of business may be established as the general partners determine.

6. **Term.** The partnership shall commence on _____ and shall continue until terminated as provided herein.

7. **Capital.** The initial capital of the partnership shall be $_____. Each of the partners shall contribute in cash or in property the amount set opposite the partner's name.

General Partners	Cash Contributions	Agreed Value of Property Contributions
	$	$
Limited Partners		

The property contributed is described in a separate instrument attached as Exhibit A.

8. **Additional Contributions to Capital.** The general partners shall make, and the limited partners each shall have the option of making, additional contributions to the capital of the partnership in such amount as the general partners deem necessary to carry on the business of the partnership.

9. **Withdrawal of Capital.** Neither a general nor a limited partner may withdraw all or any part of his or her capital contribution without the consent of all of the general partners, provided that each limited partner rightly may demand the return of all or part of his or her contribution after he or she has given six months' notice in writing to all other partners. Upon any withdrawal by a limited partner, the certificate of limited partnership shall be amended to reflect this change in his or her capital contribution.

10. **Profits and Losses.** The net profits of the partnership during each fiscal year shall be credited, and the net losses incurred by the partnership during any fiscal year shall be tentative, as of the close thereof, to the capital accounts of the partners in the proportion set opposite their respective names.

General Partners	Percentage
Limited Partners	

Notwithstanding anything to the contrary contained in this agreement, no limited partner shall be liable for any of the debts of the partnership or for any of its losses in excess of his or her capital contributions to the partnership.

11. **Capital Accounts.** An undivided capital account shall be maintained for each partner, to which shall be credited his or her contributions to capital and to which shall be convicted his or her withdrawals from capital as well as his or her share of partnership losses.

12. **Salaries.** Each of the general partners shall receive such reasonable salaries as may from time to time be agreed by the general partners. These salaries shall be treated as an expense of the partnership in determining the net profit or loss in any fiscal year.

13. **Drawing Accounts.** An individual drawing account may be maintained for each partner in an amount fixed by the general partners, but such drawing accounts shall be in the proportion to which the partners are entitled to share in the profit of the partnership.

14. **Management.** The general partners shall have equal rights in the management of the partnership business.

15. **Devotion to Business.** Each general partner shall devote all of his or her normal business time and best efforts to the conduct of the business of the partnership.

16. **Limitation on General Partner's Powers.** No general partner shall, without the written consent or ratification of the specific act by all the other partners:

(a) assign, transfer, or pledge any of the claims of or debts due to the partnership except upon payment in full, or arbitrate or consent to the arbitration of any disputes or controversies of the partnership;

(b) make, execute, or deliver any assignment for the benefit of creditors, or sign any bond, confession of judgment, security agreement, deed, guarantee, indemnity bond, surety bond, or contract to sell or contract of sale of all or substantially all profit of the partnership;

(c) lease or mortgage any part of partnership real estate or any interest therein, or enter into any contract for any such purpose;

(d) pledge or hypothecate or in any manner transfer his or her interest in the partnership, except to the parties of this agreement;

(e) become surety, guarantor, or accommodation party to any obligation except for partnership business; or

(f) do any act prohibited by law to be done by a single partner.

17. **Books of Account.** The partnership shall maintain adequate accounting records. All books, records, and accounts of the partnership shall be kept at its principal place of business and shall be open at all times to inspection by all partners.

18. **Accounting Basis.** The books of accounts shall be kept on a cash basis.

19. **Fiscal Year.** The fiscal year of the partnership shall be the calendar year. The net profit or net loss of the partnership shall be determined in accordance with generally accepted accounting principles as soon as practicable after the close of each fiscal year.

20. **Annual Audit.** The books of accounts shall be audited as of the close of each fiscal year by a certified public accountant selected by all partners.

21. **Banking.** All funds of the partnership shall be deposited in its name in such checking account or accounts as shall be designated by the general partners. Checks shall be drawn on such accounts for partnership purposes only and shall be signed by any of the general partners.

22. **Assignment by Limited Partner.** Each limited partner may assign his or her interest in the partnership, and the assignee shall have the right to become a substitute limited partner and shall be entitled to all the rights of the assignor if all of the partners (except the assignor) consent. Otherwise, the assignee shall be entitled only to receive the share of the profits to which his or her assignor would have been entitled.

23. **Retirement of a General Partner.** A general partner may retire from the partnership at the end of any fiscal year by giving at least 90 days' notice in writing to all other partners.

24. **Effect of Retirement, Death, or Insanity of a General Partner.** The retirement, death, or insanity of a general partner dissolves the partnership, unless the business is continued by the remaining partners as provided in this agreement.

25. **Distribution of Assets on Dissolution.** Upon dissolution of the partnership by mutual agreement or for any other reason, its liabilities to creditors shall be paid in the order of priority provided by law; and the remaining assets or the proceeds of their sale shall be distributed in the following order:

(a) to the limited partners in proportion to their share of the profits;

(b) to the limited partners in proportion to their capital contributions;

(c) to the general partners other than for capital and profits;

(d) to the general partners in proportion to their share of profits; and

(e) to the general partners in proportion to their capital contributions.

26. **Election of Remaining Partners to Continue Business.** In the event of the retirement, death, or insanity of a general partner, the remaining partners shall have the right to continue the business of the partnership under its present name either by themselves or in conjunction with any other person or persons they may select; but they shall pay to the retiring partner, or to the legal representative of the deceased or insane partner, as the case may be, the value of his or her interest in the partnership as provided in paragraph 28 of this agreement.

27. **Notice of Election to Continue Business.** If the remaining partners elected to continue the business of the partnership, they shall serve notice in writing of such election upon the retiring partner within two months after receipt of his or her notice of intention to retire, or upon the legal representatives of the deceased or insane partner within three months after the death of the decedent or the adjudication of insanity, as the case may be. If no legal representative shall have been appointed at the time of such election, notice shall be sent to the last known address of the decedent or insane partner.

28. **Valuation of Partner's Interest.** The value of the interest of a retiring, deceased, or insane partner shall be the sum of the partner's: (a) capital account, (b) drawing accounts, and (c) proportionate share of accrued net profits. If a net loss has been incurred to the date of dissolution, his or her share of such net loss shall be deducted. The assets of the partnership shall be valued at book value, and no value shall be attributed to goodwill.

29. **Payment of Purchase Price.** The value of the partner's interest as determined under the provisions of this agreement shall be paid without interest to the retiring partner, or to the legal representatives of the deceased or insane partner, as the case may be, in twelve (12) monthly installments, beginning on the first day of the second month after the effective date of purchase.

30. **Death of a Limited Partner.** In the event of the death of a limited partner, his or her personal representative during the period of administration of his former estate shall succeed to his or her rights hereunder as a limited partner, and this interest as a limited partner may be assigned to any member of the family of the limited partner in distribution of his or her estate, or to any person in accordance with a bequest in his or her last will and testament; and such member of the family to whom such assignment or bequest is made shall thereupon succeed to his or her interest as a limited partner and shall have all of the rights of a substitute limited partner.

In Witness Whereof, the parties have signed and sealed this agreement.

Limited Partners   General Partners

_____   _____

_____   _____

Formation

Limited partnerships have statutory requirements for formation. Most states require a limited partnership to file a **certificate of limited partnership** (see Figure 4-2). This certificate requires much of the same information as the articles of incorporation for a corporation (see Chapter 8 on incorporation).

FIGURE 4-2   Certificate of Limited Partnership

CERTIFICATE OF LIMITED PARTNERSHIP

THIS CERTIFICATE is made and filed with the Secretary of State of the State of Nebraska in compliance with Neb. Rev. Stat. § 67-240.

1. The name of the Partnership is Jelly Jeans, Ltd.

2. The address of the Limited Partnership is:

> 123 Park Avenue
> Omaha, NE 68105

3. Name and address of the agent for service of process:

> Samantha White
> 1234 Maple Drive
> Omaha, NE 68106

4. General Partner(s) of the Limited Partnership:

> Earlene Black
> 123 Park Avenue
> Omaha, NE 68l05

5. The Partnership shall dissolve no later than _____, 19____.

```
                                              Jelly Jeans, Ltd.
                                              A LIMITED PARTNERSHIP

                                 By      _____
                                         General Partner


    STATE OF NEBRASKA          )
                               ) ss.
    COUNTY OF DOUGLAS          )

        Before me, the undersigned Notary Public in and for said County and State, personally appeared
    the above-named Earlene Black known to me to be the person who acknowledged the foregoing in-
    strument and that the same was her free act and deed and who did swear that the statements con-
    tained therein are true to the best of her knowledge and belief.

        SIGNED and sworn to this _____ day of _____, 19____.


                                         _____
                                         Notary Public
```

The certificate must be filed with a state official, usually the secretary of state. Some states require the certificate to be filed with a local official as well. The statutes must be followed to create a valid limited partnership.

The certificate must contain the following information under the Revised Uniform Limited Partnership Act (RULPA):

1. Name of limited partnership
2. Address of the principal place of business
3. Name and address of agent for service of process
4. Name and address of each general partner
5. Latest date upon which limited partnership is to dissolve
6. Any other matters the general partners have determined to include.

Other information which may be required by states that do not follow the RULPA are:

1. Purpose of limited partnership
2. Location of the principal place of business
3. Names and addresses of all partners
4. Contribution made by each partner, including a description and, if not cash, the agreed values of property contributed
5. Whether and under what conditions the general partner can admit other limited partners
6. Whether a limited partner may sell her interest and substitute another limited partner
7. Whether the remaining general partner has a right to continue the business if a general partner dies, retires, or is otherwise incapable of being a general partner.

These were required under the ULPA and may still be required by some states. Required or not, it is best to put this information into a written partnership agreement. Some statutes require a formal written agreement. Even if it is not required, it is recommended, because many problems can arise without a written agreement. It is even more important with a limited partnership because of the limited liability of the limited partner. The agreement should state exactly the investment of the limited partner. It should spell out the duties and responsibilities of each general partner and of each limited partner. The limited partner has no say in the management and no control of the partnership. The only time a limited partner may get involved in management and control is if a matter directly affects his investment.

If a limited partner does involve herself in the partnership's management and control, she may become liable as if she were a general partner. The *Hommel* case illustrates this problem.

Hommel v. Micco, 602 N.E.2d 1259 (Ohio Ct. App. 1991)

The plaintiff, a subcontractor, brought an action against limited partners to recover for work performed on the limited partners' condominium project. The trial court held that the limited partners were not liable for the limited partnership's debt. The appellate court reversed.

The defendants, acting as agents for companies they worked for, formed a general partnership known as Harbor Creek Company. In turn, Harbor Creek Company became the sole general partner in a limited partnership known as Harbor Creek Limited. The defendants were shareholders in their own companies and were limited partners in Harbor Creek Limited. The limited partnership was formed to construct a condominium complex known as "Harbor Creek."

The plaintiff was an electrical subcontractor for the limited partnership. When he was no longer being paid, he brought this action. At the beginning of the project, the limited partnership hired a construction supervisor. When the limited partnership began experiencing financial difficulties, the supervisor was let go; the limited partners began supervising the construction.

The court found that by exercising control and management of the partnership, the limited partners became the same as general partners. The court held:

> Thus, even though appellees described themselves as limited partners functioning as agents of the general partner, it is abundantly evident that they were, in actuality, functioning as general partners in that they exercised to all intents and purposes total control over the limited partnership, Harbor Creek Limited.

Id. at 1262.

Name

As with a general partnership, a limited partnership can use any name that is not deceptively similar to that of another business. A limited partnership can register its official name and then do business under an assumed name. The assumed name also must be registered.

A limited partnership, however, cannot include the name of a limited partner unless it is also the name of a general partner. If Sue Smith and Dan Smith formed a limited partnership it could be called Smith Limited Partnership. Limited partners' names could be used if the business had existed before becoming a limited partnership (for example, a general partnership) and the name had included the limited partner's name at that time.

The name must include some language identifying it as a limited partnership. It must use Limited Partner, Ltd., or L.P. This puts the public on notice that it is dealing with a limited partnership.

Rights and Liabilities

General partners are personally liable to a limited partnership's creditors. Therefore, a limited partnership must have at least one general partner. This requirement can be circumvented in states that allow a corporation to be a general partner in a partnership. Because the corporation has limited liability under corporation laws, no one in such a limited partnership has personal liability.

Limited partners have essentially the same rights as general partners. They have a right of access to partnership books and to information regarding partnership business. Upon **dissolution**, limited partners are entitled to a return on their contribution. The limited partners receive their share of the profits and their capital contributions before the general partners receive anything. They also can assign their interests, if this is allowed in the certificate.

A limited partner is liable to creditors to the extent of her contribution or to the extent of her agreement to contribute. A general partner of a limited partnership has unlimited liability. The general partner owes a fiduciary duty to other general partners and limited partners. Because a limited partner has no apparent authority to represent the limited partnership, it owes no duty to the general partner or to other limited partners. A limited partner also can be a limited partner in a competitor of the first limited partnership.

Management and Control

Limited partners get the benefit of limited liability because they have no control or management rights in the limited partnership. They are investors only.

Under the RULPA, a limited partner will be liable as a general partner only if the third party had knowledge of the limited partner's management activity. However, this rule is unsettled, primarily because state statutes vary so widely. Courts have agreed that involvement in the day-to-day management of the business constitutes exercise of control.

> Sue is a limited partner in a restaurant. She can talk about the business plans with the general partner; however, it probably will be considered exercising control if she plans the menu and hires employees. To avoid allegations of control, Sue should not participate in the day-to-day operations, contribute services to the business, or allow her name to appear in the name of the business.

The RULPA allows more active involvement by a limited partner but does not allow control. A limited partner may be a contractor for an agent or employee of the limited partnership; consult or advise with the general partner about partnership business; act as a surety for the partnership; vote on changes in the partnership agreement, dissolution, and winding up; vote on changes in nature of the business; vote on removal of a general partner; and vote on sale of all or substantially all the assets of the partnership other than in the ordinary course of business.

Dissolution

A limited partnership is dissolved in much the same way as a general partnership. The resignation, retirement, bankruptcy, incompetence, withdrawal, or death of a general partner will cause dissolution.

However, limited partners can come and go. They are passive investors (RULPA §§ 801 and 802). If a limited partner withdraws, he may demand his capital contribution be returned if this is permitted in the limited partnership agreement. If there is not enough capital to return the limited partner's investment, the limited partner becomes a creditor of the partnership. The limited partnership agreement should contain a provision that addresses replacement of limited partners. If the withdrawing limited partner is the sole limited partner, he must be replaced to comply with the requirement of at least one limited partner.

A limited partnership will be dissolved pursuant to the **termination** clauses in the agreement. Also, all partners (limited and general) can vote to dissolve. Under certain circumstances, a limited partnership can be dissolved by court decree (RULPA § 802).

If there is more than one general partner, the partnership agreement can set out terms under which the limited partnership will continue in business if one general partner is no longer in the partnership. If the remaining partners vote within 90 days to name a new general partner, the limited partnership can continue business if the agreement so provides (RULPA § 801).

Based on the preceding discussion, one readily can see why it is important to have a written agreement. Limited and general partners cannot be substituted and the business cannot continue without interruption unless allowed in the partnership agreement.

Termination and Winding Up

If the limited partnership does dissolve, the business must be liquidated. Either limited or general partners may act as liquidators (RULPA § 804). Under the RULPA, priority distribution at liquidation is:

1. Creditors, which include partners who are creditors (does not include distributions under the partnership agreement)
2. Partners and former partners for distributions agreed under the partnership agreement
3. Partners for return of their contributions and then proportionate shares of excess.

The limited partnership agreement can include a preference to limited partners for distributions and return of contributions. If no such provision is made in the agreement, limited and general partners are treated equally, as in the *Loft* case.

Loft v. Lapidus, 936 F.2d 633 (1st Cir. 1991)

Edward Lapidus, a real estate developer, and Irwin Loft and Robert Stein, investors, joined to purchase property and to build condominiums as a limited partnership. Lapidus signed a contract to purchase the property on behalf of all three. Lapidus, Loft, and Stein never entered into a formal limited partnership agreement. Each of the three signed a letter of intent setting out the terms of their limited partnership, what the capital contribution of each would be, and how proceeds would be distributed. The seller of the property defaulted. Lapidus sued the seller and received the entire deposit back plus interest. Loft and Stein sued to get a share of what Lapidus had received. Lapidus argued that there was no agreement between the parties. The court disagreed.

The court held that the relationship of partners is a matter of intent, and a contract can be implied based on acts and words evidencing intent. The court held:

[t]he parties have agreed to every essential point of the limited partnership agreement, save the execution of the formal papers. ... [I]t is appropriate to treat the parties as if they actually had done what they ought to have done.

Id. at 636.

The court resolved the rights of the parties as if they were partners in accordance with the terms stated in the letter of intent.

Taxation

Limited partnerships usually are treated as general partnerships for **taxation** purposes. All income is deemed distributed to partners and taxed on their individual tax returns. An informational tax return for the partnership is filed with the Internal Revenue Service, the same as a general partnership. If the business has losses instead of profits, the losses can be taken against other income. The advantage to the limited partner is that she can take paper losses against other, passive income. **Passive income** is derived from such things as investments. At times, limited partners invest in partnerships in the hope that they can take a loss against other income. One always must research changes in tax laws to be sure the advantages still exist, because Congress historically has been hostile to tax-advantage business enterprises.

Key Terms

certificate of limited partnership	limited partnership
dissolution	passive income
limited liability	taxation
limited partners	termination

Quiz

1. Define the term "limited partnership."

2. Describe briefly what a limited partner must relinquish in exchange for the protection of limited liability.

3. Explain briefly the advantages of having a written limited partnership agreement.

4. List and discuss the requirements for names of a limited partnership.

5. To what extent are limited partners liable to creditors? Discuss briefly.

6. Describe concisely the causes for dissolution of a limited partnership.

7. If a limited partnership dissolves, it must be liquidated. List the priorities at distribution.

8. How are limited partnerships treated for tax purposes? Explain succinctly.

9. Limited partnerships have characteristics of both corporations and partnerships. Explain briefly what these characteristics are.

10. Describe what must be included in the certificate of limited partnership.

5 Joint Venture and Joint Stock Company

Like a partnership, a **joint venture** is an association of two or more persons. A joint venture sometimes is called a **joint adventure**. However, a joint venture is formed to carry out a single business enterprise for profit. The joint venture is for a limited time and purpose. Joint ventures were unknown at common law, making joint ventures a relatively new type of business organization.

Joint ventures normally are used for large-scale developments. One is most likely to see a joint venture used for the construction of public buildings, power projects, real estate subdivisions, and commercial shipping ventures. Joint ventures usually are formed for business ventures. Social or nonprofit ventures are called **joint enterprises**. Joint ventures are used quite often for multinational ventures.

Joint ventures are governed by partnership law and are created in much the same way as partnerships. A written agreement is not required, but it is advisable. The parties to a joint venture contribute money, property, effort, skill, knowledge, or other assets to the venture. Like a partnership, the parties to a joint venture can be individuals, corporations, or partnerships.

Like a partnership, the parties to a joint venture have the same rights of control and management, risk of loss, and manner in which profits are taxed. The parties also share equally in the profits, unless the agreement provides otherwise. They have a joint property interest in the subject matter of the venture.

Who holds title to the property depends on the agreement. Like a partnership, a joint venture can hold title to property if state law allows it to do so. A joint venture does not exist as a separate legal entity beyond the parties, however.

The parties have a right to an accounting of the venture, as do partners. Each party to a joint venture owes the other parties a fiduciary duty. The parties are jointly and severally liable to third persons.

Joint ventures are similar to partnerships in many ways. Unlike a partnership, however, a party to a joint venture can withdraw without causing a dissolution of the joint venture. The agreement should set out the grounds and consequences of withdrawal by a party.

A joint venture normally will terminate upon completion of the specific project. If a joint venture is formed to build a nuclear power plant, it will terminate when the plant is completed. The agreement may specify a particular time limit. Winding up is accomplished in the same way as a partnership.

Another distinguishing feature of a joint venture is the authority that a party to a joint venture has to bind the venture. It is far less than in a partnership, because of the limited nature of a joint venture. One effect of the limitation is to restrict one party of the joint venture from borrowing money on behalf of the venture.

The *Grammercy* and *W.B. Johnston* cases illustrate the similarities of and differences between a joint venture and a partnership.

Grammercy Equities Corp. v. Dumont, 531 N.E.2d 629 (N.Y. 1988)

Dumont and Russo (third party defendant) entered into an oral agreement to convert a commercial building to a residential cooperative. Russo was to provide cash only. He would receive a proprietary lease for the eighth floor and half the net proceeds. Dumont was to provide expertise and the actual work to form the cooperative and convey the building to it. The cooperative corporation, known as Grammercy Equities Corp., was formed and acquired title to the property. Dumont eventually sold all the floors. Each proprietary leasehold was to renovate its own space to meet code. Dumont represented to the purchasers that the building would qualify for a tax abatement.

Russo brought suit against Dumont for an accounting of his right as a party to a joint venture. Dumont denied the existence of a joint venture. Judgment was rendered against Dumont. The court found a joint venture and ordered monies to be held in trust for an accounting to be done.

Trouble arose between Dumont and the cooperative tenants. The work was not completed in time to receive the tax abatement. The tenants sued, seeking damages equal to the tax abatement. They also claimed fraud by Dumont. They claimed he never intended to complete the renovation in time to qualify for the abatement. Dumont filed a third-party action against Russo, saying if he was found liable to the tenants, Russo had to indemnify him for half the damages as a joint venturer. At trial, the jury found Dumont liable for fraud and breach of contract. The trial court allowed the indemnification based on partnership principles. There was no finding that Russo participated in the fraud.

> A joint venture is a special combination of two or more persons wherein some specific venture for profit is jointly sought [citation omitted]. It is in a sense a partnership for a limited purpose ... .
>
> The principle that a partnership must indemnify a partner who has incurred liabilities in the ordinary course of partnership business is not determinative where the liability is the result of unauthorized, intentional wrongdoing.

Id. at 632–33.

Because Russo did not share in the fraud and because Dumont's fraud was not within the ordinary course of business, the trial court's decision was reversed.

W.B. Johnston Grain Co. v. Self, 344 P.2d 653 (Okla. 1959)

Self was awarded worker's compensation against W.B. Johnston Grain Co. (Johnston) and its worker's compensation carrier. The carrier and Johnston appealed.

The carrier argued Self was not an employee of Johnston but, rather, of W.B. Johnston Grain Co. and Associates, a joint venture. It further argued that because a joint venture is a separate legal entity, the carrier was not liable for worker's compensation. The carrier claimed that all questions regarding a joint venture are governed by partnership laws.

The court found that not all states recognize partnerships as separate legal entities. The court stated:

> Joint adventures ... are of modern origin. The concept of such association or legal structure has been said to be purely the creatures of the American courts. The early common law recognized no relationship between persons as co-adventurers apart from that of a partnership established by proof of the existence of the requisite elements of partnership. In the course of time, however, through judicial decisions by American courts, there has been developed the concept that a status may be created by persons combining their properties or services in the conduct of an enterprise without forming a partnership, at least not a formal partnership in the legal or technical sense of the term.

Id. at 658.

The court held that a joint venture was not a separate legal entity. Therefore, Self was an employee of each of the parties forming the joint venture. Each joint venturer was jointly and severally liable for the worker's compensation award.

It is advisable to research state statutes for laws governing joint ventures. If there are none, or if joint ventures are not allowed under a particular state's law, the parties can accomplish basically the same type of business organization with a partnership.

Joint Stock Company

A **joint stock company** is an unincorporated association of individuals for the purpose of carrying on a business for profit. It is not a separate legal entity. Some states regulate joint stock companies by statute. If there are no statutes in your state, then the company will be governed by the agreement entered into by the owners. Some states require **articles of association** to be filed, much like articles of incorporation for corporations.

A joint stock company has many of the characteristics of a corporation, but also can resemble a partnership. It is like a corporation because ownership is in stock, which is transferable. It is managed by directors and officers and has a perpetual existence. Different from a corporation, a joint stock company is organized, not incorporated, and it derives its existence from the contract among the shareholders, whereas a corporation gets its existence from statutes. Stockholders are not agents of a joint stock company.

Like a partnership, a joint stock company is formed by agreement (not by statute); property usually is held in the names of the members, who have personal liability; and the company generally is not treated as a legal entity for purposes of a lawsuit.

The *U.S. Express* case illustrates the nature of a joint stock company.

State v. U.S. Express Co., 83 N.W. 465 (Minn. 1900)

The plaintiff, a regulatory body, sought information regarding the defendant railroad company's interstate and intrastate business and property. The defendant responded with intrastate information but nothing about its interstate business and property. The plaintiff instituted a mandamus action to compel the information. The trial court found that the defendant was a joint stock company, not a separate legal entity.

> It was organized by an agreement among its members and is not a corporation. We hold with the trial court that the defendant is not a corporation, but that it is in fact and law a partnership, having many of the characteristics of both a corporation and the essential features of a common-law partnership. It is not, however, a legal entity, and has no existence apart from its members.

Id. at 466.

The court further found that as a partnership the defendant had a right to do business within the state without the state's permission and free from control as any individual or partnership. However, because it was a common carrier, the plaintiff was entitled to intrastate information regarding the defendant's business and property. As the defendant had already answered those questions, the appeal was dismissed.

Key Terms

articles of association   joint stock company

joint adventure   joint venture

joint enterprise

Quiz

1. Briefly define the term "joint venture."

2. Describe the typical situations in which joint ventures are formed.

3. Discuss briefly the similarities and differences between joint ventures and partnerships.

4. List the situations under which a joint venture will terminate.

5. Define the term "joint stock company."

6. Describe briefly the way(s) in which a joint stock company is similar to a) a corporation and b) a partnership.

6   Limited Liability Company

The **limited liability company** is a relatively new type of business organization in the United States. In 1977, Wyoming became the first state to enact a limited liability company statute. This legislation was a result of the desire of an oil exploration company (which used Panamanian limited liability companies) to form a joint venture for oil and gas exploration in the North Sea, operating through a United States entity. The company drafted legislation for limited liability companies and presented it to the Wyoming legislature. It was adopted. It took the Internal Revenue Service eleven years to issue a revenue ruling, Rev. Rul. 88-76, stating that a Wyoming Limited Liability Company would be treated as a partnership for federal tax purposes. Prior to the issuance of this revenue ruling, Florida adopted the Florida Limited Liability Act for business dealings with Central and South America.

Almost every state and the District of Columbia have adopted limited liability company acts.

There is not yet a uniform law governing limited liability companies as there is for partnerships, limited partnerships, and corporation. In 1995, the commission that proposes uniform laws adopted a Proposed Uniform Limited Liability Act. For the time being, each state is adopting its own act and seeking IRS approval.

Limited liability companies are not new to the business environment in Europe and Latin America. In 1892, Germany enacted the first statutes allowing limited liability companies. The late nineteenth century brought limited liability companies to the United States, with Pennsylvania, Virginia, New Jersey, Michigan, and Ohio being the first states to permit them. However, their statutes were restrictive. In 1977, Wyoming passed the first true limited liability legislation. Wyoming, like most states, allows any business except banking and insurance to form a limited liability company.

Since issuing its revenue ruling in 1988 to allow limited liability companies to be taxed as partnerships under the Wyoming legislation, the IRS has issued a series of other rulings. To be taxed as a partnership, the IRS has ruled that a limited liability company cannot have more than two of the four corporate elements. Those elements are:

- continuity of life
- centralization of management
- limited liability
- free **transferability of interest.**

These elements are discussed in detail throughout this chapter. Not all states tax limited liability companies as partnerships; thus, it is important to check the laws of each particular state. For example, Florida still taxes limited liability companies as corporations.

Limited liability companies combine the flexibility of a partnership with the limited liability of a corporation. Corporations have the advantage of limited liability for shareholders. However, double taxation can be a disadvantage of corporations. Double taxation occurs when the corporation pays taxes on profits. If the profits then are passed to shareholders in the form of dividends, shareholders are taxed on the dividends as personal income. Partnerships have the tax advantage of passing through all income to the partners, but the disadvantage of unlimited liability. Limited partnerships provide the tax advantage of partnerships and the limited liability advantage of corporations for the limited partners.

However, if limited partners participate in the management of the business, they can lose their limited liability protection.

Limited liability companies combine all of these advantages. Income is passed through to members, there is limited liability for all members, and members can participate in the management of the business. Disadvantages are few for the limited liability company. One major disadvantage is that uniform statutes have not been adopted. Therefore, a company could have limited liability and tax advantages in one state but not in another. Also, because limited liability companies are relatively new, there is very little case law to review and analyze when law firms advise their clients.

Owners are **members**. Members can be individuals, partnerships, or corporations. All members of a limited liability company are granted limited liability, unlike limited partnerships. Members' liability is limited to their investment.

The characteristics of a limited liability company are much like those of a corporation. It is a separate legal entity apart from its owners. It can hold title to property and can transact business in its own name. A limited liability company has statutory powers and can function only through statutes or through authority granted in the **articles of organization**. It is formed for a certain duration, and it is responsible for its own debts and liabilities.

Statutory powers that most states grant to limited liability companies are:

1. Can sue and be sued, participate in legal proceedings in its own name
2. Purchase, receive, lease as lessee or lessor, pledge, acquire, own, hold, sell, mortgage, transfer, or encumber real and personal property in its own name
3. Have a seal
4. Lend money and assist its employees
5. Purchase, take, receive, own, hold, vote, use, mortgage, sell, lend, or otherwise use or dispose of interests or shares in other limited liability companies, corporations, general partnerships, or limited partnerships
6. Incur liabilities, borrow money, make contracts
7. Invest funds of the company
8. Elect managers, appoint agents, and set their compensation
9. Make or alter one or more operating agreements
10. Establish deferred compensation plans, pension plans, profit-sharing plans, and other incentive plans
11. Exercise any and all other powers necessary for the purposes for which the limited liability company is organized.

Some states allow limited liability companies to be a partner of a general partnership, limited partnership, joint venture, or another limited liability company.

A limited liability company requires more formality in formation (discussed later in this chapter) than a partnership. Members are allowed to participate in management as do partners. Members, however, do not lose their limited liability protection as limited partners would if they participated in management.

If there are many owners, a limited liability company may not be practical. In this situation, it may be better to form a corporation to take advantage of all four characteristics of a corporation, particularly full transferability of interest and continuity of life.

Ownership and Management

The owners of a limited liability company are called members. The members contribute capital in exchange for **membership interest**. The members may be passive investors, much like shareholders in a corporation. This type of member is called an owner of economic interest.

Some states require the members to manage the company. Other states allow the members to elect **managers**. The managers can be either members or outside managers.

Members have the ownership right to vote. They vote for managers, transfer of membership interest, and whether to continue the business after statutory dissolution. Their right to manage is equal to their percentage of contribution. However, the operating agreement can alter this result in any way that is agreed to by the members.

Members may resign by giving written notice to the other members. The resigning member has a right to his distribution as set out in the agreement. However, creditors must be protected. The member will not receive his distribution if it would cause the company to dissolve. The death, retirement, withdrawal, or expulsion of a member may cause dissolution of the limited liability company in states that attribute partnership characteristics to the entity. Because of this, a limited liability company lacks the corporate characteristic of **continuity of existence.**

Ownership interest also gives members the right to remove a manager. This should be stated in the **operating agreement**. The members have a right to inspect the books and records of the company. Members also have the right to attend meetings of the membership.

Members are agents for the limited liability company. Therefore, they have a fiduciary obligation to the company.

Managers

One corporate characteristic that limited liability companies usually have is centralized management. This is especially true when there are several owners. It would be cumbersome to have all owners vote on management decisions. Therefore, most limited liability companies elect managers to run the business.

A limited liability company can have one or more managers. Managers are like general partners or the board of directors of a corporation. The operating agreement or articles of organization prescribes the duties and responsibilities of the managers, as well as the specific term for which they can be elected. Some states require the managers to be natural persons.

Managers may be removed by a majority of the members. Vacancies can be created by the removal, resignation, death, or retirement of a manager. Vacancies are filled by a majority of the remaining managers.

Managers are considered agents of the limited liability company. They can legally bind the company if they are acting within the scope of their authority. Managers must act in good faith and with the best interests of the company. Refer to Chapter 1 on the duties of an agent. Managers are not liable for the obligations of the limited liability company.

Transferability of Membership Interest

Another corporate characteristic that most limited liability companies lack is the free transferability of a member's interest. Usually, state statutes require that the company have restrictions on the transferability of interest.

A member's membership interest is personal property, so it may be transferred or assigned. The operating agreement should state the rights regarding transferability. States that treat a limited liability company as a partnership require unanimous, written consent before a member can transfer or assign his interests. The member is an integral part of the company, as a partner is to a partnership. New members are not allowed without unanimous consent.

Formation

The formation of a limited liability company requires documents similar to both partnerships and corporations. The articles of organization that must be filed with the state are much like articles of incorporation. Most states require two or more persons to form a limited liability company. Sole proprietors do not form limited liability companies. The management of the company is stated in the operating agreement, which is similar to a partnership agreement.

As with other business organizations, any name may be used for a limited liability company as long as it is not the same or deceptively similar to the name of another business. The name must include "Limited Liability Company." Some statutes allow abbreviations to be used, such as L.L.C., L.C., or Limited Company. The name can be reserved before the articles of organization are filed. One should do this if it will be a few months before filing. Also, limited liability companies may use assumed names; these usually must be registered with the state and local authority.

Some states limit the purpose for which a limited liability company can be organized. The limitations usually are designed to prevent banking and insurance industries from using this form of business entity. However, the IRS does not have any similar restrictions.

Companies may contract to do business in other states. The company must comply with the statutes for foreign limited liability companies. Also, there may be local licensing and other regulations that must be met for the particular type of business in which the company is engaged. For example, if the company plans to run a gambling parlor, gaming licenses must be obtained before commencing operation.

State statutes govern what must be included in the articles of organization. The usual requirements are:

1. Name
2. Principal place of business
3. Purpose for which the company was organized
4. Name of the registered agent and the address of the registered office
5. If it is to be managed by manager(s), the name(s) and business address(es) of the initial manager(s)
6. If it is to be managed by the members, the names and addresses of the initial members
7. The latest date when the company will be dissolved and other events that could cause dissolution
8. The names and addresses of each organizer
9. Capital contributions of the members
10. Right of the limited liability company to admit new members
11. Right to continue business if a member leaves
12. Any other provisions that members wish to include.

Members may decide they want the right to continue the business if it must be dissolved because of death, retirement, resignation, expulsion, or bankruptcy or dissolution of a member. This must be set out in the articles of organization. Also, the articles should state how the company will purchase the membership interest owned by a member who is deceased, retired, resigned, expelled, or bankrupt.

Always research state statutes and check with the secretary of state for rules governing filing requirements, forms, fees, use of trade names, and causes of dissolution.

To keep the articles of organization flexible for a changing business, keep nonessential provisions to a minimum. Include them in the operating agreement instead. The operating agreement is much like a partnership agreement. There are some differences, however.

One difference is that managers elected by the members can make decisions in a limited liability company. In a partnership, the partners control and manage the business. The operating agreement must be consistent with the articles of organization.

Some states also prescribe what must be included in an operating agreement. This agreement sets out the internal management of the limited liability company. It must be in writing and must be signed by all members.

Requirements may include how the members will share assets and earnings; rights of the members to assign all or a portion of their interests in the company and the procedure for doing so; when an assignee of a member's interest may become a member of the company; whether the company will issue certificates showing membership interest; and the procedure to amend the operating agreement.

Optional provisions may include:

1. The right of the company to borrow money from members or third parties
2. Requirements to make additional capital contributions by members mandatory
3. Maintaining capital and income accounts for each member; allocation of profits, gains, cash, or losses among the members
4. Distribution of assets to members
5. Admission of new members; voting of members, including whether a member can vote by proxy
6. Setting the place, time, and manner of meetings of the members
7. What constitutes a quorum for member meetings
8. Duties and powers of the managers
9. Qualifications of the managers
10. The number and term of each manager and how managers are elected
11. Meetings of the managers
12. Location of the records and books of the company
13. Causes of dissolution
14. Distribution of assets if the business is terminated
15. Whether the company will buy life insurance on all members to facilitate purchasing their interests upon death.

These are just some of the provisions that can be included in an operating agreement. The agreement should be tailored to fit the company. The more detailed the agreement, the fewer problems there will be from disagreements among the members.

The articles of organization must be filed with the state; however, the operating agreement need not be filed. In most states, there is a filing fee for the articles of organization. Once the articles have been filed and the fees paid, the state will issue a **certificate of organization**. This should be kept with the books and records of the limited liability company.

If the company will be managed by managers, there should be an organizational meeting of the managers. This is much like the organizational meeting of the directors of a corporation. The organizational meeting is used to adopt certain actions formally.

Finance

Members' contributions can be made in cash, property, or services. Some states set requirements for the contributions. For example, a particular state may require a written contribution agreement to be signed that is irrevocable for six months. The contribution agreement is a contract that can be enforced. This may mean that if the member does not pay his contribution, he can be sued by the company. Specific requirements vary from state to state.

If the contribution is property or services, their value must be stated in the operating agreement, as one would do in a partnership agreement. The value of a member's contribution affects his interest in the company; therefore, it should be agreed at the outset. Any number of methods can be used to value a member's contribution. If the contribution is property, the company can obtain an appraisal and use that value. Alternately, the members can vote on a particular value. If the contribution is services, the members will have to agree on the value and set it out in the operating agreement. Some states require that the value be set out in the articles of organization.

Members are entitled to distributions as established in the operating agreement and the articles of organization. Once a member is entitled to receive distributions, she is considered a creditor of the company until her distributions are paid in full.

Duration and Dissolution

The articles of organization must state the duration of the limited liability company. Most statutes limit the duration, usually thirty years. This is to preserve the partnership tax status of the company. A limited liability company cannot have a perpetual existence, as a corporation does, or it may be subject to double taxation. The duration of a limited liability company is specified in the articles of organization.

As with all business entities, a limited liability company can be dissolved in a variety of ways. Like a partnership, a limited liability company can be dissolved by unanimous, written agreement of all the members. A limited liability company can be dissolved by court order. The death, retirement, resignation, expulsion, bankruptcy, dissolution of a member, or any other event that terminates the membership of a member can dissolve the limited liability company.

The remaining members may continue the business if the operating agreement allows. However, if the business is not continued, the company must wind up its affairs. The company must file with the state a statement of intent to withdraw. This notifies creditors that the company will dissolve. Like all other business entities that dissolve, creditors must be protected. Creditors are paid first; then assets are distributed to the members pursuant to the operating agreement. State statutes differ on whether capital contributions are paid first, followed by distribution of the remaining assets, or whether all remaining assets are distributed after creditors are paid.

Once the company's affairs are wound up and the assets are distributed, the company must file articles of dissolution. Usually, the company must give advance notice of the dissolution to creditors for their protection.

Some states allow general partnerships and limited partnerships to convert to a limited liability company. The conversion can be accomplished by filing articles of organization as a limited liability company. Some statutory schemes also allow limited liability companies to merge with another limited liability company, a limited partnership, a general partnership, or a corporation. This is unique to limited liability companies. Most states do not allow one partnership to merge with another; neither do they allow partnerships to merge with corporations.

Taxation

The IRS taxes limited liability companies as partnerships if the statutes correctly establish the formation of these companies. The IRS requires that a limited liability company can have only two of the four characteristics attributed to a corporation. If a limited liability company has more than two of these characteristics, it will be considered a corporation for tax purposes and may be subject to double taxation. These corporate characteristics are:

- perpetual existence
- free transferability of interest

- limited liability
- centralized management.

Most state statutes do not allow a limited liability company to have perpetual existence. Usually, limited liability companies are not allowed to exist for more than thirty years. Also, a limited liability company usually dissolves upon the death, bankruptcy, resignation, expulsion, or dissolution of a member. It is easy to provide continuity of life and still follow the statutes, however. A limited liability company can adopt a provision to continue the business with consent of the members, like a partnership or limited partnership. By including this provision, it takes on a perpetual existence. The IRS will not allow majority consent; it must be unanimous consent. Priv. Ltr. Rul. 90-10-027 (Dec. 7, 1989).

The purpose of forming a limited liability company is to take advantage of its limited liability. Neither the members nor the elected managers are liable for the company's debt. Also, most organizational agreements and state statutes allow centralized management. Unless the company is managed by all members, it will have centralized management. Having all members of a limited liability company manage the business can be quite cumbersome; therefore, most are run by elected managers. These are the two corporate characteristics usually found in limited liability companies: limited liability and centralized management.

The last corporate characteristic, free transferability of interest, usually is lacking in state statutes that authorize the formation of limited liability companies. **Free transferability** means members have a right to transfer their interests without consent of other members. Corporations are the only business entities that may have this feature. Most statutory schemes require unanimous written consent of members before a member can sell or otherwise transfer her interests. Members are allowed to withdraw at any time. This can force the company to dissolve.

If the limited liability company qualifies under IRS rules to be taxed as a partnership, there is no double taxation. The profits and losses of the company are passed through to the members and are taxed on their individual tax returns. They are taxed whether or not they actually receive the profits, just as in a partnership. The distributions of the company are made pursuant to the operating agreement. The members can agree on any formula for the distribution. If the operating agreement is silent, the distributions are based on the members' contributions.

In the past, the IRS has considered this type of distribution to be passive income or loss, because it is not wages. Because the IRS requires that passive losses be offset only by passive income, investment in a limited liability company may not meet a member's needs unless passive income or losses are available to offset her investment. The federal tax code is ever changing, however, and should be consulted before investing in a limited liability company.

A limited liability company is a noncorporate business. Therefore, it has limited liability, single taxation, and members can participate in management. The IRS has ruled the statutes in Virginia and Colorado qualify to be taxed as a partnership. Rev. Rul. 93-5, 1993-3 I.R.B. 6; Rev. Rul. 93-6, 1993-3 I.R.B. 8.

The Commerce Clause of the United States Constitution requires states without limited liability company statutes to allow such companies to do business within the state. However, nothing in the Constitution requires those states to tax limited liability companies as partnerships or to give the company limited liability. Therefore, statutes and case opinions for the state in which a limited liability company will do business as a foreign entity must be researched for liability and tax consequences. It may be advisable in states without authorizing statutes to form a corporation if the investors seek limited liability. If their primary aim is tax advantages, a partnership or a limited partnership may be the right choice. These are things to consider when forming a limited liability company that will conduct business in more than one state.

Liability

The very nature of a limited liability company is limited liability. However, if members act beyond their authority, they may become personally liable. The operating agreement should state exactly what each member's authority is and what liability the company is willing to accept.

A member's personal creditors can reach a member's economic interest in a limited liability company. Because members have no right to specific property, creditors can reach only the economic interest of a member. They cannot reach specific property.

Limited liability companies have been compared to Subchapter S corporations, which are not subject to double taxation. Most Subchapter S corporations are of limited duration. A Subchapter S corporation dissolves upon the death, expulsion, retirement, bankruptcy, or withdrawal of a shareholder. However, Subchapter S corporations have restrictive requirements for formation, making limited liability companies more flexible than Subchapter S corporations.

The nature of certain types of businesses makes them good candidates for the limited liability company structure. A limited liability company can hold and pass title to property, so it is a good business structure for real estate development. Because members can be involved and still enjoy limited liability, it is favorable for almost any development activities. General and family businesses often make good candidates for the limited liability company structure. They have limited liability, usually are taxed as partnerships, and do not have to worry about the requirements of Subchapter S statutes.

Some states allow professionals to form limited liability companies. Utah and Kansas are examples. Utah Code Ann. § 48-2b-105(l)(R) (Supp. 1991); Kan. Stat. Ann. § 17-760333 (Supp. 1991).

Questions to consider when forming a limited liability company are:

1. Whether this is a new entity or a conversion of an existing entity
2. Number of members and type of members
3. Name of the company
4. Who will be the registered agent and her address
5. What type of business this will be
6. What type of management to choose, whether a group of managers, a single manager, or management by members
7. What type of authority the managers will have regarding this business
8. Manager qualifications
9. Election procedure, filling vacancies, removal of managers, and compensation
10. What type of voting rules the company should have, whether super majority, simple majority, or variable, depending on the issue (amending the articles of organization, amending the operating agreement, or electing new managers)
11. How many votes each member will have, whether equal or based on contributions.

The operating agreement provisions also must be considered. These might include items such as recordkeeping; value of contribution; distribution; admission of new members; assignability of interest; dissolution causes and right to continue the business; winding up of the business upon dissolution; and distribution of assets at dissolution. All of these decisions should be made prior to filing the articles of organization and adopting the operating agreement. Doing so avoids many of the problems found in the *Abu-Nassar* case.

Abu-Nassar v. Elders Futures Inc., 1991 WL 45062 (S.D.N.Y. 1991)

The owners (Abu-Nassar) of a Lebanese limited liability company, Infovest, sued a registered futures commission merchant, Elders, for commissions due Infovest. Elders counterclaimed, stating Infovest owed it money to cover deficits of customers and seeking to pierce the corporate veil. Elders alleged Infovest was the alter ego of the owners and not a separate company; therefore, the owners should have personal liability for the debts.

Abu-Nassar argued Lebanese limited liability law should apply. The Lebanese code in Art. 7 requires a minimum capitalization. Infovest initially was capitalized in excess of the minimum, but then it was undercapitalized for over three years. Art. 7 can impose personal liability for undercapitalization. It is considered deceit under Lebanese law.

Lebanese law also requires annual meetings. Infovest did not hold formal, annual meetings. Abu-Nassar used "LTD" instead of Limited Liability Co. Also, Lebanese law states that a company must put notification of funding on all documents. Infovest did not. The Lebanese Code states that personal liability comes into play if there are damages to a third party because of non-compliance.

> [S]ummary judgment cannot be entered in favor of the plaintiffs insofar as Lebanese law may be applicable ... . Infovest has not, by its summary judgment motion, put into issue the question of whether Infovest's alleged violations of the Lebanese Code caused injury to Elders. Accordingly, Elders has not been called upon on this motion to establish causation, and cannot be denied the opportunity to do so at an appropriate time.

Id. at 10.

Even if the corporate form was preserved under Lebanese law, the corporate veil could be pierced under New York law.

> The corporate form may be pierced when it can be demonstrated that the [corporate] form has been used to achieve fraud, or when the corporation has been so dominated by an individual ... and its separate identity so disregarded that it primarily transacted the dominator's business rather than its own and can be called the other's alter ego.

Id. at 10 [citations omitted].

Factors that are considered to pierce the corporate veil are 1) intermingling of corporate and personal funds and siphoning of corporate funds by the principal; 2) failure to observe corporate formalities; 3) failure to pay dividends; 4) inadequate capitalization; 5) insolvency; 6) perpetuation of fraud by a shareholder. This is not an exhaustive list; equity is also considered.

Elders alleged deposits of profits and investments of Infovest were deposited in a personal account for the plaintiffs. Infovest commingled personal and corporate money and loans were made by plaintiffs to Infovest to cover debts. Abu-Nassar argues that the political climate in Lebanon required them to deposit funds in personal accounts.

There is not sufficient evidence to determine whether there are complete and accurate corporate records regarding meetings and declaring dividends. Undercapitalization and insolvency are not enough to pierce the veil, but they are additional factors.

Elders also claims fraud in the plaintiffs' failure to state the extent of capitalization on all Infovest documents and payment by plaintiffs of corporate obligations and transfer of Infovest assets to a similar corporate entity controlled by plaintiffs. This made Infovest an empty shell to defraud creditors.

The court finds the Elders allegations that Infovest failed to state its capitalization adequately, that it has shut down except for purposes of this litigation, that its liabilities have exceeded its assets for at least three and one-half years, and that it has had to borrow funds from plaintiffs to meet its obligations—when viewed in conjunction with the facts underlying Elders' claim of domination and abuse of the corporate from by plaintiffs—are sufficient to raise a triable issue of fact as to whether plaintiffs fraudulently perpetuated Infovest's corporate form.

Id. at 21.

Key Terms

articles of organization	managers
certificate of organization	members
continuity of existence	membership interest
free transferability	operating agreement
limited liability company	transferability of interest

Quiz

1. Identify the four corporate characteristics.

2. Identify the number of corporate characteristics a limited liability company can possess without losing its status as a limited liability company.

3. What are the most common characteristics found in a limited liability company?

4. The owners of a limited liability company are considered members. Is membership restricted to natural persons? Explain briefly.

5. Limited liability companies take advantage of characteristics of other forms of businesses. Describe succinctly these characteristics.

6. Explain briefly some of the disadvantages of limited liability companies.

7. What ownership rights do members have in a limited liability company? Describe briefly.

8. Describe the event(s) that may terminate the existence of a limited liability company.

9. Explain briefly the term "centralized management" as it applies to limited liability companies.

10. Explain concisely how a limited liability company is financed.

11. List and describe briefly the event(s) that may cause dissolution of a limited liability company.

12. How are limited liability companies viewed by the IRS in terms of their tax treatment?

13. Describe briefly the steps that must be taken to form a limited liability company.

14. Describe briefly the types of provisions that should be included in an operating agreement.

7 Corporations

A **corporation** is a business organization that is a separate entity and has an existence apart from its owners. Most corporations are small businesses; they are not the major companies that generally come to mind, such as General Electric or Ford Motor Company. A corporation is created under the laws of a state to conduct business. Therefore, state law governs a corporation just as it governs partnerships, limited partnerships, and limited liability companies. Because a corporation exists apart from its owners, the owners (shareholders) can come and go, unlike in other business entities. A change in shareholders does not affect the corporation's existence. A corporation is considered a "person" under state and federal law; therefore, it enjoys the same rights and protections that individuals do within the United States.

There are several types of corporations. **Public corporations** are created by legislation. The management answers to a governmental authority. Entities such as an airport authority, a municipal corporation, and some school districts are public corporations. Another type of corporation is a **public service corporation**. Public utilities are public service corporations.

Private corporations are the type discussed in this text. Private corporations can be either for profit or nonprofit. The stock of a private corporation can be publicly traded or privately held. Publicly traded stock is bought and sold on the New York Stock Exchange. Most corporations are small businesses with privately held stock.

A corporation is a **domestic corporation** in the state where it is incorporated. It is a **foreign corporation** in all other states in which it does business. A corporation from another country doing business in the United States is an **alien corporation**.

New Jersey and Delaware always have had very favorable corporate statutes; therefore, many corporations are incorporated in these two states. There is a uniform law for corporations: the Model Business Corporation Act (MBCA). Many states have adopted all or part of this uniform law. More recently, a majority of states have adopted the Revised Model Business Corporation Act (RMBCA).

Corporations are given statutory powers by the state law that governs them. The Model Business Corporation Act, at § 3.02, sets out these corporate powers:

1. To sue and be sued, complain, and defend in its corporate name.

2. To have a corporate seal, which may be altered at will, and to use it, or a facsimile of it, by impressing or affixing it or in any other manner reproducing it.

3. To make and amend **bylaws**, not inconsistent with its articles of incorporation or with the laws of the state, for managing the business and regulating the affairs of the corporation.

4. To purchase, receive, lease, or otherwise acquire, and own, hold, improve, use, and otherwise deal with real or personal property, or any legal or equitable interest in property, wherever located.

5. To sell, convey, mortgage, pledge, lease, exchange, and otherwise dispose of all or any part of its property.

6. To purchase, receive, subscribe for, or otherwise acquire; own, hold, vote, use, sell, mortgage, lend, pledge, or otherwise dispose of, and deal in and with shares or other interests in, or obligations of, any other entity.

7. To make contracts and guarantees, incur liabilities, borrow money, issue its notes, bonds, and other obligations (which may be convertible into or include the option

to purchase other securities of the corporation), and secure any of its obligations by mortgage or pledge of any of its property, franchises, or income.

8. To lend money, invest and reinvest its funds, and receive and hold real and personal property as security for repayment.

9. To be a promoter, partner, member, associate, or manager of any partnership, joint venture, trust, or other entity.

10. To conduct its business, locate offices, and exercise the powers granted by this Act within or without the state.

11. To elect directors and appoint **officers**, employees, and agents of the corporation, define their duties, fix their compensation, and lend them money and credit.

12. To pay pensions and establish pension plans, pension trusts, profit-sharing plans, share bonus plans, share option plans, and benefit or incentive plans for any or all of its current or former directors, officers, employees, and agents.

13. To make donations for the public welfare or for charitable, scientific, or educational purposes.

14. To transact any lawful business that will aid governmental policy.

15. To make payments or donations, or do any other act, not inconsistent with law, that furthers the business and affairs of the corporation.

The **articles of incorporation** may be drafted so that these powers are restricted. One must decide if the corporation is to have broad or restrictive powers. However, the corporation cannot broaden its powers beyond those allowed by the state law that authorizes it to exist.

The Model Corporation Business Act allows a corporation to incorporate for any lawful purpose. States may restrict those powers in their respective statutes. The business of the corporation is defined in the articles of incorporation as the *corporate purpose*. The corporate purpose could be operating a restaurant, a telemarketing firm, a bank, or the like. Because the Model Corporation Business Act allows corporations to be formed for any lawful business, one is not required to be specific in defining the corporate purpose.

Corporations are allowed to exist perpetually under the MBCA. Most states also allow a corporation to exist perpetually. However, this does not mean that a corporation cannot limit its existence. A corporation may be created to exist for a specific period of time. In that case, the limited time must be included in the articles of incorporation.

In every state, corporations are allowed to own real property in the corporate name. Some states restrict this ownership right to real property necessary to further the corporate purpose.

As enumerated earlier, corporations have the power to lend money to assist employees. This power varies from state to state. Corporations also have the power to make donations, to become a partner or member of another business, and to establish pension plans.

An important power that corporations have is the power to act in an emergency. A corporation is a separate legal entity; however, it can act only through the resolutions of the **board of directors** and officers. Directors act at regularly scheduled meetings where a quorum is present. If there is an emergency and if the directors cannot meet as required, the Model Business Corporation Act provides separate emergency powers that can be used in case of a disaster or a catastrophic event. The Act allows the board to modify lines of succession to accommodate incapacitated corporate employees, relocate the principal office, and/or have a meeting with directors by whatever means they can be reached; it further provides that any action taken in good faith will not result in liability to corporate employees who had to make the decisions.

If a corporation acts outside its powers, the act is considered **ultra vires**. An *ultra vires* act can be one that exceeds the corporate powers or one that is contrary to law. An *ultra vires* act can result in personal liability for the officers or directors. The Model Business Corporation Act upholds the validity and enforceability of an *ultra vires* contract as between the parties involved, subject to the following rights:

1. The right of shareholders on behalf of the corporation to bring an action to obtain an injunction and damages.
2. The right of the corporation itself to recover damages from the officers and directors who caused the *ultra vires* transactions.
3. The right of the attorney general of the state to institute a proceeding to obtain an injunction against the *ultra vires* transactions or to institute dissolution proceedings against the corporation for *ultra vires* acts.

Ownership and Control

A corporation is owned by shareholders. A **shareholder** owns an interest in a corporation by purchasing shares of stock. However, the corporation is managed by the board of directors and the officers. The directors are elected by the shareholders. The officers are appointed by the board of directors.

Shareholders

Shareholders are owners of a corporation and have certain **ownership rights**. Ownership rights are limited by statute. Those rights may include the right to vote, the right to a return on the investment, and the right to share in the assets upon liquidation. Shareholders do not have day-to-day involvement in the corporation, but they do elect the board of directors.

The board of directors of a corporation determines current ownership interests by setting a **record date**. A **holder of record** is a shareholder who owned shares of stock on the record date. A corporation usually sets the record date several weeks before a shareholder meeting or before the declaration of a dividend so the corporation can determine who the record owners are.

Very rarely are certificates (see Figure 7-1) issued for stock in publicly traded companies. To do so would be a paperwork nightmare. Computers can determine the owners very quickly and efficiently.

Shareholder Rights   Those shareholders who are holders of record have rights. Shareholders may be allowed cumulative voting rights. Cumulative voting is a way in which directors can be elected for a corporation. The authorization of cumulative voting rights may vary. Some states have constitutional provisions; others require that a corporation specifically authorize cumulative voting in its articles of incorporation. The Model Business Corporation Act states that the authorization must be in the articles of incorporation and can be used only if the notice for the meeting to elect directors says that cumulative voting will be allowed and only if at least one shareholder gives the corporation notice that he intends to exercise this right.

Cumulative voting allows shareholders to concentrate their votes for one or more nominees. Each share of stock, which normally entitles a shareholder to one vote, is multiplied by the number of directors to be elected.

> Corporation X will elect five directors to its board. Shareholder A has 100 shares of stock. If the corporation allows cumulative voting, shareholder A will have 500 votes that she can cast. Shareholder A will be allowed to concentrate those 500 votes in any way she wants.

Cumulative voting allows minority shareholders to elect one or more directors to the board when they otherwise would not have a voice in the election.

Another right shareholders have is to amend the articles of incorporation. The procedure to amend the articles usually requires a resolution from the board of directors stating what amendment is needed, which then is approved by the shareholders at their next meeting. A change in the articles might be required if the corporation needs to authorize

FIGURE 7-1   Stock Certifiate

more shares of stock, authorize a new class of stock, change the corporate name, change the registered agent and address, or amend the duration or purpose, if these were restricted in the original articles.

Shareholders have a right to inspect the corporate books and records. However, state statutes often restrict this right somewhat. The Model Business Corporation Act does not allow the articles or bylaws to abolish or restrict shareholder rights to inspect the corporate books and records. Some states try to protect a corporation from being harassed by a shareholder who bought a share for the sole purpose of harassing the managers. Those states limit the right to inspect, for example, by requiring a proper purpose for the request or by not allowing shareholders to inspect the records or books until they have held their shares for a certain length of time.

Shareholders also have the right to vote on extraordinary matters. These are transactions that are outside the normal scope of business activities. A corporate merger, consolidation, transfer of stock, sale of substantially all of the corporate assets, and dissolution are the types of activities that fit this category.

The articles of incorporation can give shareholders **preemptive rights**. This right allows a shareholder to purchase newly issued stock to retain the same percentage of ownership.

Shareholder B holds 10% of the issued and outstanding stock of a corporation. The corporation decides to issue additional authorized stock. If the articles grant preemptive rights to shareholders, shareholder B will be allowed to purchase 10% of the new issue before it is sold to outsiders. Shareholder B does not have the right to purchase more than 10% of the new issue.

Preemptive rights do not attach to a new class of stock, however.

Preemptive rights are important to small corporations. Preemptive rights allow shareholders to keep their percentages of ownership and control if they so choose. Statutes may vary in relation to preemptive rights. Some states grant preemptive rights automatically unless the articles of incorporation specifically prohibit preemptive rights. Other states and the Model Business Corporation Act require that the articles of incorporation provide specifically for preemptive rights if they are to exist.

Another right that shareholders have is a right to distribution, which applies to both dividends and distribution at liquidation. Shareholders have a right to dividends only if dividends are declared by the board of directors. Once declared, the shareholders become creditors of the corporation until the dividends are paid. Shareholders also have a right to the remaining assets after liquidation and payment of all creditors. If there are unpaid dividends, those are paid first; then the assets are distributed pursuant to each shareholder's interest in the corporation.

Limited Liability The most attractive characteristic of a corporation may be its **limited liability**. A shareholder risks only the amount of her investment. A corporation is a separate legal entity. Historically, limited liability was the main reason the corporate form was chosen over other business entities. The advent of the limited liability company may change this.

In a new corporation, the protection of limited liability may be eroded by contractual obligations. Creditors are not readily amenable to lending money to a new business that has few assets and no proven track record. Therefore, shareholders and directors may have to guarantee loans personally.

Corporations are subject to the legal concept of **piercing the corporate veil**. This doctrine is imposed by courts on corporations that do not follow the formalities of corporate law. The corporation affords shareholders protection through limited liability. If courts find abuse of this protection, they will "pierce the corporate veil," thus allowing creditors to hold shareholders or directors personally liable for the corporation's liabilities.

The most common abuses are failing to fund the corporation adequately, failing to observe certain formalities, or forming the corporation to perpetuate a fraud. Most states require that the corporation be funded at a certain level at the time of incorporation. The Model Business Corporation Act requires the funding to be $1,000. This means that at least $1,000 of stock must be sold when the corporation is formed. This money is put into the capital account of the corporation.

The formalities that a corporation must observe are:

1. Hold shareholder and director meetings, keep minute books, and have a registered agent and office.
2. Operate as a separate business and financial entity, with separate books, records, and accounts. There should be no intermingling of accounts and funds with the shareholders, officers, directors, or other affiliated corporations.
3. Do not hold out to creditors or to other third parties that this business is being operated as anything other than a corporation, such as a partnership or sole proprietorship (these entities do not provide limited liability for their owners).
4. Have adequate capital to meet its obligations.

If a court finds that one or more of these formalities has not been observed, or that a fraud has been perpetuated, it will decree that there is no corporation; the shareholders then will be treated as partners, with unlimited personal liability to creditors.

Most often, this problem arises in corporations with only one or two shareholders, who are also the directors and officers. In this situation, it is very easy to use corporate assets for personal use, commingle funds, or forget to have formal director and shareholder meetings. If someone sues the corporation and if it is determined that the corporate assets are not adequate to compensate him, the court will look behind the corporate veil. If formalities have not been followed, the court may pierce the veil.

Board of Directors

The board of directors is elected by the shareholders to manage the corporation. The articles of incorporation may set the number of directors for the corporation. If not, the number will be set in the bylaws. To keep a corporation flexible, it is better to set the number of directors in the bylaws. A change to the articles of incorporation requires a vote by the shareholders; the bylaws can be changed by the board of directors alone.

Directors have certain rights and responsibilities. They have the right to participate in meetings, the right to inspect the corporate books and records, and the right to make decisions regarding the management of the corporation. Directors' responsibilities include making corporate policy decisions, appointing officers, and making financial decisions (for example, declaring dividends and issuing additional shares of authorized stock).

Directors owe a fiduciary duty to the corporation. This includes the duty of due care and the duty of loyalty. The duty of due care requires directors to use reasonable business judgment in conducting corporate affairs. The duty of loyalty implies faithfulness to the corporation. It prohibits directors from using corporate funds or information for personal gain. It also requires directors to disclose any conflicts of interest.

Some states require that the corporation state the names and addresses of the initial board of directors in the articles of incorporation. The Model Business Corporation Act does not require this. If the initial board is not stated in the articles, the incorporators will elect the board at the organizational meeting.

The Model Business Corporation Act allows corporations to have as few as one director. Many states require a minimum of three directors. The bylaws set the qualifications for board members. There is no age requirement under the Model Business Corporation Act. Some states impose requirements concerning age and other matters. There should be a provision to indemnify the directors for any acts within the scope of their authority. Directors are protected from personal liability for corporate acts. The bylaws also establish the duties and responsibilities of the directors; compensation, if any; and other requirements.

Large corporations have several members on the board of directors. Directors usually are elected because of who they are, such as presidents of other major corporations. Sometimes their only compensation is for expenses. These directors consent to serve because of the business contacts and other benefits they achieve by serving on several boards. The corporate powers are exercised by the board of directors; however, the board may delegate its authority to an executive committee, officers, and employees.

Shareholders can remove directors with or without cause unless the articles of incorporation provide that directors can be removed only for cause. If a director was elected by cumulative voting, she can be removed only by cumulative voting. Otherwise, the majority shareholders could undo what the minority shareholders had accomplished by cumulative voting.

Officers

The board of directors appoints the officers to run the corporation on a day-to-day basis. The board sets the requirements for the officers in the bylaws. Also stated in the bylaws are the duties and responsibilities of the officers, as well as the type and number of officers. The usual officers are president, vice president, secretary, and treasurer. The board can appoint officers or other agents as needed. A small corporation may not need vice presidents. In addition, the authority each officer possesses is set by the board in the bylaws.

Because officers are responsible for the corporation on a day-to-day basis, they hire employees, purchase office equipment and supplies, sign contracts, and do anything else within their authority that is needed for the corporation to do business. The Revised Model Business Corporation Act allows one person to hold all offices.

Officers owe the same fiduciary duties of due care and loyalty to the corporation as do directors.

Continuity of Existence and Dissolution

An advantage of corporations is their ability to exist perpetually. A corporation's existence is not affected by the death of a shareholder. This is one characteristic that sets a corporation apart from other business organizations. However, the articles of incorporation can set a specific term for the corporation to exist.

Of course, a corporation can be dissolved at any time if the owners no longer wish to have a corporation. Also, the courts and the state may dissolve a corporation for certain reasons. Minority shareholders can force a dissolution if they are being prejudiced by the shareholders who are in control.

If the corporation decides to dissolve voluntarily, the board of directors passes a resolution to that effect. At the next meeting of the shareholders, the dissolution is approved. The Model Business Corporation Act requires only a majority vote to dissolve a corporation. Some states require a unanimous vote or a two-thirds vote of the shareholders. If approved by the shareholders, the corporation must file **articles of dissolution** with the secretary of state. The corporation also must notify all creditors. Creditors are paid first. Then stockholders receive the remaining assets according to their proportionate ownership interests.

The court or the state can dissolve a corporation involuntarily. Some reasons are for failure to observe the legal formalities of a corporation, illegal activity, creditor lawsuit, or a shareholder lawsuit. These are discussed more fully in later chapters.

Taxation

There are tax advantages and disadvantages to the corporate structure. Corporations are subject to federal, state, and local taxes. Corporations can deduct expenses from income prior to paying corporate income tax. Expenses include salaries, rent or mortgage, office equipment and supplies, and benefits for employees over and above their salaries. These benefits could include insurance premiums, bonus programs, and incentive programs.

A tax disadvantage of corporations is called **double taxation**. First, a corporation pays taxes on its income as corporate income tax. If a dividend is declared and paid to shareholders, the shareholders must include this dividend on their individual income tax returns. In effect, the income of the corporation is taxed twice. To avoid this situation, some corporations do not pay dividends to the shareholders. The value of the stock increases, and no taxes are paid until the shareholder sells the shares. Then she must pay capital gains tax. A corporation whose officers are also shareholders can pass income to the officers in the form of salary or bonus. If the officers are also the only shareholders, the IRS may scrutinize salaries and bonuses to determine if they are a sham to avoid double taxation.

Certain types of corporations receive special tax treatment for income or capital gain on the sale of stock. Some of these corporate forms are Subchapter S, Subchapter C, and corporations with Section 1244 stock.

The *Gross* case is an example of the court forming a corporation by law.

Gross v. Kentucky Board of Managers of World's Columbian Exposition, 49 S.W. 458 (Ky. 1899)

The state of Kentucky passed legislation to build a building to collect and exhibit the resources of Kentucky and run a restaurant at the World's Columbian Exposition. To carry out the work, a board was set up. The board was given the power to employ agents and employees. The state specifically stated that it would not assume any debts of the board. The board contracted with the plaintiff to run the restaurant. The board failed to comply with the contract. The plaintiff sued. The board demurred, saying it could not be sued because it was an agent of the state.

> The question presented was whether the board was vested by the legislature with the character of a corporation. "Its character depends upon the powers given it, and not upon the name by which the legislature may call it." *Id.* at 459. Given the fact that the state will not assume the debt, the state must have contemplated that the board would be responsible.
>
> Because the power to contract was expressly conferred on the board, the power to be sued or sue on these contracts was necessarily vested in the board.

Key Terms

Alien corporation	Holder of record
Articles of dissolution	Officers
Articles of incorporation	Ownership rights
Board of directors	Piercing the corporate veil
By-laws	Preemptive rights
Corporation	Public corporation
Cumulative voting	Public service corporation
Domestic corporation	Record date
Double taxation	Shareholder
Foreign corporation	*Ultra vires*
Limited liability	

Quiz

1. Briefly define what a corporation is.

2. What powers typically are given to corporations under state law? Describe briefly.

3. Briefly define the rights of shareholders as owners of the corporation.

4. Briefly define the concept of "piercing the corporate veil."

5. Briefly explain the requirements under the Model Business Corporation Act to qualify as a director for a corporation.

6. Briefly describe the rights and duties of the directors as the managers of the corporation.

7. Who manages the corporation on a day-to-day basis?

8. Briefly explain the major tax disadvantage of corporations.

9. For what purpose(s) may a business incorporate, and where is the purpose stated?

10. Briefly explain the concept of shareholder preemptive rights.

11. Briefly explain the major advantage of a corporation.

8 Incorporation

Several things must be decided once a business decides to incorporate. A jurisdiction in which to incorporate must be selected. In this jurisdiction, the corporation will be known as a *domestic corporation*. If the corporation transacts business in other states, the corporation will be a *foreign corporation*, subject to those states' laws. To determine which state in which to incorporate, several factors must be considered. If the corporation does not plan to do business in more than one state, it probably would incorporate within the state where it will do business. Other factors include the corporation statutes, taxes, and court opinions regarding the treatment of corporations and shareholders in a particular state. One must consider such items, as listed in Figure 8-1.

FIGURE 8-1 Corporate Formation: Checklist for Selection of Corporate Jurisdiction (Reprinted with permission from Henn & Alexander, *Handbook of the Law of Corporations and Other Business Enterprises* 175–85 (3d ed. West 1983).

1. Are there provisions for preincorporation share subscriptions?
2. May a corporation be formed for either perpetual or limited duration?
3. How restrictive are the laws on corporate names?
4. Can you reserve a corporate name? How is it done? For how long?
5. Is a single incorporator permissible?
6. What are the qualifications required for incorporators?
7. May a corporation serve as an incorporator?
8. Are there restrictions on the purpose for incorporation?
9. Must the purposes be set out in the articles of incorporation?
10. Are there restrictions on corporate ownership of real property? Personal property? Shares in other corporations? Limitations on the amount of debt?
11. Are there express provisions on the *ultra vires* doctrine? (a corporation acting without authority to do so)
12. How broad are the statutory general corporate powers? Must they be set out in the articles of incorporation?
13. What are the filing fees for the articles of incorporation?
14. What are the organization taxes? Other taxes? Are shares without par value treated differently?
15. Are there filing delays caused by administrative scrutiny?
16. Is there a state stamp tax on the issuance of securities? (sale of stock in a business entity)
17. Are blue sky law requirements burdensome? (laws of a state regulating the purchase and sale of stock in a business entity)
18. What is the minimum authorized or paid-in capital requirement? What happens if there is noncompliance?
19. What qualitative and quantitative consideration requirements apply to par-value shares? Does the true value or good faith rule apply to the valuation of property or services?

20. Can a portion of the consideration received for shares be allocated to capital surplus? To what extent and within what period of time?

21. May partially paid shares be issued? May fractions of shares be issued? (scrip)

22. If there are two or more classes of stock, must the provisions affecting the shares be stated on the certificates?

23. Are divided preferences allowed? Liquidation preferences?

24. When two or more classes of shares are authorized, must the provisions concerning them be stated or summarized on the share certificates?

25. Are express provisions made for issuing preferred or other "special" classes of shares in the series? What are the limitations on permissible variations between series of the same class?

26. To what extent may preferred shares be redeemed? To what extent may common shares be redeemed?

27. To what extent may shares be made convertible?

28. What are the record date provisions? Are bearer shares permissible? What rights attach to them?

29. What are the express statutory provisions for, and judicial and administrative attitudes toward, close corporations?

30. To what extent may voting rights of shareholders be denied or limited? Absolutely? Contingently? May shares carry multiple votes? Fractional votes?

31. What are the minimum quorum requirements for shareholder action?

32. Are there express provisions permitting greater-than-normal requirements for shareholder quorum or shareholder votes?

33. Are there express provisions for holding shareholder meetings out of state? On dates to be set by board of directors? What are the notice requirements?

34. Are there express provisions for informal action by shareholders? Unanimously? By required percentages?

35. Is cumulative voting permissive or mandatory?

36. What are the provisions for shareholder class voting for directors?

37. Are there express provisions for shareholder voting agreements?

38. Are there express provisions permitting shareholder control of directors?

39. Are there express provisions for irrevocable proxies?

40. Are there express provisions for voting trusts, permitting closed voting trusts and renewals?

41. Are there express provisions for purchase and redemption by the corporation of its own shares, including use of stated capital if the purchase is made for a specified purpose?

42. Are there provisions concerning the validity and enforceability of agreements by the corporation to purchase its own shares?

43. Is insolvency, either in the equity or in the bankruptcy sense, a limitation on the redemption or purchase by the corporation of its own shares?

44. Are there express provisions for rights and options to purchase shares, including the issuance of shares and the share certificates for them, even partly paid, to directors, officers, and employees? What are the judicial attitudes with respect to these?

45. Is shareholder approval required for the issuance of share options, either generally or to directors, officers, and employees?

46. Do preemptive rights exist or not exist without a provision in the articles of incorporation? Are they adequately defined? May they be denied, limited, amplified, or altered in the articles of incorporation?

47. What is the minimum number of authorized directors?

48. What are the qualifications required of directors with respect to residence, citizenship, shareholding, age?

49. May the board of directors be classified? Staggered?

50. What are the minimum quorum requirements for action by the board of directors?

51. Are there express provisions permitting greater-than-normal requirements for board of directors quorum? Board of directors vote?

52. Are there express provisions for holding board of director meetings outside the state?

53. Are there express provisions for informal action by the board of directors? By telephone conference or some comparable communication technique?

54. What are the provisions for removal of directors? For cause? Without cause?

55. Are there express provisions for filling vacancies on the board of directors? By shareholder action? By board action?

56. Are there provisions for increasing the size of the board of directors? By shareholder action? By board action?

57. Are there provisions for filling newly created director positions? By shareholder action? By board action?

58. Are there express provisions for executive committees of the board of directors? Other committees of the board of directors? Informal action by committees? What powers may be exercised by committees? What is the minimum number of committee members?

59. Are there express interested directors/officers provisions?

60. What corporate officers are required?

61. May the same person hold more than one office?

62. What are the required qualifications of the various officers with respect to residence, citizenship, shareholding, being a director, age, or other?

63. Are there provisions for the election of officers by shareholders? For the removal of officers by shareholders?

64. To what standards are directors and officers held accountable? Standard of care? Fiduciary standards? Statutory duties? What are the possible liabilities of directors? Officers?

65. To what extent may directors immunize themselves from liability by filing their written dissents? By reliance on records?

66. What are the express provisions for deadlock, arbitration, and dissolution; and what are the judicial attitudes toward these?

67. Are cash and property dividends payable out of surplus? Capital surplus? Earned surplus? Net profits?

68. Is insolvency, either in the equity sense or in the bankruptcy sense, a limitation on cash or property dividends?

69. Are unrealized appreciation and depreciation recognized in computing surplus? Capital surplus? Earned surplus?

70. Are there express "wasting assets" corporation dividend provisions?

71. Are there express provisions for share dividends? Share splits? Other share distributions?

72. To what extent do statutory requirements of notice or disclosure to shareholders apply in the event of cash or property dividends or other distributions from sources other than earned surplus? Share distribution? Reduction of stated capital by cancellation all of reacquired shares? Reduction of stated capital made by board of directors? Elimination of deficit in earned surplus account by application of capital surplus ("quasi-reorganization")? Conversion of shares? Who will be liable for noncompliance? Corporation? Directors? Officers?

73. What are the provisions for shareholder class voting for extraordinary corporate matters? May filings affecting extraordinary corporate matters have delayed effective dates?

74. What shareholder approval is required for a sale, lease, exchange, or other disposition of corporate assets?

75. What shareholder approval is required for a corporate mortgage or pledge?

76. What shareholder approval is required for a corporate guaranty?

77. Do the statutory provisions provide for expeditious amendment of the articles of incorporation? Including elimination of preemptive rights? Elimination of cumulative voting? Elimination of cumulative preferred dividend arrearages? Making nonredeemable shares redeemable? Are there provisions for "restated" articles of incorporation?

78. What are the statutory provisions permitting merger or consolidation?

79. Are there provisions for short-merger of a subsidiary into a parent corporation? Of a parent into a subsidiary corporation?

80. What are the statutory provisions concerning nonjudicial dissolution?

81. What are the statutory provisions concerning judicial dissolution?

82. How extensive are the appraisal remedies afforded to dissenting shareholders? To what extent are appraisal remedies exclusive?

83. What are the express provisions relating to shareholder derivative actions?

84. Are there express provisions for derivative actions by a director? By an officer? By a creditor? By others?

85. Is there statutory differentiation between shareholder derivative actions and other actions brought by shareholders?

86. What are the provisions for indemnification for litigation expenses of directors? Of officers? Of other corporate personnel? Are there provisions for insurance?

87. Are the statutory indemnification provisions exclusive or not with respect to directors? Officers? Other corporate personnel?

88. What books and records must be kept within the state?

89. What are the requirements with respect to annual and other reports?

90. What are the annual franchise tax rates?

91. Are nonresident security holders subject to local taxes? Personal property taxes? Inheritance taxes?

92. Are there express provisions to accommodate small business investment companies?

93. Are there express provisions to accommodate open-end investment companies ("mutual funds")?

94. To what extent are foreign corporations doing business in the state subject to the corporate statutes' regulatory provisions? Local "blue sky" laws? Local fees and taxes?

95. To what extent has the corporate statute been construed by the courts? Are judicial and administrative attitudes sympathetic?

96. Does the state have a statute or regulation similar to Chapter S?

The next step is to select a corporate name and to reserve it with the secretary of state before incorporation. Most states have prohibitions against using the same or deceptively similar names as existing corporations. Therefore, if the corporation intends to do business in more that one state, the name should be reserved in each state. The same corporate name may not be available in each state. Some states will allow corporations to have almost the same name.

> The corporate name is ABC, Inc. ABC, Inc. incorporated in Nebraska but also wants to do business in Iowa. Iowa already has an ABC, Inc. The laws may allow the corporation to use ABC, Inc. of Iowa or ABC, Inc. of Nebraska.

The secretary of state sometimes answers informal inquiries concerning availability of a specific name. With computers, it usually is simple to find out whether a name is available before preparing the documents. Each state has its own form to reserve a name, and the forms are readily obtainable from the state. The period for which a name can be reserved varies anywhere from one month to twelve months. If the corporation wishes anonymity until it is incorporated, an attorney can reserve the name and transfer it when it is time to incorporate.

As with other business entities, a corporation is allowed to do business under an assumed name or trade name. Some states require that the assumed name also be registered with the secretary of state. The official corporate name is used on all documents filed with the state as well as all contracts and other legal documents.

Foreign corporations can register their names. However, some states require a foreign corporation to renew the registration each calendar year.

The corporation may not be in a financial position to incorporate until it has investors, investigates the business opportunities, acquires property, and hires personnel. These things can be done before incorporation. Some would-be corporations hire what is called a **promoter**. This is an agent (refer to Chapter 1 on agency) or a group of agents who promote the business. They find investors, look at the feasibility of the business venture, perhaps locate office space, negotiate leases, obtain equipment, and hire personnel.

The Model Business Corporation Act requires $1,000 paid-in **capital** to commence business. That is not a requirement under the revised act (RMBCA). However, some states still require paid-in capital. Investors may be needed to provide this and to provide the capital to start the business. If the business will not be incorporated until the necessary capital is obtained, potential shareholders can sign **preincorporation share subscriptions**. These are offers to purchase shares in a corporation prior to its formation. Share subscriptions are legally binding and enforceable contracts. Persons who enter into share subscription agreements are called **subscribers**.

The Model Business Corporation Act makes share subscriptions irrevocable for a period of six months. If the corporation is formed during this period, the corporation can require the subscriber to purchase stock. Usually, the board of directors calls the subscriptions due at its organizational meeting. Because share subscriptions are contracts, the subscriber could be liable for breach of contract if she defaults.

Share subscriptions are assignable. A potential investor may change her mind and find someone else to take over the contract. Several subscribers may sign one share subscription for a certain amount of shares, or it can be signed by one subscriber for herself alone.

Some states require **incorporators** to be subscribers. This could be a factor in deciding what jurisdiction to select for incorporation.

A promoter may enter into contracts on behalf of the corporation. A promoter can be held personally liable on any preincorporation contracts. The promoter will be personally liable until the corporation is formed and the contracts are assumed by the corporation.

Articles of Incorporation

Once the business is ready to incorporate, **articles of incorporation** (see Figures 8-2 and 8-3) are filed with the appropriate state office, which typically is the secretary of state. The articles of incorporation create and define the corporate structure. The articles can be thorough and very detailed or can contain only the minimal information required by law.

FIGURE 8-2   Articles of Incorporation (detailed)

**ARTICLES OF INCORPORATION
OF
CRITTERS, INC.**

The undersigned natural persons of majority age, acting as the incorporators of a corporation under the Nebraska Business Corporation Act, adopt the following Articles of Incorporation for such corporation:

Article I

The name of the corporation formed hereby is Critters, Inc.

Article II

The period of the corporation's duration is perpetual.

Article III

The purpose or purposes for which the corporation is organized is any lawful purpose or purposes; the transaction of any and all lawful business; to promote the interests of the corporation or enhance the value of any of its properties; and to do any and all things and to exercise any and all powers which it may now or hereafter be lawful for the corporation to do or to exercise under the laws of the State of Nebraska and that may now or hereafter apply.

Article IV

The business of the corporation shall be managed by the Board of Directors, except as otherwise provided by statute or by the Certificate of Incorporation.

The Board of Directors shall consist of five members. Except as provided in the Certificate of Incorporation, this number can be changed only by the vote or written consent of the holders of 90 percent of the stock of the corporation outstanding and entitled to vote. This number cannot be changed by amendment of the bylaws of the corporation. No director is required to be a stockholder.

Article V

The corporation shall have a President, one or more Vice Presidents, a Secretary, a Treasurer, and such other officers, agents, and factors as may be deemed necessary.

Article VI

The annual meeting of the stockholders for the election of directors and for the transaction of such other business as properly may come before such meeting shall be held at 3:00 in the afternoon on the second Monday of June in each year, if not a legal holiday, or, if a legal holiday, then on the next succeeding day that is not a legal holiday.

A special meeting of the stockholders may be called at any time by the President or by the Board of Directors, and shall be called by the President upon the written request of stockholders of record holding in the aggregate one-fifth or more of the outstanding shares of stock of the corporation entitled to vote, such written request to state the purpose or purposes of the meeting and to be delivered to the President.

Article VII

The aggregate number of shares which the corporation shall have authority to issue is 1,000 shares of common stock, and the par value of each such share shall be $1.00.

Article VIII

Each stockholder shall have preemptive right to acquire issued shares of the corporation stock, equal to shares issued as incentives to employees and approved by the Board of Directors, whether now or hereafter authorized, unissued, or issued.

Article IX

To the extent permitted by law, the corporation shall have the power to purchase and to maintain the insurance on behalf of any person who is or who was a director, officer, employee, or agent of the corporation against any liability asserted against him or her and incurred by him or her in such capacity or arising out of his or her status as such, whether or not the corporation would have the power to indemnify him or her against such liability.

Article X

The corporate seal, subject to alteration by the Board of Directors, shall be in the form of a circle, shall bear the name of the corporation and the year of its incorporation and shall indicate its formation under the laws of the State of Nebraska. Such seal may be used by causing it or a facsimile thereof to be impressed or affixed or reproduced or otherwise.

Article XI

The address of the initial registered office of the corporation is 1234 Luck Street, Omaha, Nebraska 68100. The name and address of its initial registered agent is Dan D. Duck, 1234 Luck Street, Omaha, Nebraska 68100.

Article XII

The principal place of business of the Corporation shall be located at 234 Fawn Parkway, Omaha, Nebraska 68110.

Article XIII

The names and addresses all of the incorporators are:

Dan D. Duck   Amy Nalastik
1234 Luck Street   234 Fawn Parkway
Omaha, NE 68100   Omaha, NE 68110

Article XIV

The existence of this corporation shall commence at the time of the filing of these Articles in the office of the Secretary of State of the State of Nebraska.

Article XV

We, the undersigned, being all of the incorporators of said corporation, to hereby execute the Articles of Incorporation, hereby declaring and certifying that the facts herein stated are true and, accordingly, have hereunto set our respective hands this _____ day of _____, 19____.

_____
Incorporator

_____
Incorporator

FIGURE 8-3   Articles of Incorporation (minimal)

ARTICLES OF INCORPORATION
OF
FLORA & FAUNA, INC.

We, the undersigned natural persons of the age of twenty-one years or more, acting as incorporators of a corporation under the Nebraska Business Corporation Act, adopt the following Articles of Incorporation for such corporation:

I.

The name of the corporation is FLORA & FAUNA, INC.

II.

The period of duration is perpetual.

III.

The purpose or purposes for which the corporation is organized is to grow and sell floral species and supplies at wholesale and retail and for any other lawful purpose or purposes; the transaction of any and all lawful business; to promote the interests of the corporation or to enhance the value of any other properties; and to do any and all things and to exercise any and all powers which may now or hereafter be lawful for the corporation to do or to exercise under the laws of the State of Nebraska that may now or hereafter apply.

IV.

The aggregate number of shares which the corporation shall have authority to issue is 176. Such shares are to consist of one class only. The par value of such shares is $10.00 per share.

V.

Provisions for the regulation of internal affairs of the corporation, including provisions for the distribution of assets on dissolution or financial liquidation, shall be set forth in the bylaws of the Corporation.

VI.

The street address of its initial registered office is 2916 Daisy Drive, Omaha, Nebraska 68112; and the name of the registered agent at such address is Frances Flowers.

VII.

The name and street address of the incorporator is:

Isadora Rose
2907 Thornbush Street
Omaha, NE 68233

Dated: _____, 19____.

_____
Incorporator

There is more flexibility if the articles contain only the bare essentials. Otherwise, the articles must be refiled each time the corporate structure is changed in any way.

The Model Business Corporation Act requires very little to be included in the articles of incorporation:

- Corporate name
- Number of shares the corporation is authorized to issue
- Name of the initial registered agent and address of initial registered office
- Name and address of each incorporator.

Permissible information that may be added to the articles under the Model Business Corporation Act includes:

1. Names and addresses of the initial board of directors
2. Purpose for which the business was organized
3. Management and regulation of the affairs of the corporation
4. Powers of the corporation, board of directors, and shareholders
5. Par value of the stock
6. Language imposing personal liability on the shareholders for the debt of the corporation
7. Any other provision that could be set out in the bylaws.

As one can see, very little is required to be stated in the articles of incorporation. Over the years, states have relaxed their requirements also. Additional information that may be required in a particular state could include: the period of duration (which can be perpetual); designation of each class of stock and the rights of each class; whether preemptive rights are allowed; and whether cumulative voting will be allowed by the shareholders.

Items to consider when drafting articles of incorporation are:

1. *Corporate name:* Is it acceptable to the secretary of state of the state of incorporation and other states? Is a trademark search or a trade name filing needed?
2. *Location of the registered office:* It does not have to be where the business is operated.
3. *Location of the principal office.*
4. *Purpose of the corporation,* whether general or specific.
5. *Powers of the corporation:* One can set out the statutory powers if desired, but it is not required; it can make the articles very long and cumbersome. If one wishes to restrict the corporate powers, the restrictions must be set out in the articles.
6. *Stock,* including the total number of shares the corporation will be authorized to issue, how many classes of stock, par-value stock, no-par-value stock, price at which the stock will be sold.
7. *Preferred stock:* What preferences, if any, there are for this class of stock. Types of preferences could be guaranteed dividends, cumulative dividends, redemption terms, or conversion rights.
8. *Minimum amount of capital* for the corporation to commence business. Check the state statutes to see if there is a minimum requirement.
9. *Incorporator(s):* The names and addresses of incorporators must be set out in the articles of incorporation.
10. *Existence:* Will the corporation have perpetual existence, or will it exist for a fixed duration?
11. *Preemptive rights:* Will the corporation allow or deny preemptive rights to the stockholders?

12. *Voting:* Will any type of transaction require more than a majority vote by the stockholders?

13. *Restriction on transfer of stock:* When forming either a close corporation or a professional corporation (discussed in later chapters), the transfer of stock must be restricted, and the restriction must be stated in the articles of incorporation.

14. *Voting rights:* Any limitation on the right of one vote for each share must be stated, as well as whether preferred stock will have voting rights on any or all issues.

15. *Director powers:* Limitations on authority must be stated if they are desired.

This is not an all-inclusive list of things that may be included in the articles of incorporation. Some of the more important items for consideration, as well as the items usually required by state statutes are discussed in the following subsections.

Name   The name of the corporation is important. Some businesses choose a very simple, almost generic, name for the corporation and do business under a more colorful assumed name (ABC Inc., doing business as "Denise's Bistro," for example). A corporation cannot use a name that is already in use or one that is similar or deceptively similar to another name. There are many lawsuits and court opinions regarding the use of corporate or trade names that are similar.

The Model Business Corporation Act and most state statutes require that some form of the word "incorporation" be used after the name. This lets the public know that the business is a corporation and that the owners have limited liability. The variations commonly allowed are Inc., Corp., and Incorp.

Stock   The next item required by the Model Business Corporation Act and by many statutes is the number and types of classes of stock. Shares of stock are equity securities. The number of shares that a corporation is allowed to issue is set out in the articles of incorporation. The corporation is limited to this number unless the articles of incorporation are amended. Therefore, the articles of incorporation should authorize a sufficient number of shares. If the corporation plans to issue more than one class of stock, authority to issue preferred stock should be included in the articles. All of the rights given to preferred stock must be stated in the articles as well. The corporation must have at least one class of stock that has unlimited voting rights and is entitled to receive net assets of the corporation upon dissolution. This class of stock usually is common stock. All corporations have common stock. The decision to issue different classes of stock usually depends upon the investors.

The stock authorized in the articles must be given a value. This can be either **no par value** or **par value**. If the stock has a par value, it cannot be sold for less than that value. Small corporations generally select a low value for par, such as $10 per share, so there is never a question of selling the stock for less than par value. The capital that is generated by selling par-value stock is called **stated capital**.

If the stock is without par value, the board of directors sets the value at which the stock will be sold. This value is called **stated value**. The capital generated by selling no-par stock is **capital surplus**. Capital surplus can be used to pay dividends and for repurchase of shares by the corporation.

The requirement to maintain a registered agent and a registered office are universal, imposed for legal and official matters. Under the Model Business Corporation Act, failure to maintain a registered agent and office for sixty days is grounds to dissolve the corporation. States have dissolved corporations for this reason. Each state imposes its own requirements and sanctions. Consider the *Partridge* case.

Incorporators   The incorporators are the persons who form the corporation. They are required to sign the articles of incorporation. Their names and addresses usually are required to appear as well. The incorporators are responsible for holding the organizational meeting to elect the board of directors and for initially setting up the corporation. It is

---

Partridge v. Associated Cleaning Consultants & Services, Inc., 424 S.E.2d 664 (N.C. 1993)

Plaintiff slipped and fell on a wet floor in a restroom at an airport. The defendant was the cleaning company that cleaned the restrooms. Plaintiff filed suit against the defendant. Service of process was sent to the registered agent's address. The summons was returned. Service was then perfected on the secretary of state. A default judgment was entered against the defendant.

Defendant appealed to set aside the judgment, claiming that the failure to maintain a registered agent and notify the secretary of state of the address change was excusable neglect. The court found:

> A corporation doing business in North Carolina "which fails to pay due attention to the possibility that it could be involved in litigation ... by failing to take steps to ensure that it is notified of claims pending against it, is guilty of inexcusable neglect."
> *Id.* at 668.

---

permissible to name the initial board of directors in the articles of incorporation. If that is done, then the incorporators do not hold the organizational meeting of the corporation; that is handled by the initial board of directors instead.

Duration   The period of duration in not required to be stated, but normally is included in the articles, nonetheless. An advantage the corporate form has over the limited liability company is that a corporation can exist perpetually. Of course, the articles can contain a specific period of duration. A corporation does not have to exist perpetually just because the articles are set out that way. A corporation can dissolve at any time.

Purpose   Another permissible item for the articles of incorporation is the statement of purpose of the corporation. This is another place where the articles can be very flexible or quite restrictive. Most states allow corporations to exist for any lawful purpose. To be most flexible, the articles do not have to state the exact purpose for incorporating. If the articles are general, the business can expand into other areas without having to amend the articles. Some states do not allow incorporation of certain professions, such as law or medicine. States that do allow professionals to incorporate govern them under professional corporation statutes (discussed in Chapter 10). Some states also have special corporate forms for other industries, such as banks and insurance companies.

Preemptive Rights   Preemptive rights come from common law. This allows the shareholder to maintain the same proportionate share of ownership. If the corporation decides to issue more shares of stock, a shareholder is allowed to purchase the same ownership percentage before the shares are sold to third parties.

> Shareholder A owns 10% of the shares of stock in a corporation. The corporation issues 1,000 more shares of authorized stock. Shareholder A will be allowed to purchase 100 shares prior to sale of shares to any third parties. Shareholder A must purchase 100 shares if she buys at all; she cannot purchase more or less than this number.

Preemptive rights keep the ownership interest the same. If preemptive rights are to be granted, most states require this to be included in the articles of incorporation. The right can be limited.

Cumulative Voting   Cumulative voting is another shareholder right that must be included in the articles of incorporation if it is to be allowed. Cumulative voting allows minority shareholders to vote representation onto the board of directors. Using cumulative voting, a shareholder is allowed to vote the number of shares she owns times the number of directors to be elected.

> Shareholder B has 500 shares of stock of Apex Corporation. At the annual meeting, the shareholders will elect five directors. If cumulative voting is allowed, Shareholder B will have 2,500 votes to cast. Shareholder B can vote all of her shares for one director or can split her votes among several directors.

If a group of shareholders joins to pool votes, they may be able to elect at least one board member. This is an advantage for minority shareholders.

Other Provisions   There are some provisions that usually are included in the articles of incorporation, even though they are no longer required by the Model Business Corporation Act. The initial board of directors can be stated in the articles. There are no required qualifications for directors. There is no age requirement, citizenship requirement, or business requirement. Directors do not have to be shareholders. However, state statutes may have restrictions and qualifications for directors.

Other provisions can be included in the articles of incorporation as well. The Model Business Corporation Act allows the articles of incorporation to regulate the internal affairs of the corporation. These provisions are optional. The more regulation of internal affairs in the articles, however, the less flexible the articles become. It usually is better to regulate the internal affairs of the corporation through the **bylaws**.

One optional provision is limitation of director liability. Court decisions have made the cost of director and officer insurance prohibitive. Therefore, the Model Act allows a corporation to limit a director's liability. Corporations also are allowed to indemnify directors.

Another optional provision allows corporations to repurchase shares from shareholders. Most states allow this. Usually, a corporation is restricted to repurchasing shares only if it has funds that are unreserved and unrestricted in earned surplus. **Earned surplus** is the accumulated profits that have not been designated for other purposes. The articles of incorporation may provide for capital surplus funds to be used. *Capital surplus* is the amount collected over par value or the amount designated as capital surplus from no-par shares.

In addition, the articles may allow shareholders instead of directors to fix the consideration for shares of stock to be issued, the number of shareholders and directors needed for a quorum, and the vote required. Normally, a quorum for a meeting is the majority of shareholders or directors, and the affirmative vote of the majority of the quorum will pass a resolution. However, the articles may change the requirement for the vote or for the quorum. Some actions of the corporation may require more than a majority, such as a resolution to dissolve the corporation. The Model Business Corporation Act still allows a simple majority vote, although some states require two-thirds or a unanimous vote.

Finally, the articles may include the qualifications and compensation for directors, as well as stating whether the corporation can enter into transactions with interested directors. At common law, a director could not have any interest in a business transaction involving the corporation. The Model Business Corporation Act allows directors to have such an interest as long as it is disclosed.

The preceding provisions are optional under the Model Business Corporation Act. Some states require one or more of these provisions to be included in the articles of incorporation. To maintain flexibility in the articles, a corporation should include only the minimum requirements.

Formalities

After the articles of incorporation have been drafted, they must be filed with the secretary of state. The articles must be signed by the incorporators. Some states require the signatures of the incorporators to be notarized. Other formalities that may be required are filing with a local authority, publication in a newspaper of general circulation within the county of the registered office, (sometimes) filing of other documents. Finally, many states require that a minimum amount of capital be put into the corporation to commence business.

A corporation usually begins to exist when the **certificate of incorporation** is issued by the secretary of state. Some states deem a corporation to exist when the articles of incorporation are filed. After the articles are filed, there must be an organizational meeting (discussed in Chapter 9). Corporate supplies must be gathered: the minute book, corporate seal, stock transfer ledger, and stock certificates. There are firms from which these supplies can be ordered with the corporate name printed on them.

If the procedures for incorporation are not followed, the existence of the corporation may be challenged. A third party or a creditor could seek to hold the shareholders personally liable for a contract, for example. Alternately, if the corporation attempts to enforce a contract, a third party may be able to avoid liability.

Bylaws

The *bylaws* are the rules that regulate and govern the internal affairs of the corporation. Bylaws are much easier to amend than the articles of incorporation. Therefore, it is better to set out provisions in the bylaws instead of the articles of incorporation. Bylaws can be changed by the board of directors at its regular meetings or by a unanimous, written consent of the board of directors. Amendments require neither approval of the shareholders nor filing with the secretary of state. The Model Business Corporation Act provides that the initial bylaws are to be adopted by the incorporators or by the initial board of directors if named in the articles of incorporation. Some states may require that the shareholders adopt the initial bylaws. The jurisdiction of incorporation should be researched to determine specific requirements.

Standard bylaws contain the following provisions:

- Location of the principal office of the corporation
- Location of the registered office of the corporation
- Board's authority to change these offices
- Time and place of the shareholders' annual meeting
- Procedure for sending notices of meetings and the appropriate time frame
- Procedure for preparing and examining voting lists.

If the corporation plans to allow meetings without notice, the authority to do this must be stated in the bylaws. The procedure for calling special meetings of the board of directors and shareholders also are stated in the bylaws.

Bylaws regulate the number of shares required to constitute a quorum for shareholders' meetings and the number of directors to constitute a quorum for board meetings. Voting requirements are regulated by the bylaws. These include whether voting by proxy or cumulative voting will be allowed, and which classes of stock are entitled to vote on matters.

The duties and responsibilities of the board of directors are contained in the bylaws. The bylaws authorize the board to manage the business. The number, tenure, and qualifications of the directors are included. The procedure to fill vacancies, to remove directors, to set their compensation, and the like are set out in the bylaws. Authority to act without a meeting must be given in the bylaws if it is to exist. Any authority, duty, or responsibility of the board should be stated in the bylaws.

Important provisions in the bylaws are those governing the officers of the corporation. The authority of the board of directors to appoint officers is contained in the bylaws. The number, procedure for election, term of service, and compensation are stated here. The duties and responsibilities of the officers are also delineated in the bylaws, as is the procedure to fill a vacancy or to remove an officer. The board usually authorizes the officers to enter into contracts on behalf of the corporation, because the officers run the corporation on a day-to-day basis and must have to authority to act.

Finally, the bylaws should include:

1. Fiscal year for the corporation; either a calendar year or another twelve-month period (for example, October 1 through September 30)
2. Authority to declare and pay dividends
3. A description of the corporate seal
4. Provisions for adopting emergency bylaws and for amending, altering, repealing, or adopting new bylaws.

Key Terms

Articles of incorporation	No-par-value stock
Bylaws	Par-value stock
Capital	Preincorporation share subscriptions
Capital surplus	Promoter
Certificate of incorporation	Stated capital
Earned surplus	Stated value
Incorporator	Subscribers

Quiz

1. Briefly describe the primary decisions that must be made before incorporation.

2. Concisely explain the role of a promoter in relation to a corporation.

3. List and briefly describe the steps for incorporation.

4. Briefly describe what must be included in the articles of incorporation under the Model Business Corporation Act.

5. Briefly define the term "share subscriptions."

6. Briefly explain the concept of cumulative voting.

7. Briefly describe the purpose and the type of information that generally is contained in the bylaws of a corporation.

8. Explain briefly why is it better to keep the articles of incorporation simple and to include most organizational items in the bylaws.

9 Internal Organization of a Corporation

Once the business has been incorporated, other formalities must be undertaken to complete the organization process. Primary among them are the various organizational meetings that are held and documented in the corporate records.

Organizational Meetings

The first meeting typically is the **organizational meeting** of the incorporators. If the articles of incorporation set out the initial board of directors, the incorporators will not meet. Instead, the initial board of directors will hold the organizational meeting. Actions taken at the organizational meeting include:

1. Acceptance of the certificate of incorporation or articles of incorporation
2. Acknowledgment of the payment of any taxes
3. Election of the initial board of directors
4. Authorization of the board of directors to issue shares
5. Adoption of bylaws
6. Acceptance of share subscriptions
7. Any other business that appropriately comes before the meeting.

Once the directors are appointed by the incorporators, they preside over the remainder of the organizational meeting. Additional items to be acted upon at the organizational meeting include approval of actions taken at the previous incorporators' meeting. If payment was not tendered for share subscriptions, the directors must pass a resolution to call for payment. A share subscription is a contract and is enforceable by the corporation. The board of directors then must authorize the officers to issue the share certificates to subscribers.

The board of directors also authorizes payment of expenses incurred in the formation of the corporation. This may include any taxes and fees as well as reimbursement to persons for out-of-pocket expenses. The corporation may have had a promoter who performed significant amounts of work in setting up the corporation. If so, the corporation (principal) owes the promoter (agent) for reimbursement.

If no-par-value stock is issued, sold, or given in exchange for subscriptions, or if par-value stock is sold in excess of its value, the board of directors should allocate the excess consideration to capital surplus. Capital surplus can be used to repurchase shares of stock or to issue dividends.

The board of directors must adopt any preincorporation agreements that may have been made by the promoters or organizers of the corporation. These types of agreements may be a bank loan to set up the business, a lease for office space, or the purchase or lease of equipment. Each agreement should be adopted in a separate resolution. The resolution should set out the terms of the agreement and should show clearly the approval by the board of directors.

An important item completed at the organizational meeting is election of officers. The officers run the day-to-day affairs of the corporation. The board also will establish compensation. There may be employment contracts with the officers. These contracts are adopted by resolution. The bylaws state the duties and responsibilities of each officer and which officers the corporation will have. When forming a corporation, a president, secretary, and treasurer may be the only officers needed.

The board of directors will need to adopt a bank resolution. This resolution prescribes the authority to maintain a bank account and the names of the persons who will have authority to obligate the corporation in banking matters. The bank will supply the resolution form that it requires. The board should complete this form and attach it to the **minutes** of the meeting. The resolution in the minutes authorizes the opening of the account and adopts by reference the provisions in the bank resolution.

Other items to be handled at the organizational meeting include adoption of a resolution to apply for admission and qualification as a foreign corporation in another jurisdiction, if the corporation plans to do business in another state. Also, the appointment of the registered office and agent should be ratified by the board of directors. The registered office and agent are set out in the articles of incorporation; however, the appointment should be ratified. The board of directors may designate an attorney to act as corporate counsel and also may designate an accountant.

If the corporation will do business under an assumed name, the board must adopt a resolution authorizing the use of a specific name. Then the officers will file a statement of assumed name with the secretary of state and with any local clerk's office, as required.

If the corporation decides to make a Subchapter S election or to authorize adoption of a Section 1244 stock plan, these resolutions also should be adopted at the organizational meetings. (These concepts are discussed in Chapter 10.)

The directors who are present at the organizational meeting can set the dates of their regular board meetings and can delegate authority to the officers. Once these items are finished, the meeting can be adjourned. The secretary signs the minutes.

The formalities of the initial meeting are crucial, as discussed in the *Duck River* case. The legal status of the corporation may depend on them.

There are several documents that should be attached to the minutes of the organizational meeting:

Duck River Preservation Ass'n. v. Tennessee Valley Authority, 410 F. Supp. 756 (E.D. Tenn. 1974)

The plaintiff brought an action against the defendant challenging compliance with the National Environmental Policy Act. The defendant challenged the plaintiff's capacity to sue because it had failed to hold an organizational meeting. Instead, it had held a general membership meeting at which the constitution and bylaws were approved and the directors were elected. After the lawsuit was filed, the directors approved the bylaws and constitution effective as of the date of the general membership meeting. The court held that the plaintiff was a viable legal entity.

> The capacity of a corporation to sue ... shall be determined by the law under which it was organized .... It is stipulated that a charter of incorporation of the plaintiff was filed by the secretary of the state of Tennessee on April 26, 1971. The corporate existence of a Tennessee corporation begins when the charter of the corporation is filed by the secretary of state.

(citations omitted) *Id.* at 757.

The evidence shows that at the special meeting of the board of directors, the corporate charter was approved and ratified as of the date of filing the charter of the corporation with the secretary of state; the bylaws and constitution were approved and ratified; the institution and continuation of this action was ratified; and all previous actions taken by officers, incorporators, attorneys, and members of the board of directors were approved and ratified.

"[T]he plaintiff is now a viable legal entity which commenced this lawsuit and whose directors have ratified the commencement and continuation hereof." *Id.* at 757.

Its act in commencing this lawsuit is not invalidated by the fact that the plaintiff may not have been so empowered or capacitated at the time this lawsuit commenced.

- Notice or waiver of notice of the meeting
- Articles of incorporation (and certificate of incorporation, if received)
- Minutes of incorporators' meeting
- Bylaws
- All contracts approved by the board
- A specimen of the share certificates
- Written stock subscriptions
- Bills for expenses of organization
- Banking resolution
- Internal Revenue Service forms if Subchapter S status is elected.

Regular and Special Meetings

The bylaws set the procedure for holding a regular meeting and for calling a **special meeting** of the board of directors. The Model Business Corporation Act defers to the bylaws in regulating these meetings. Therefore, bylaws must be drafted carefully to specify the desired procedures or notice for meetings.

The Model Business Corporation Act states that the quorum required for the board to take action is a majority of the number of directors stated in the bylaws or in the articles of incorporation. The articles or the bylaws may require a greater number than a majority but cannot require less than the number required by law. States may require more than a majority for a quorum. The Model Business Corporation Act further states that a board action can be approved by a majority of the members present. Therefore, if the board of directors consists of five members, a quorum exists if three members attend the meeting. Using this example, it would take the vote of only two to take action. Corporations want directors to attend the meetings.

In today's world of electronics and multimedia, the Model Business Corporation Act allows board members to attend by telephone or by other communication devices, as long as each director can hear all other directors simultaneously. It is necessary that all directors be able to participate in the meeting by hearing all comments of all other directors and to communicate their comments to all other directors.

At the regular meetings, the board can take action on any matters necessary to manage the corporation. These may include the approval of contracts, appointment of officers, salaries for employees, and other such matters.

Special meetings may be called by the board if some urgent matter arises that cannot wait until a regular meeting. Some boards of directors meet only once a year, at the same time as the stockholders' meeting. A special meeting would be called if there were a threat of a hostile takeover, expansion of the company, bankruptcy of the corporation, or a vote to dissolve. The bylaws specify the procedure for calling a special meeting.

All meetings, regular or special, of the board of directors require that advance notice be given. However, if the bylaws so provide, a waiver of notice can be signed by each director at the meeting prior to conducting any business. The waivers should be attached to the minutes of the meeting and kept in the official corporate minute book.

Shareholder Meetings

Shareholders also must meet at least annually. Shareholders must elect the board of directors on an annual basis. The directors' terms may be staggered in such a way that not all directors are elected each year; however, some always will be elected. Shareholder meetings are more regulated by statute than are director meetings. This is to ensure that shareholders have a voice in corporate affairs. Shareholders can obtain court enforcement of shareholder meetings if the corporation does not set the meetings.

Normally, all actions of the shareholders are to be approved by a majority vote. The bylaws can require a greater-than-majority vote for all matters or for selected matters.

Sometimes, votes on extraordinary matters require more than the majority vote. Extraordinary matters include such things as dissolution, merger, consolidation, or an exchange of assets. (These are discussed in Chapter 11.) The Model Business Corporation Act requires only a majority vote on all matters before the shareholder meetings.

As with board of directors meetings, the electronic age allows a shareholder to attend and to participate in meetings without being there in person. The bylaws must provide for this type of attendance, however.

The bylaws also contain the procedures for the shareholder meetings, the place of the regular meeting, the call and procedure for special meetings, and the **notice of the meeting**. The notice states when the meeting is, how it will be held, and why it is needed. In the case of a special meeting, the notice may state that the meeting will be held as a conference call. Also, the bylaws will set the method of voting, including whether proxy voting is allowed. In the case of special matters, such as a vote to dissolve, the bylaws may provide that proxy voting is not permitted. The corporation may believe certain matters should be voted on personally by the shareholders.

Special meetings can be called by the board of directors or by one-tenth of the shareholders. The call for a special meeting is addressed to the secretary of the corporation. Then the procedure in the bylaws for calling a meeting is followed, and the meeting takes place.

A notice must be sent to the shareholders. Publicly traded stock can change hands very quickly. How does a corporation decide who should receive notice of a meeting? The board of directors must set the **record date** or close the stock transfer ledger. The board decides that whoever owns stock on a certain date will be entitled to vote at the next election. Even if a stockholder sells her stock after the record date, she can vote at the meeting.

The record date is set far enough in advance of the meeting to give the corporation time to organize the meeting. A list of the record owners must be compiled. This is called a **voting list**. The voting list must be alphabetical, and contain the addresses of the stockholders and the number of shares they own. The purpose of the voting list is to allow shareholders to contact each other prior to the meeting.

After the record date is set and the voting list is prepared, notice to each shareholder must be sent not less than ten days, nor more than sixty days, prior to the meeting. The Model Business Corporation Act allows more time if extraordinary matters will be considered at the meeting. If notice is not proper, it renders the meeting invalid; any action taken at an invalid meeting can be challenged.

Some corporations, particularly small corporations with very few shareholders, simply have the shareholders sign a waiver of notice at the beginning of the meeting. The waiver of notice must be kept in the minute book. If there are few shareholders, a record date is not needed.

For the publicly held corporation, substantial lead time is required to organize a shareholder meeting. The preparations for the next year begin right after the annual meeting is over. The best thing to do is to create a timetable and a checklist and to adhere to them. Things that must be done include:

1. Ordering supplies, such as envelopes for mailing the notices and proxies
2. Preparing and distributing proxy materials for both directors and shareholders
3. Reserving a meeting place
4. Determining availability of nominees
5. Notifying interested parties of the record date (banks, brokers, proxy agents, nominees)
6. Mailing documents and filing fees to the Securities and Exchange Commission
7. Mailing proxy material, the annual report, and an agenda to the shareholders, other interested parties, and the Securities and Exchange Commission
8. Holding the annual meeting
9. Sending postmeeting reports to the shareholders.

Arranging and holding an annual meeting of a publicly held corporation is a monumental task. The chairperson sometimes uses a script so that all necessary items are considered in an orderly fashion. The script should anticipate questions and should have answers summarized. This portion of the script is used merely as a guide for the chair.

Each outstanding share of stock is entitled to one vote unless the articles of incorporation state otherwise. The articles may have established **weighted voting**, whereby certain classes of stock may have more or less than one vote–one share. Shareholders also may be put into voting groups based upon the type of stock they hold. For example, preferred stock may be given voting rights on certain matters or may have been given greater voting rights. This, of course, must be set out in the articles of incorporation.

One of the most important business items at a shareholder meeting is the election of directors. The articles of incorporation can leave other matters to the shareholders to decide as well. In a close corporation, the shareholders may act as the board of directors and thus make all decisions regarding the corporation.

A corporation may allow the election of directors by cumulative voting. This allows minority representation on the board (see prior discussion and Chapter 7). With cumulative voting, each share carries as many votes as there are vacancies on the board. If four directors will be elected and if a shareholder has 100 shares of stock, she has 400 votes to cast. These 400 votes can be cast in any way the shareholder decides. Thus, if several minority shareholders combine in a voting trust or agreement, they may be able to elect at least one director to the board.

Shareholders can remove directors with or without cause. Bases to remove directors should be included in the bylaws. If the directors were elected by cumulative voting, they must be removed in the same manner. Otherwise, a director elected by minority shareholders could be removed by the majority shareholders immediately after the election.

Shareholders have the right to vote on such matters as mergers, consolidations, dissolution, or other structural changes to the corporation. These matters affect their ownership interest in the corporation. Amendment of the articles of incorporation is also a structural change. The Model Business Corporation Act historically required a two-thirds vote for such actions, but now requires only a majority vote. State law determines the required vote, particularly for dissolution. Also, the corporation's bylaws can set the vote required for unusual matters.

The Model Business Corporation Act permits action to be taken by the board of directors or shareholders without a meeting. The Act sets up a written consent procedure. However, this consent must be unanimous. The Act permits the articles of incorporation to restrict this procedure for directors, but it does not allow restriction of this procedure for shareholders. Most states have some comparable procedure.

The requirements to use this type of procedure are that it must be a matter that properly could have been before a regular meeting and that unanimous, written consent must have been given. Some states allow less than unanimous consent or allow the articles to provide for less than unanimous consent.

For large corporations with many shareholders, this procedure would be impractical and burdensome. For them, the vote must be unanimous, and the signature of each shareholder must be obtained.

Minutes

Minutes must be kept for all meetings of the corporation, whether directors or shareholders, special or regular. The secretary of the corporation is responsible for maintaining the minute book. Some corporations have the corporate attorney keep the minutes.

The minutes of each meeting should reflect that all statutory requirements were met. The minutes should contain:

1. Name of the corporation
2. Date of the meeting

3. Place where the meeting was held

4. Under what authority the meeting was called (whether by the articles, bylaws, or statute)

5. Persons present, absent, and shares represented in person or by proxy

6. Statement that the meeting is being held pursuant to a notice or waiver of notice (attach the waivers to the minutes)

7. Nature of the meeting (whether regular or special)

8. Approval of the previous meeting minutes

9. Substance of the matters presented and how and by whom they were presented

10. Decision made on each matter in resolution form

11. Copies of all reports, if submitted in writing, or a summary of reports if submitted orally

12. Summary of any other business submitted at the meeting.

For the directors' meetings, it is important to record in the minutes how each director voted on each resolution.

As previously stated, the corporate minute book should contain the articles of incorporation that were filed with the secretary of state, the bylaws, the bank resolution, and the minutes of all organizational meetings of the incorporators and initial board of directors. Minutes are important, as shown in the *Freestate Land* case.

Freestate Land Corp. v. Bostetter, 440 A.2d 380 (Md. 1982)

Action by executors of the estate of a corporate promoter against the corporation and individuals to declare null and void certain actions by the officers and alleging fraudulent conveyance of real estate.

Freestate Land Corp. was set up by Bostetter to take title to a farm Bostetter was selling as assignee of a mortgage. Bostetter was the assignee for purposes of foreclosure and collection. The incorporators of Freestate were to be the initial directors until the first annual meeting. No minutes of an organizational meeting have ever been found. Bostetter told Oliver he was president, and Oliver signed a note on behalf of Freestate to Bostetter for the farm. Rents were collected from the farm and deposited in Bostetter's trust account. Bostetter wrote checks to Freestate and delivered records of Freestate to Oliver. Freestate never issued stock until after Bostetter's death.

After Bostetter's death, his son, the personal representative of the estate, sued the corporation on the note. Judgment was entered in favor of the estate. His son held an organizational meeting of the corporation and procured a conveyance of the farm to himself individually.

Subsequent to this, Freestate sued Bostetter's son, seeking an injunction against the son to refrain from acting in the name of the corporation, to declare the deed to the son a nullity, and an accounting. The trial court found that the estate was the owner of Freestate.

The maxim that all things shall be presumed to have been rightly and correctly done, until the contrary is proved, extends to the organization proceedings, and hence the corporation will be presumed to have been duly organized where it proceeds to act as a corporation.

Id. at 385.

The real question is who is entitled to own the stock of Freestate. We come down to the fact that there is no proof here in any way that Bostetter either divested himself of the right to be a stockholder or divested himself of stock. In light of the concessions made, it follows that Bostetter's estate is the owner of the corporation and that stock should be issued accordingly.

Key Terms

Minutes	Record date
Notice of meeting	Special meeting
Organizational meeting	Voting list
Quorum	Weighted voting

Quiz

1. Briefly describe what transpires at the organizational meeting of the incorporator(s) and directors.

2. Describe what is meant by a record date and its effect for purposes of shareholder meetings.

3. List those matters on which shareholders have the right to vote.

4. List the documents that generally should be attached to the minutes of the organizational meeting.

5. Briefly define and explain what a voting list is.

6. Describe the procedure and timeline for organizing a shareholder meeting.

10 Other Corporate Forms

Previous chapters reviewed the basic corporate form and structure. This chapter examines different corporate forms that do not always conform to the standards for corporations, such as close corporations, professional corporations, Subchapter S corporations, Subchapter C qualified stock, and Section 1244 stock.

Close Corporations

A **close corporation** is owned by a small group of shareholders. Close corporations are sometimes referred to as privately held, closely held, or family corporations. Shareholders often are friends or relatives. Family businesses typically are close corporations. They operate with substantial shareholder participation. However, the business enterprise operated by a close corporation is not necessarily small—it may be quite lucrative.

A close corporation is formed and operated under the corporate statutes. Therefore, close corporations must be allowed by statute in a particular state before this structure can be used. The flexibility in the statutes for close corporations allows the corporation to dispense with formal shareholder meetings and to dispense with the board of directors. Shareholders are given management authority in the articles of incorporation. Also, statutes usually require greater than the normal voting requirements. A two-thirds or three-quarters vote is most often required.

There are certain requirements set out in the Statutory Supplement to the Model Business Corporation Act that a close corporation must observe to maintain its status. The articles of incorporation must state that it is a close corporation. There must be fifty or fewer shareholders, and the shares of stock cannot be publicly traded. The words "close corporation" must be placed on each certificate.

The shares of a close corporation are subject to restrictions on transfer. The Model Business Corporation Act provides that shareholders can transfer their shares to other shareholders, other family members, or persons approved in writing by the other shareholders. The Act also allows transfers to executors when a shareholder dies, to trustees in the event of a bankruptcy of a shareholder, in mergers and other business combinations where stock usually is exchanged, and as collateral for a loan. Otherwise, a shareholder must offer the shares to the corporation first. If the corporation does not purchase the shares, then they can be offered to an outsider. However, the outsider must be eligible to become a shareholder. A close corporation can provide in the articles of incorporation that the corporation *must* purchase the shares of a deceased shareholder. This ensures that the status of the close corporation cannot be defeated by heirs of the deceased shareholder.

There are fundamental, statutory differences between a corporation and a close corporation. Most states require at least a two-thirds majority vote. This is because shareholders actively participate in the decisions of the corporation, and shareholders usually have management authority. Also, shareholders have authority to dissolve the corporation at will or upon the happening of some specific event. The statutes governing close corporations protect the corporation from piercing of the corporate veil because of failure to follow certain formalities. The Model Business Corporation Act allows close corporations to suspend the normal formalities. The Act also protects close corporations from having personal liability imposed on the shareholders.

A close corporation is managed like a sole proprietorship or a partnership. However, because it is a corporation, it still must meet the statutory requirements of corporations.

Some states have enacted statutes that specifically dispense with some of the legal requirements for a close corporation.

There may be more judicial supervision with a close corporation. Because of shareholder management, there may be more disputes and court actions in a close corporation (see the *Industrial Equipment* case, for example).

Industrial Equipment Co. v. Montague, 80 S.E.2d 114 (S.C. 1954)

This is an action by a corporation against a former officer and stockholder for alleged conversion of corporate funds, alleged unauthorized salary payments, alleged personal debt due the corporation, and for alleged sale of automobiles to the corporation at a price above their value. The trial court found for the defendant, and the corporation appealed.

Industrial was formerly a partnership of three individuals, one of which was the defendant. It was incorporated, and the partners became the stockholders in the same proportion of ownership that they had as partners. The defendant owned 45% of the corporation. The court found that this corporation was "a close corporation in the popular sense of that term." *Id.* at 115.

This action alleged that the defendant converted to his own use bonus volume checks issued to the corporation, withdrew money from the corporation as unauthorized salary, incurred personal debt to the corporation, and sold used automobiles to the corporation for an exorbitant price. Defendant alleges that the bonus volume checks were used to pay dividends to all stockholders and to pay a bank note; that he received no salary; that he repaid his debt to the corporation on a monthly basis; and that there was no sale of automobiles.

The court found that the funds were the property of the corporation, and the recipients were the stockholders who were the real owners of the funds. In a close corporation, the directors are the stockholders and, therefore, the fiduciary duty of holding corporate property in trust for the owners does not apply. The directors were the owners and could not hold property for themselves in trust. The court did not discuss the legality of paying a dividend that was not declared as such.

Some states require the corporation to elect its close corporation status and continuously qualify as a close corporation. This can make the process difficult for these types of corporations. There may be better alternatives than a close corporation. If the shareholders want management and supervision, a partnership could be more flexible than a close corporation. Alternately, the limited liability company structure may be better suited for the business, because the shareholders would have management control as well as limited liability.

Professional Corporations

Most professions were at one time prohibited from operating as corporations. This was due mostly to that fact that states did not want professionals to shield themselves from liability through a corporation. States began allowing **professional corporations** in 1961. However, the Internal Revenue Service (IRS) did not recognize professional corporations until 1969 for tax purposes. In 1979, the Model Professional Corporation Act was adopted.

Professional corporation statutes were enacted to allow professionals to establish pension and retirement plans that were available only to corporate employees. However, tax code changes in the 1980s eliminated this need. Changes such as individual retirement accounts and Keogh plans now offer the same benefits.

Professional corporation statutes vary widely from state to state. Some states include the authority to incorporate with other business regulation statutes. Other states include these regulations in their supreme court rules.

All states allow the creation of professional corporations for attorneys, physicians, and dentists. Most states include accountants, veterinarians, psychologists, engineers, and architects. A few states also allow registered nurses, physical therapists, pharmacists, and marriage counselors to incorporate.

Only those persons licensed in a profession may form a professional corporation. The purpose of the professional corporation is to practice a single profession. The Model Business Corporation Act allows for joint professions to incorporate if allowed by state statute.

A professional corporation has most of the same powers as a regular corporation; however, a professional corporation cannot be a general partner, a promoter, or an entity associated with a partnership, joint venture, or trust. A professional corporation can engage only in the business stated in the articles of incorporation, which is the business of the specific profession.

Like a corporation or other business entity, most states require that the professional corporation designate that it is a professional corporation. Designations such as "Professional Corporation," "Professional Association," "Service Corporation," or the abbreviations P.C., P.A., or S.C. are allowed.

Share ownership is restricted to persons in the profession. Shares can be transferred only to those licensed within the profession. The share certificates must state on their face that this is a professional corporation, just like the close corporation.

Most states do not allow professionals to hide behind the corporate structure to defeat or limit malpractice claims. States require professionals to be personally liable for improper acts. (See the *Bar Association of Hawaii* case.) However, the other shareholders usually are protected from the malpractice of one shareholder.

Petition of the Bar Association of Hawaii for Adoption of a Rule Permitting Professional Incorporation of Attorneys, 516 P.2d 1267 (Haw. 1973)

The Supreme Court of Hawaii adopted the bar association's petition to allow attorneys to incorporate.

> We are mindful that petitioner's principal motive in seeking permission for its members to incorporate is to enable the attorneys of this State to qualify for the federal tax advantages which would accompany such incorporation.

Id. at 1268.

The court did not allow the rule on limitation of liability. The court found that the Code of Professional Responsibility did not permit the limitation of an attorney's individual liability to his client. The court further found that this absence of limitation of liability should not affect the corporate nature for tax purposes. It went on to set out the new rules for professional corporations.

Most state statutes and the Model Business Corporation Act provide that any privilege that exists between a professional and a client or a patient is preserved in the professional corporation. This privilege extends to the professional corporation as a whole.

All directors and officers of a professional corporation must be licensed to practice the particular profession. For example, in a professional corporation formed by lawyers, only lawyers can own shares of stock, sit on the board of directors, or hold an office in the corporation.

Professional corporations have all the same rights and responsibilities as a normal corporation. The professional corporation must keep its professional status and purpose. The professional corporation must also observe the requirements for shareholder qualifications. A professional corporation can evolve into a normal corporation if it ceases to render professional services.

The Model Business Corporation Act allows foreign professional corporations. The foreign professional corporation, of course, must comply with all state laws governing professional corporations and regular corporations.

Subchapter S Corporations

A **Subchapter S corporation** is a small business corporation. Subchapter S refers to the IRS Code sections that regulate this type of corporation for tax purposes: 26 U.S.C. §§ 1361–1379. A Subchapter S corporation is formed, operated, and dissolved in the same way as a regular corporation. If the corporation meets certain requirements, it may notify the IRS of its election to be taxed as a partnership. Income is passed through directly to the shareholders and taxed as personal income, so there is no double taxation. This is beneficial when the individual shareholder's tax rates are lower than the corporate tax rates. However, profits, whether distributed or not, must be claimed as income to the individual shareholders.

There are IRS requirements that must be met to qualify as a small business corporation:

- It must be a domestic corporation.
- There can be no more than seventy-five shareholders (a husband and wife count as one shareholder for this calculation).
- All shareholders must be natural persons.
- The corporation can issue only one class of stock.
- The corporation cannot have nonresident aliens as shareholders.
- The corporation cannot hold more than 80 percent of another corporation's stock.

Shareholders must make an affirmative election to be a Subchapter S corporation (see Figure 10-1). The resolution for the election usually is voted on at the organizational meeting of the board of directors and presented to the shareholders for their approval. This election must be done right away after the business is incorporated. If the corporation decides to withdraw its Subchapter S election, it cannot reelect to be a Sub S until five years have passed.

A Subchapter S designation is economically beneficial if there are losses. Most small business are not profitable right away. Therefore, if the shareholders have other income, it can be advantageous to pass through losses to the shareholders. The losses can be offset against other income pursuant to current IRS tax provisions. Another advantage of Subchapter S designation is that if the shareholders' tax rates are lower than the corporate rate, the corporation's income is taxed at the lower rate. This is because the income is taxed directly to the shareholders rather than to the corporation. The shareholders are taxed whether or not they actually receive the profits. However, the shareholder's lower tax bracket is advantageous if the corporation wants to accumulate profits for some future business purpose.

The Subchapter S designation terminates if the corporation ceases to qualify as a Subchapter S corporation or by a majority vote of the shareholders. Also, a corporation ceases to be a Subchapter S corporation if it receives 25 percent or more of its income for three consecutive years from passive income. *Passive income* includes such things as royalties, rents, dividends, or interest.

Section 1244 Stock

Section 1244 stock is another type of election for special tax treatment. It applies to shares issued by a small corporation that qualifies for ordinary loss treatment. Section 1244 refers to the section of the Internal Revenue Code that regulates this type of election: 26 U.S.C. § 1244.

A share of stock is a capital asset and may result in taxable gain or loss when sold. Usually, a capital loss on the sale of stock can be offset only against any capital gain that a taxpayer has in the same tax year. To some extent, capital losses can be offset against ordinary income for individual taxpayers, but some of the loss must be carried forward. By

FIGURE 10-1   Subchapter S Election form

| Form **2553**
(Rev. February 1987)

Department of the Treasury
Internal Revenue Service | **Election by a Small Business Corporation**
(Under section 1362 of the Internal Revenue Code)
▶ **For Paperwork Reduction Act Notice, see page 1 of instructions.**
▶ **See separate instructions.** | OMB No. 1545-0146

Expires 1-31-89 |

Note: *This election, to be treated as an "S corporation," can be approved only if all the tests in Instruction B are met.*

Part I   Election Information

Name of corporation (see instructions)	Employer identification number (see instructions)	Principal business activity and principal product or service (see instructions)
Number and street		Election is to be effective for tax year beginning (month, day, year)
City or town, state and ZIP code		Number of shares issued and outstanding (see instructions)

Is the corporation the outgrowth or continuation of any form of predecessor? . . . . ☐ **Yes**   ☐ **No** | Date and place of incorporation

If "Yes," state name of predecessor, type of organization, and period of its existence ▶ . . . .

A   If this election takes effect for the first tax year the corporation exists, enter the earliest of the following: (1) date the corporation first had shareholders (2) date the corporation first had assets, or (3) date the corporation began doing business. ▶

B   Selected tax year: Annual return will be filed for tax year ending (month and day) ▶ . . . .

See instructions before entering your tax year. If the tax year ends any date other than December 31, you must complete Part II or Part IV on back. You may want to complete Part III to make a back-up request.

C Name of each shareholder, person having a community property interest in the corporation's stock, and each tenant in common, joint tenant, and tenant by the entirety. (A husband and wife (and their estates) are counted as one shareholder in determining the number of shareholders without regard to the manner in which the stock is owned.)	**D** Shareholders' Consent Statement. We, the undersigned shareholders, consent to the corporation's election to be treated as an "S corporation" under section 1362(a). (Shareholders sign and date below.)"	**E** Stock owned		**F** Social security number (employer identification number for estates or trust)	**G** Tax year ends (month and day)
		Number of shares	Dates acquired		

*For this election to be valid, the **consent of each shareholder**, person having a community property interest in the corporation's stock, and each tenant in common, **joint tenant**, and **tenant by the entirety** must either appear above or be attached to this form. (See instructions for Column D, if continuation sheet or a separate consent statement is needed.)

Under penalties of perjury, I declare that I have examined this election, including accompanying schedules, and statements, and to the best of my knowledge and belief, it is true, correct, and complete.

contrast, Section 1244 stock can be offset against ordinary income without having to carry it forward. Therefore, the individual taxpayer can deduct the entire capital loss in the same tax year against ordinary income.

Qualifications for small business stock are different than for Subchapter S corporations. Designation as Section 1244 stock depends on the amount of money to be raised by the sale of stock and the amount of existing equity. The amount of stock offered and the amounts received as contributions of capital or paid surplus cannot exceed $1 million.

To qualify, a corporation must acquire more than 50 percent of its income from other than passive income. Passive income is derived from such sources as royalties, rents, dividends, and interest. The business must comply with this provision after the stock is issued and for five years before an investor sustains a loss. The Internal Revenue Code (IRC) has repealed the provision requiring a small business to have a written plan before issuing Section 1244 stock. However, it is always a good idea to have a written plan or a resolution specifically stating that the stock is being issued pursuant to Section 1244.

If all requirements of the Code are met, capital loss on the stock will receive ordinary loss treatment if a loss is incurred when the stock is sold. This, of course, can be very advantageous to a individual stockholder.

Qualified Small Business Stock

Section C of the Internal Revenue Code provides for qualified small business stock. This section is found at 26 U.S.C. § 1202.

A **qualified small business** is called a **Subchapter C** corporation. A Subchapter C corporation must have less than $50 million of aggregate capital on the date the shares are issued. At least 80 percent of the value of the corporate assets must be used in an active trade or business. Usually, an active trade or business does not include a corporation whose principal asset is the skill of one or more of its employees. Therefore, a professional corporation will not qualify as a Subchapter C corporation.

If a corporation qualifies as a Subchapter C corporation, it can issue qualified small business stock. Individual shareholders can hold this stock for more than five years and exclude one-half of any gain from the sale or exchange of the shares. The other one-half of the gain is taxed at the normal capital gains tax rate. The net effect is the shareholder pays only half the tax rate. This is a major tax advantage if the company grows during those five years and if the value of the stock increases.

Subchapter C corporations still have the same tax advantages of regular corporations. Necessary expenses can be deducted by the corporation. These types of expenses may include incentive programs or fringe benefits for the corporation's employees. *Fringe benefits* are such things as health, life, and accident insurance; qualified pension and profit-sharing plans; and share options. These expenses can be deducted even if the employees are also shareholders.

Also, the tax disadvantages of corporations fall to some of these corporations as well. As discussed previously, the major tax disadvantage is double taxation. The corporation pays income taxes; if the corporation declares a dividend, the shareholder pays income tax on the dividend.

Key Terms

Close corporation

Professional corporation

Qualified small business

Section 1244 stock

Subchapter C

Subchapter S corporation

Quiz

1. Briefly define and describe the characteristics of a close corporation.

2. Describe the way(s) in which close corporations differ from standard corporations.

3. What are the requirements to establish a professional corporation? Explain briefly.

4. How is the liability of professionals who incorporate limited? Discuss briefly.

5. Define a Subchapter S corporation and discuss the requirements for its creation.

6. Briefly describe Section 1244 stock.

7. Briefly explain the nature of and requirements to create a Subchapter C corporation.

11 Extraordinary Corporate Matters

A corporation may want to change its corporate structure in some way. A corporation even may dissolve its corporate status. When a corporation changes its structure, this is called **extraordinary corporate activity**. It is outside the scope of normal corporate business or routine. Extraordinary activity includes amending the articles of incorporation, merger or consolidation, sale or mortgage of assets, and dissolution. Shareholders may have the right to vote on these matters, as their ownership rights will be affected.

Amendment of the Articles of Incorporation

A corporation can make any amendment to its articles of incorporation that would have been permitted in the original articles. Some amendments can be accomplished by the board of directors alone. Others must be approved by vote of the shareholders. The Model Business Corporation Act allows the following to be done without shareholder approval:

1. Delete the original directors
2. If there has been a change in the registered agent and the change is on file with the secretary of state, the board may delete the original registered agent
3. Extend the duration of existence
4. Change the corporate name by substituting *company, corporation,* or *incorporated,* or an abbreviation of any of these words
5. Change issued and unissued authorized shares of an outstanding class of stock into a greater number of whole shares if the corporation has only one class of stock outstanding
6. Make any other changes permitted by statute by the board of directors.

The incorporators of the corporation may decide that shareholders should approve all changes to the articles. If so, the articles of incorporation must deny the board of directors the power to adopt such amendments.

The board of directors adopts a resolution stating the specific amendment to the articles. The resolution also will state that it is to be submitted to the shareholders at a special meeting or annual meeting. Those shareholders who own stock with voting rights on the record date are allowed to vote. However, a class of stock without voting rights is allowed to vote on any amendment that would affect those shares of stock.

Some state statutes provide that shareholders can initiate a change to the articles of incorporation. A specific number of shareholders is required (10 or 15 percent, for example). They can petition the board to adopt a resolution to put the amendment before the shareholders or can request the president to call a meeting of the shareholders.

The articles of incorporation may contain a provision that requires a greater percentage of approval than normal on routine matters. It could be two-thirds or three-quarters. Also, a particular state statute may require a higher percentage for approval. The Model Business Corporation Act requires only a majority vote.

All changes to the articles of incorporation must be filed with the secretary of state. If the original articles had to be filed with any local government agency, the changes must be filed there also. If the original articles have been changed several times, the corporation can file a **restatement of the articles of incorporation**. This makes it easier to determine what a corporation's articles currently state without having to go through many amendments. Many states require shareholder approval to file a restatement.

The requirement for shareholder approval, combined with these procedures, demonstrates why the original articles of incorporation should be as broad as possible.

Disposition of Substantially All Assets

A corporation is allowed to sell, mortgage, or otherwise dispose of its assets. However, a corporate shell exists if substantially all assets are sold other than in the ordinary course of business. This is a structural change that requires shareholder approval.

The Model Business Corporation Act provides for certain dispositions of assets that do not require shareholder approval. A corporation can mortgage property without approval. A corporation can dispose of substantially all of its assets in the normal course of business without approval. For example, a manufacturing company that sells its inventory routinely disposes of its assets. The inventory is the greatest asset of the company, but the company is in the business of selling its inventory. The following transactions do not require shareholder approval:

- Corporation A transfers all its assets to corporation B when corporation B owns all the shares of corporation A.

- A parent corporation transfers all its assets to a subsidiary.

The Act requires shareholder approval for the **disposition of substantially all the corporation's assets** not in the ordinary course of business.

The procedure for obtaining approval in this situation is the same as for obtaining approval of amendments to the articles of incorporation. The board adopts a resolution and sends it to the shareholders for approval.

The Uniform Commercial Code (UCC) regulates **bulk transfers** of goods. The UCC contains procedures that protect creditors from a corporation transferring its inventory. The corporation must prepare a list of all creditors, including the amount owed each creditor and each creditor's address, and the property being transferred. The creditors must be notified in writing. The purchaser of the property must keep the property for six months. This is to ensure that the creditors are paid. Bulk sale statutes vary from state to state. Some states do not required notice to be given to creditors (Texas, for example). Investigation of appropriate state statutes is needed to ensure proper compliance.

Merger, Consolidation, or Exchange

A corporation may extend or reorganize its business through merger, consolidation, or exchange of assets with another corporation. The corporations involved are called **constituent corporations**.

A **merger** takes place when one or more corporations merge into another corporation. The corporation that merges into the other corporation ceases to exist. The merged corporation becomes the surviving corporation and continues to exist. Corporation A merges into B; B still exists. The surviving corporation takes over the assets, liabilities, business activities, and stockholders of the merging corporations; however, exact details depend entirely upon the business regulations and upon the structure of the deal. Usually, the surviving corporation issues shares of stock and pays consideration to the shareholders of the corporation that ceases to exist.

A **consolidation** occurs when two or more corporations form a new corporation. For example, corporations A and B consolidate to form corporation C. The Model Business Corporation Act makes no reference to consolidation. In the modern business environment, it generally is more advantageous to have one corporation continue to exist. However, most states still refer to consolidations in their statutes.

An **exchange** takes place when two or more corporations exchange some or all of their stock with each other. All corporations continue to exist. By this method, at least one corporation seeks a controlling interest in the other corporation(s).

The IRS treats mergers, consolidations, and exchanges as reorganizations. A **type A reorganization** is a statutory merger or consolidation; a **type B reorganization** is an exchange; and a **type C reorganization** is when stock is traded for assets, which is not considered an exchange.

Consolidations, mergers, and exchanges affect shareholders, who receive either stock in the new corporation or money. Thus, they have a right to approve these structural changes.

The procedure begins when the boards of directors for all corporations involved adopt a resolution. The resolution must state the names of all the corporations, the terms, how shares will be converted, and any changes to the articles of incorporation for the surviving corporation. It often takes months or years of negotiations before the boards adopt the necessary resolutions. Also, letters of intent are exchanged between constituent corporations. Then, as for other structural changes, the resolution is submitted to the shareholders of each corporation at a special or annual meeting. The vote required could be a majority vote or more, depending on the statutes of the jurisdiction.

The Model Business Corporation Act requires shareholder approval unless it is either a small impact merger or a short-form merger. A **small impact merger** occurs when the surviving corporation does not change its articles of incorporation or the shares of stock owned by its shareholders and does not increase its outstanding stock by more than 20 percent as a result of the merger. The shareholders of the surviving corporation are not required to vote, because the merger has such a small impact on their rights. At most, the ownership interests will be decreased by 20 percent, they are otherwise unaffected.

A **short-form merger** takes place between a parent corporation and a subsidiary in which the parent owns at least 90 percent of the shares of the subsidiary. The parent is allowed to merge the subsidiary into the parent without shareholder approval from either corporation. The vote would be meaningless in any event, as the parent corporation would vote at least 90 percent of the subsidiary's stock.

Mergers, consolidations, and exchanges necessarily require amendments to articles of incorporation. **Articles of merger, consolidation, or exchange** must be filed with the secretary of state after shareholder approval is obtained. The articles should include the terms and conditions of the plan, approval of the shareholders or a statement that no approval was required, and the number of votes cast for and against the plan. Once each corporation has filed its articles, the state will issue the respective certificate.

The constituent corporations become a single entity. The surviving or new corporation has all the powers, assets, and liabilities (see the *Steele* case, for example).

Steele v. Missouri Pacific Railroad, 659 P.2d 217 (Kan. 1983)

This action started as an eminent domain proceeding. The railroad was acquiring property in Kansas. The plaintiffs had sought an injunction but failed. In this action the plaintiffs allege that the railroad did not follow the procedures for merging and, therefore, had no authority in Kansas to acquire property. The Missouri corporation merged into a Delaware corporation.

The Kansas statutes governing the sale of railroads require the corporation to file a certified copy of a resolution of its board of directors designating a resident process agreement and stipulating that said company shall be subject to the provisions of the statutes. The trial court found that there was a merger, not a sale. "Under Kansas law, a merger of two corporations results in a transfer of the property to the new corporation which retains the name and corporate identity and assumes the rights and responsibilities of the former corporation." *Id.* at 223. The court found there was no sale and, therefore, compliance with the provisions of the statutes was unnecessary.

Recently, many corporations have decided to revert to private ownership from public ownership, using **leveraged buyouts**. The management of a corporation purchases all outstanding shares held by the public, thereby gaining control over the corporation. This is a risky transaction. It usually requires incurring a large debt by borrowing against the assets of the corporation. This can be done through issuance of bonds or through a bank or investment loan. Some corporations do not survive a leveraged buyout.

Hostile Takeovers

Not all mergers, consolidations, or exchanges are achieved through negotiation. A corporation or individual may try to take over the operation of a corporation by using statutory rules against the will of the corporation and its shareholders. This is known as a **hostile takeover**.

A corporation may be perceived as profitable, or an individual or corporation may want to change management. If a stock is publicly traded, enough stock must be purchased to gain a controlling interest in the corporation. Once there is control, a new board of directors is elected; thereafter the business is managed and controlled according to the wishes of the controlling interest.

A unique vocabulary has developed to describe the dynamics of a hostile takeover. The investors who purchase controlling shares to cause corporate action are called **sharks**. A shark often seeks control of a corporation to cause a merger or exchange. The new, controlling investors can abuse their power by selling back the shares of stock at a premium. This is known as **greenmail**. Because they now control the corporation, they frequently can make a substantial return on their investment, particularly if the acquired corporation is profitable.

There are defenses a corporation can take to stop a hostile takeover or to make the corporation not as attractive to others. The first are corporate structure defenses. A corporation, if it perceives a threat of takeover, can alter its stock structure to give existing stockholders extra rights. This is called a **poison pill**. Only existing shareholders get these rights. A corporation would issue a new class of stock with greater rights and would issue these to existing shareholders through a stock dividend. This new class of stock could be bought back by the corporation (neutralizing the poison) if there is a friendly takeover.

Another corporate structure defense is the **people pill**, also known as a **suicide pact**. Management agrees that if anyone is fired or demoted, management will resign. It could be devastating to a corporation if all knowledgeable managers leave at the same time.

State statutory rules also can protect a corporation from hostile takeovers. These rules are called **shark repellent**. One such statutory scheme does not allow the new owners of the controlling shares to vote unless the other shareholders agree. **Controlling shares** are the shares that have voting power sufficient to allow the owner to control the affairs of the corporation, usually a percentage of voting power. It could be triggered at 20 percent, 30 percent, or even 50 percent. It is possible, in a publicly held corporation, that 20 percent of the shares could control the corporation.

Other rules could allow a corporation to buy back control shares at fair market value. This allows a corporation to buy out a hostile investor. Thus, the investor cannot vote the shares to the detriment of the other shareholders.

Another statutory scheme involves affiliated corporations. An **affiliated corporation** is one that owns a sufficient number of shares in another corporation to control the vote. Some state statutes do not allow a merger or consolidation with affiliated corporations unless there is a two-thirds majority approval by the shareholders. This gives existing shareholders protection, as the shark must acquire many more shares in the corporation to effect the takeover. Additionally, a corporation could look for a **white knight**. This is an investor (a person or a corporation) who can buy the corporation on more acceptable terms.

A **tender offer** is another avenue for hostile takeover. The corporation seeking a controlling interest in another corporation is called the aggressor. The corporation to be acquired is known as the target corporation.

The aggressor makes a public offer to all shareholders of the target corporation to purchase shares. **Public offer** means it is advertised and addressed to all shareholders. This offer is a tender offer and usually is higher than the market value. The higher price is used as an inducement to shareholders to sell. The tender offer can be for stock in the aggressor corporation instead of cash. Generally, tender offers are contingent on obtaining a specific number of shares by a specified date. Federal securities laws control tender offer terms and duration.

There are responses the corporation can make against tender offers. The directors can make a recommendation to the shareholders as to whether rejection or acceptance of the offer would be more beneficial. Also, the corporation could make a tender offer to its own shareholders. The corporation also may seek an injunction against the acquiring corporation, if it believes the offer violates antitrust laws.

The period from 1967 to 1970 saw a wave of mergers and acquisitions. Congress responded by adopting the Williams Act of 1968. The Williams Act was a series of amendments to the 1934 Securities Act and was designed to make corporate acquirers or raiders reveal their position. The Act added the requirements that when anyone acquires more than 5 percent of any class of stock of a company registered with the Securities and Exchange Commission (SEC), she must file what is called a Schedule 13D statement. It must describe the purchaser's identity and background, the source of the funds for the purchase, and the purchaser's reasons for acquiring the securities and intentions as to the issuer. The Williams Act requires the same filing for tender offers.

Dissenting Shareholders

What happens to shareholders who do not want to merge, consolidate, or exchange shares or who do not want to sell or mortgage the corporation's assets? Almost one-half of all voting shares can vote against the action, and the action still could be approved. The Model Business Corporation Act gives dissenting shareholders the right to have their shares appraised and purchased by the corporation in certain circumstances. This is called the **right of appraisal**. Most states include rights to dissent and receive payments within the corporate statutes.

The Model Business Corporation Act allows the **right to dissent** in cases of mergers, exchanges, and the sale of substantially all assets not in the ordinary course of business. Also, the right to dissent is allowed when the articles of incorporation are amended and the rights of the shareholders are affected. These changes could be such things as eliminating a preferential right, preemptive rights, redemption rights, or voting rights. The articles, bylaws, or board of directors resolution must provide dissenter rights.

There are important limitations on the rights of dissenters. Shareholders of a surviving corporation whose votes were not necessary to approve the merger are not entitled to the right of dissent and appraisal. The right of appraisal is not offered to holders of shares registered on the national securities exchange under the Model Business Corporation Act. Some states have this same exclusion. The rationale for this rule is that shares registered on the national securities exchange can be readily sold, so the appraisal process is not necessary to establish value.

To dissent and to receive the right of appraisal, the shareholder must follow a specific procedure. The notice of the shareholders meeting must state that shareholders may have the right to dissent and must be accompanied by a copy of the applicable state statute. Then the shareholder must give written notice of her intention to demand payment for shares before the vote is taken at the meeting. Some states require the written notice by the shareholder to be given before the meeting; other states require the notice of dissent to include a demand for appraisal and purchase of the shares. A shareholder who has given notice of dissent cannot vote in favor of the transaction, of course.

Some states have elaborate procedures. If they are not followed exactly, a shareholder will lose the right to dissent and appraisal.

Once the transaction is approved at the shareholder meeting, the dissenting shareholder must make a demand for payment of the fair value of the shares. Each state has a specific time period within which the demand must be made. This demand should be addressed to the surviving corporation in a merger or to the new corporation in a consolidation. A shareholder will lose her right to payment if she does not follow the procedure. She then is bound by the corporate action.

Fair value of the shares must be determined. The Model Business Corporation Act defines *fair value* as the value immediately before the transaction, excluding appreciation or depreciation in anticipation of the transaction. This requires the difficult task of evaluating the impact of publicity surrounding the transaction on the value of the shares. Many states do not follow this evaluation procedure.

Ideally, the corporation and the shareholder will agree on the value. If not, the corporation pays the shareholder what it believes is the fair value plus interest. The payment must include the corporation's financial statement, explanation of how interest was calculated, and a statement of the dissenter's rights.

The corporation looks at when the shares were purchased. If the shares were purchased after the transaction became public, the corporation may not be required to purchase the shares. This prevents shareholders from buying shares just before an extraordinary transaction, purely for the purpose of having an instant market for their shares through dissenter's rights.

If the shareholder disagrees with the corporation's valuation, the shareholder may file her own estimate within thirty days. If the demand is not settled within sixty days, it can be settled through court action. The corporation must file the petition. All dissenters are made parties to the action.

Corporations prefer to have unanimous approval of extraordinary corporate actions. The appraisal process can be very time-consuming and cumbersome for both the corporation and the shareholder.

Voluntary Dissolution

The ultimate extraordinary corporate transaction is the decision to dissolve. Shareholders must approve a voluntary dissolution. A **voluntary dissolution** is the decision by the incorporators, directors, or shareholders to dissolve. Corporations also can be dissolved by the courts or by the state. This is known as an **involuntary dissolution** (discussed later in this chapter).

If the corporation has been incorporated but has not yet transacted any business, the incorporators may dissolve it by filing **articles of dissolution** with the state.

After business has commenced, the decision to dissolve must originate with the board of directors or with the shareholders. If it is the shareholders who wish to dissolve, their unanimous, written consent usually can initiate the dissolution process. All shareholders, whether they generally have voting rights or not, typically participate in the decision to dissolve. This can be an easy procedure, particularly for small corporations that have few shareholders.

Otherwise, the board of directors adopts a resolution in the same manner required for other extraordinary transactions and sends the matter to the shareholders for approval. The Model Business Corporation Act requires only a majority vote by the shareholders to dissolve. Some states require a two-thirds or three-quarters vote.

Most states require a corporation to give advance notice to outsiders of its intent to dissolve. Written notice must be given to creditors. Usually, a statement of intent to dissolve must be filed with the secretary of state. Some states require newspaper publication of the dissolution as well. Once the transaction has been approved, the articles of dissolution are filed. The Model Business Corporation Act requires only the articles of dissolution to be filed; no notice is required. Most states do not allow the filing of the articles of dissolution until the corporation finishes winding up the business. The secretary of state then issues a **certificate of dissolution**.

Shareholders or incorporators can revoke the dissolution. They would follow the same procedure as to dissolve. The shareholders, if they gave written consent to dissolve, must give written consent to revoke. This can be done anytime before the secretary of state issues the certificate of dissolution. If the dissolution was accomplished by resolution of the board of directors and submission to the shareholders, the same procedure is used for its revocation. The corporation must file a **statement of revocation** of the voluntary dissolution.

A dissolved corporation continues to exist until **liquidation** is completed. The corporation usually has business affairs to conclude. It must collect all of its assets and liquidate the business. Creditors already have been put on notice, so they should have filed claims. Creditors must be paid. If a corporation is dissolving because it is insolvent, creditors' claims should be resolved through negotiation.

All expenses of the corporation also should be taken care of during the winding-up process. All contracts must be terminated. If the corporation no longer exists, a contract cannot continue.

Finally, the remaining assets are distributed to the shareholders. These are called **liquidating distributions**. If dividends were declared to a class of stock, but were not paid, those shareholders are creditors to the extent of the accrued and unpaid dividends. These dividends must be paid prior to distribution to shareholders. In addition, there may be preferred stockholders with preferential liquidating distribution rights. If so, they must receive their distribution before common or other stockholders. Whatever assets remain are distributed to shareholders pursuant to their ownership shares in the corporation.

Preferred stockholders could receive more than one distribution at liquidation. The preferential treatment may include a set liquidation distribution, after which the preferred stockholders receive a distribution along with all other shareholders.

In a voluntary dissolution, the liquidation is accomplished by the corporation's management. In a judicial (involuntary) dissolution, the liquidation is handled by a receiver appointed by the court.

Involuntary Dissolution

Involuntary dissolution can be caused by the state, by creditors, or by shareholders through judicial action. The state may force dissolution because the corporation failed to file required documents, such as annual reports; failed to pay fees; or exceeded the authority provided by law. Some states dissolve a corporation for failure to maintain a registered agent, insolvency, antitrust violations, failure to begin the business, or if the corporation's existence is contrary to the public interest. Also, if the articles of incorporation were achieved through fraud, the state can dissolve the corporation.

The Model Business Corporation Act allows the secretary of state to send a notice to the corporation at its registered office or principal place of business. The notice states the alleged violation of state law. The state usually gives the corporation time to cure the defect prior to dissolution. If the corporation does not respond or does not cure the defect, the secretary of state administratively dissolves the corporation and issues a certificate of dissolution. Some states do not allow the corporation to cure the defect; it is simply dissolved.

Shareholders can apply to the court for liquidation. There are several grounds for shareholder actions against the corporation:

- A deadlock of the board of directors that is unbreakable. The shareholders must show irreparable harm to the corporation.

- Oppressive, illegal, or fraudulent acts by the board of directors (this can also be a basis for court liquidation).

- Shareholder deadlock that has caused the corporation not to elect board members for at least two years.

• A Showing of a waste of corporate assets.

If the court determines that the corporation should be dissolved, it will issue a **decree of dissolution** and will appoint a receiver. A **receiver** collects assets, pays creditors, and manages the business during liquidation. The liquidation procedures set out earlier in this chapter will be followed.

In addition, creditors can dissolve a corporation involuntarily. If a creditor has an undisputed claim and the corporation is insolvent, the creditor can go to court and force judicial liquidation. The *Chicago* case shows the interplay of creditors' rights, dissolution, and corporate existence.

Chicago & Northwestern Railway v. Hospers Packing Co., 363 F. Supp. 697 (N.D. Iowa 1973)

This is an action by a railway company to recover freight charges incurred by the defendant, a shipper. The defendant alleges that it had been dissolved and the court has no jurisdiction because of its nonexistence. The defendant alleges that the dissolution was effected by filing the notice of intent to dissolve with the secretary of state and the disposition of substantially all of its assets.

The court found that the Iowa statutes provide that a corporation is not dissolved until a certificate of dissolution is issued by the secretary of state or a decree is entered by a court dissolving the corporation. Neither of these two requirements has happened.

The court further found that this argument is irrelevant because the Iowa statutes governing survival of actions provides that dissolution of a corporation does not take away the rights of a creditor against the corporation if the claim existed, as long as the action was commenced within two years of the dissolution. This action was commenced within the two-year statute of limitations. The claim by the railway was allowed.

Key Terms

Affiliated corporation	Merger
Articles of dissolution	People pill (suicide pact)
Articles of merger, consolidation, or exchange	Poison pill
Bulk transfer	Public offer
Certificate of dissolution	Receiver
Consolidation	Restatement of articles of incorporation
Constituent corporations	Right of appraisal
Controlling shares	Right to dissent
Decree of dissolution	Shark repellent
Disposition of substantially all assets	Sharks
Exchange	Short-form merger
Extraordinary corporate activity	Small impact merger
Greenmail	Statement of revocation
Hostile takeover	Tender offer
Involuntary dissolution	Type A reorganization
Leveraged buyout	Type B reorganization
Liquidating distributions	Type C reorganization
Liquidation	Voluntary dissolution
	White knight

Quiz

1. Briefly explain what is meant by the term "extraordinary corporate matters."

2. List the types of activities that are considered extraordinary in relation to corporations.

3. How does the Uniform Commercial Code protect creditors when a bulk transfer occurs? Explain briefly.

4. Define: (a) merger; (b) consolidation; and (c) exchange.

5. Briefly explain the terms "small impact merger" and "short-form merger."

6. Define the following terms: (a) shark; (b) greenmail; (c) poison pill; (d) people pill; (e) shark repellent; and (f) white knight.

7. Briefly explain what a tender offer is.

8. What can shareholders who do not want to merge, consolidate, or exchange do to protect themselves? Explain briefly.

9. Briefly outline the procedure for voluntary dissolution.

10. Which person(s) or entities can initiate an involuntary dissolution?

12 Financial Structure of a Corporation

Corporations run on capital obtained primarily from investors, creditors, or shareholders. A corporation can borrow money from investors or creditors, or can sell stock to investor shareholders.

When a corporation sells stock to shareholders, the stock is called **equity securities**. When a corporation borrows money, it may issue **debt securities** to the creditor. Both types of securities are discussed in this chapter. The corporation has an obligation to repay debt securities. There is no obligation to pay equity securities.

Equity Securities

Equity securities are intangible personal property evidenced by a stock certificate. The equity securities of a corporation are bought as an investment. An investor can make money either from dividends or from growth of the company.

One who purchases shares in a corporation becomes a part owner of that corporation. When shares are issued, a capital account is created and the money is deposited. In return for their investment, shareholders receive dividends. **Dividends** are income paid on equity securities. In contrast, *interest* is income paid to holders of debt securities (discussed later in this chapter).

If an investor wants earnings (dividends), he will buy stock in an established, publicly traded company that has a history of paying dividends. In contrast, if an investor is interested in what he ultimately can sell the stock for, he will buy stock in a company that is growth-oriented.

Investors also may purchase equity securities for control of the corporation. Investors may want the ability to declare dividends and have a voice in the direction the company takes.

The Securities and Exchange Commission (SEC) regulates publicly traded securities. There are two federal securities acts that regulate the issuance and sale of securities. The Securities Act of 1933, 15 U.S.C. § 77a, establishes the disclosure requirements for the public sale of shares or bonds. The Securities Exchange Act of 1934, 15 U.S.C. § 78a, protects potential investors by making sure they are fully informed about the investment and regulates the information so that no misleading or untrue statements are made concerning the securities. Most states have what are known as **blue sky laws**. These laws also govern the sale of public shares to protect the potential investor.

Becoming an equity security holder gives the investor ownership rights. These rights include the right to dividends if declared by the board, the right to a distribution of corporate assets upon dissolution, and the right to vote on corporate matters.

A corporation's articles of incorporation will state the number of shares that the corporation has authority to issue. The number stated in the articles is called **authorized shares**. A corporation does not have to issue all of its authorized shares. To keep the articles flexible, a corporation may want to authorize more shares than it intends to issue initially. Once shares have been purchased by shareholders, the shares are issued and outstanding. Shares that are fully active (carrying the rights to receive dividends, vote, and distribution at liquidation) are authorized, issued, and outstanding.

The articles of incorporation may state a par value for the shares of stock. Many small corporations use a low par value. Stock must be sold for at least the par value stated in the articles. If it is sold for less than the stated par value, it is **watered stock** or **discount stock**. Shareholders could become liable for the difference between what they paid and the par value. The Model Business Corporation Act does not require a specific value that must be stated as par value in the articles; however, some states do require a statutory minimum par value.

Shares may be repurchased by a corporation. If so, the shares become authorized and issued, but not outstanding. These shares are called **treasury shares**. Treasury shares can be sold again to shareholders. The board of directors sets the value for treasury shares. This is known as **stated value**.

The board of directors can set the value of all shares. Shares can be sold at higher than par value. However, the corporation must take care not to dilute its shares. **Diluted shares** are those sold at a higher price than the most recent price.

> Sue Smith buys stock in Corporation A for $100 a share. The corporation finds another equity investor, Jennifer Adams, who is willing to pay $110 a share. Jennifer Adams has now purchased diluted shares. She paid more than Sue Smith, but she does not get any more or greater rights of ownership.

The corporation may be liable to Jennifer Adams for her diluted shares. However, if Sue and Jennifer did not buy their shares at the same time, the corporation may be able to justify the difference in price due to an increase in the value of the shares between the time of one purchase and the time of the other. Of course, this does not apply to stocks traded on an exchange. The market and other economic influences determine the price of shares sold on the exchange.

When setting the par value in the articles of incorporation, the tax laws of the state of incorporation must be taken into account. Some states charge fees, known as *franchise fees*, based on the aggregate authorized capital. The aggregate capital is the amount stated in the articles. If the par value set in the articles is no par, some states will set an arbitrary value. If this value is low, such as $1 for no par, a corporation could authorize more shares. For example, a corporation could authorize 10,000 shares at no par, which would be assessed the same fee as 1,000 shares at $10. Some states discourage the use of no par value by setting the value much higher. If that is not the case, it may be more advantageous, for tax purposes, for a corporation to have more authorized shares at a lower par value.

Several types of accounts exist on a corporation's ledger. The **stated capital account** is where the capital generated from the sale of stock appears. The par-value amount is put into this account. The excess that is collected over par value goes into an account called **capital surplus**. Most states require that a corporation have money in its capital surplus account before it can buy treasury shares. Therefore, this may be an account that a corporation sets up early. The Model Business Corporation Act does not include this requirement.

The **earned surplus account** is where the profits of the corporation appear. The obligations of the corporation are paid from this account. Also, if there is preferred stock that requires periodic dividends, this amount is restricted earned surplus. Most states require that there be unrestricted funds in this account before a dividend is declared by the board of directors.

Share Certificates   When shares are sold, certificates usually are issued to represent ownership of those shares. Some stock is uncertificated. This means that ownership will appear on the books of the corporation, but no document will be issued to the shareholder. Some stock that is publicly traded can be bought and sold numerous times, even on a single trading day. It would be a bookkeeping nightmare if certificates had to be issued for each shareholder. However, because most corporations are small businesses, and their stock is not traded on the exchange, the shareholder usually receives a certificate evidencing their ownership.

The Model Business Corporation Act requires that each certificate must be signed by two officers and bear the seal of the corporation. These officers who can sign may be authorized in the bylaws or may be designated by the board of directors. The Act permits either manual or facsimile signatures. In addition, each certificate must bear the name of the corporation, the name of the state in which the corporation was organized, and the number and class of shares the certificate represents. If there are several classes and a series within the class of stock, this also must be designated on the shares. The rights given to each class and series must be designated on the shares as well.

Common Stock   Common stock is the basic class of stock. If a corporation has only one class of stock, it will be common stock. One class of stock must have full voting rights; usually, it is common stock. Other classes of stock can be issued, typically called **preferred stock**, which give preferred treatment for dividends, voting, or distribution. If there is more than one class of stock, they must be authorized in the articles of incorporation. See the *General Investment* case.

General Investment Co. v. Bethlehem Steel Corp., 100 A. 347 (N.J. 1917)

Defendant corporation promulgated a plan to issue common stock without voting rights. Plaintiff purchased stock in the corporation after the plan was announced but before a vote. Plaintiff then sought a restraining order against defendant, alleging that issuing common stock without voting rights was against public policy.

Plaintiff argued that the privilege of voting is necessary to common stock. The court held that it is a matter of contract law whether persons who purchase the stock choose to do so without voting rights:

> Every corporation organized under this act shall have power to create two or more kinds of stock, of such classes, with such designations, preferences and voting powers or restrictions or qualifications thereof as shall be stated and expressed in the certificate of incorporation or in any certificate of amendment thereof.

Id. at 350.

The court did not find any public policy that prohibited issuing a class of common stock without voting powers. "The matter is one for the stockholders to determine by their contract." *Id.*

Holders of common stock have rights incident to their ownership. First, and probably the most important, are voting rights. In general, there is one vote for each share owned. However, the articles can provide for cumulative voting (discussed in Chapters 7 and 8).

If corporations have circular holdings, the Model Business Corporation Act does not allow those shareholders to vote. **Circular holdings** exist when Corporation A owns a majority of the stock in Corporation B, and Corporation B owns a majority of the stock in Corporation A. In this situation, the minority stockholders would never have a voice in the corporations. Because the shares owned by circular holdings cannot be voted under the Act, the minority shareholders would control the election of the board of directors.

Another right that holders of common stock may have is a preemptive right. This is a right to purchase proportionate shares of newly issued stock. Holders of common stock also have the right to dividends or other distributions if declared by the board. For any distribution declared but not paid, stockholders become creditors to the extent of the distribution.

Finally, owners of common stock have liquidation rights. Once a corporation is dissolved, all assets are collected, and creditors are paid, the remaining assets are divided among the stockholders according to their percentage of ownership.

Preferred Stock   Certain investors may want preferential treatment. The holders of preferred stock are granted a preference with respect to their shareholders' rights. They may want guaranteed dividends or preferred treatment at liquidation. An investor looking for income will purchase preferred stock with a guaranteed dividend. The articles of incorporation must authorize preferred stock if it is to be issued by the corporation. Therefore, if organizers did not contemplate a new class of stock when the corporation was formed, the articles must be amended. Also, the share certificates must set out completely the preferred rights given to this class of stock.

The most common preference is for distribution. Preferred stockholders will have a priority to distribution before other stockholders. The distribution can be a predetermined amount to be given at certain times (quarterly, for instance). The distribution can be cumulative or noncumulative. If it is cumulative, the preferred stockholders are entitled to the dividend whether it is paid or not. Therefore, once the dividend is declared, all back years are due and owing if unpaid. Shareholders become creditors of the corporation to the extent there are unpaid distributions owed to them. If it is noncumulative, dividends are owed only to preferred stockholders once the dividend is declared by the board of directors. Back years (when a dividend was not declared) will not be due and owing to the preferred stockholders.

The distribution also can be cumulative to the extent earned. This means the distribution is cumulative if the corporation earned enough money to have declared a distribution. The dividends are owed to the preferred stockholders even if not declared by the board of directors.

Another common preference is participation. A preferred stockholder can participate in other distributions that are declared in addition to the guaranteed distribution.

> Sue owns 50 shares of preferred stock with a $2 a year preference and participating. The company declares a $1 per share dividend. Sue will receive $100 for her preference and $50 for participation.

Preferred stockholders also may receive liquidation preference. The preferred stockholders are paid a specific amount at liquidation plus accrued distributions that have not been paid. The specific amount usually is based on a fixed sum or on a fixed percentage of par value. Outside creditors still have priority at liquidation, but the preferred stockholders with liquidation preference are be next in line.

A corporation must have at least one class of stock with full voting rights. This usually is common stock. Preferred stock most typically does not have voting rights. A corporation may want investors, but the current owners do not want to dilute their ownership interests by having more voting stock owned by others. The Model Business Corporation Act requires that preferred stockholders be allowed to vote on matters that affect their interests. If there is nothing in the articles of incorporation regarding voting rights for preferred stockholders, they will be allowed one vote for each share.

The Model Business Corporation Act allows a corporation to establish separate voting groups. There must be a quorum of the separate voting group at a shareholder meeting before that group can vote. Section 10.04 of the Act specifies when a separate voting group is entitled to vote as a class. They can vote on a proposed amendment that would:

1. Increase or decrease the aggregate number of authorized share of the class
2. Effect an exchange, reclassification, or cancellation of all or part of the shares of the class
3. Effect an exchange, or create a right of exchange, of all or any part of the shares of another class into the shares of the class
4. Change the designation, preferences, limitations, or relative rights of the shares of the class
5. Change the shares of the class into the same or a different number of shares of the same class
6. Create a new class of shares having rights and preferences prior, superior, or substantially equal to the shares of the class

7. Increase the rights and preferences or the number of authorized shares of any class having rights and preferences prior, superior, or substantially equal to the shares of the class

8. Limit or deny any existing preemptive rights of the shares of the class

9. Cancel or otherwise affect distributions or dividends on the shares of the class that have accrued but have not been declared.

Some states also may have requirements regarding the voting rights of stockholders.

Preferred stockholders may have been given **redemption rights** for their shares. *Redemption* is the right of a corporation to reacquire shares of preferred stock. A corporation may want to do this if the preferred stock has a high distribution right (a high percentage for dividends, for example). The corporation may want to pay this dividend only for a set number of years. The redemption clause must appear on the stock certificate and must be authorized in the articles of incorporation. This clause includes:

- A date when the stock will be redeemable by the corporation
- The price at which the stock is redeemable
- Persons and period of time for which a notice of redemption will be given
- Where and when payment will be made
- Whether the board of directors has the right to accelerate payment
- How to surrender certificates
- Cancellation of the rights of the shareholders
- Provision regarding the procedure if a shareholder refuses to surrender certificates

Some corporations create a sinking fund to pay for redemption. A **sinking fund** is an account into which the corporation periodically deposits money, so that when the redemption date occurs, the corporation has the money to redeem the shares.

Redeemed shares usually are canceled. The shares then are restored as authorized but unissued shares. The Model Business Corporation Act allows restoration of shares to be automatic unless the articles of incorporation state otherwise. If the shares are to be canceled and not restored, the corporation must file a statement of cancellation with the secretary of state. The cancellation will change the authorized number of shares of the corporation. Generally, however, cancellation does not require shareholder action even though it effectively is an amendment to the articles.

The Model Business Corporation Act previously did not allow corporations to redeem shares under certain circumstances. The revised Act no longer has any restrictions. However, some states continue to restrict the redemption of shares. For example, if the corporation is insolvent or if the redemption will render the corporation insolvent, redemption is not allowed. States that restrict redemption rights do not allow redemption if it will reduce net assets below what is owed to holders of shares having prior or equal rights to the assets of the corporation upon involuntary dissolution.

Another preference that can be given to preferred stockholders is a conversion privilege. This allows a preferred stockholder to convert her shares of stock to another class at a specific rate and at a specified time. If a corporation's growth is good, this can be beneficial to both the corporation and the stockholder. The corporation no longer has to pay a higher or guaranteed distribution to the preferred stockholder. Also, if the corporation is growing, the preferred stockholder could convert to common stock to have a vote on corporate matters and also be entitled to any distributions declared for the common stock.

As with all preferred stock, this right must be set out in the articles of incorporation and must appear on the certificate. The clause should include the conversion rate, the number of shares of common stock into which each share of preferred stock is convertible, provision for fractional shares that may result, the procedure for redemption (including notice), and reservation of an adequate number of shares of common stock (keeping in mind that all conversion privileges may be exercised). The corporation may want to include a provision to make adjustments to the conversion rate. This is necessary if there is a stock split, stock dividend, or other action that changes the character of the common shares.

The Model Business Corporation Act allows different series of stock within the same class. This alleviates the difficulty of amending the articles of incorporation to create a new class. The series shares are the same class of stock, but with different rights. The articles of incorporation must give the board of directors the authority to issue series of stock within a particular class. The board then issues the series by resolution that establishes the rights associated with that series.

The articles of incorporation may grant extensive decision-making powers to the board. However, the board's power to choose may be limited by federal and/or state law, as it was in the *Roper* case.

Roper v. South Carolina Tax Commission, 99 S.E.2d 377 (S.C. 1957)

Plaintiff brought action to recover income taxes paid under protest. Plaintiff was the sole stockholder of a corporation. The corporation issued preferred stock as a dividend to the plaintiff. Plaintiff did not report the stock dividend as income. The Tax Commission assessed taxes, which were paid under protest by plaintiff.

The trial court found that the stock dividend was income. Plaintiff argued that stock dividends are not income under the federal income tax laws and that South Carolina had adopted the federal income tax laws.

The court found that South Carolina had enacted a new tax law and no longer follows the federal income tax law. Dividends are income under South Carolina law.

Dividends are the appropriate fruit of stock ownership, are commonly reckoned as income, and are expended as such by the stockholder without regard to whether they are declared from the most recent earnings, or from the earnings of the past, or are based upon the increased value of the property of the corporation.

Id. at 382.

Fractions of Shares   A corporation sometimes must issue a **fractional share**. A corporation has authority to issue fractional shares only if state statutes allow. A fractional share may be required when a stock dividend is declared.

> Apex Corporation declares that for each 50 shares, a stockholder will receive one share. Sue owns 75 shares. She is entitled to receive one and one-half shares of stock.

If the state permits fractional shares, the corporation may issue a stock certificate for one-half of a share. Some states authorize **scrip** instead of fractional shares. Scrip is a certificate that represents a percentage of a share. The holder is entitled to receive a full share once she has accumulated enough scrip to equal a full share. Fractional shares also can be created in stock splits and at redemption, depending on the redemption rate.

Under the Model Business Corporation Act, if fractional shares are issued, the holders are entitled to a fractional vote, fractional share of dividends, and fractional participation in the liquidation of the corporation. The holder of scrip usually is not entitled to these rights. States treat fractional shares and scrip quite differently.

Consideration   **Consideration** is what is paid or exchanged for shares of stock in a corporation. What is required for consideration depends on whether the stock has a par value or is no par value. Shares that have a par value cannot be sold for less than par value. The value of no-par stock is set by the board of directors or by shareholders, depending on the statutes and articles of incorporation. Therefore, the consideration given for shares of stock must be at least equal to the par value or equal to the stated value of no-par stock.

When the consideration is money, it is easy to determine that the minimum value has been given. If services or property are given as consideration, the value of the consideration must be determined. There are basically three rules of law in determining the value of property or services:

- *True value rule*—The property or services must be appraised at the time of the issuance of shares. It must have an actual value equal to or greater than the minimum required for par value or stated value.
- *Absence of fraud rule*—This rule requires the board of directors to evaluate and determine the value of the property or services adequate for the required consideration. The board of directors' evaluation will be accepted absent any fraud.
- *Model Business Corporation Act rule* (the most flexible)—It provides that the board of directors simply must declare the consideration to be adequate.

For the second and third rules, the board of directors should go on record with its evaluation.

These three rules address the amount of consideration but do not address the quality of the consideration. Most statutes specify what can be given as consideration for shares of stock. Consideration typically is limited to money, property (tangible or intangible), or services actually performed for the corporation. Some states allow promissory notes to be given as consideration for shares. Future services or services performed before incorporation rarely are adequate consideration under a particular state's statutes.

The Model Business Corporation Act allows tangible or intangible property, cash, promissory notes, services already performed for the corporation, contracts for services to be performed, or other securities as adequate consideration for the exchange of shares of stock. Shares of stock are issued but held in escrow until the promissory note is honored or until the services are performed. If the promises are not kept, the shares in escrow are canceled.

When the consideration has been received by the corporation, the shares are considered fully paid and nonassessable. If the shares are not fully paid but issued, the shareholder becomes liable to creditors for the unpaid consideration. The directors may be in violation of their fiduciary duty to the corporation if they issue shares that are not fully paid.

Transfer Agents   Somehow, a corporation has to keep track of the record owners of its shares of stock. Corporations must designate a **transfer agent** by resolution. Small, privately held, or close corporations are not required to designate a transfer agent. Most banks or other financial institutions have departments to keep these records for corporations. A transfer agent issues the certificates. If the corporation also has a registrar, the registrar records who owns the certificates. The records must be kept either at the corporation's place of business or at the transfer agent's offices.

The Model Business Corporation Act allows facsimile signatures of the officers on the certificates. This makes it convenient for the transfer agent to keep blank certificates with printed signatures at her office. If a registrar is used, the transfer agent will send prepared certificates to her office for registration and signature. The registrar must keep a stock ledger to record all certificates. The transfer agent then issues the certificates to the shareholders.

Debt Securities

As discussed, a corporation can generate capital by issuing equity securities (ownership interests in a corporation). However, the corporation may not want to issue equity security for some reason. By statute, a corporation is allowed to borrow money, to mortgage property, and to exercise other rights afforded persons as long as it is for corporate purposes. Therefore, a corporation may generate money by issuing debt security instead of equity security. *Debt securities* are loans made to the corporation. Holders of debt securities are creditors of the corporation instead of owners. In return for the loan, creditors are paid interest. Creditors with debt security sometimes are promised assets upon dissolution of the corporation.

Debt securities may be either unsecured and secured. An unsecured loan is a **debenture**. It is unsecured because only a promissory note is signed by the corporation. Most debt securities are secured and are called **mortgage bonds**. A **bond** always states the principal amount owed by the corporation, the repayment date, and the periodic interest rate. If an investment is attractive, the bonds may be sold at an amount higher than the principal amount. If so, they are sold at a premium. If the investment is not attractive, the bonds may have to be sold for a discount, which is less than the principal amount.

Bonds usually are offered and sold under an agreement with the corporation, a lender, and a trustee. The trustee is generally a financial institution. This agreement is called an **indenture**. The indenture sets out the rights and obligations of the corporation and the bond holders. The trustee is appointed for the bond holders. The trustee then executes all of the documents and makes the purchase of the bonds. This allows bond holders to remain anonymous if they wish.

The corporation pledges property—either real estate or personal property—as collateral. If personal property is used as collateral, the transactions are governed by the Uniform Commercial Code (UCC). A security agreement must be signed and filed if personal property is to be used as security for a debt.

To make them more attractive to investors, debt securities can have various privileges. One investor may be given priority over the debt of another, making the other debt subordinate to the new one. Another privilege is redemption. The debt security, usually bonds, is redeemable at a certain time and at a specified rate. Municipal bonds are usually set up this way.

> An investor buys municipal bonds at $100 a bond for 30 years at 5% interest. The investor is paid 5% each year for 30 years; and at the end of 30 years, the bonds will be redeemed by the seller for a stated amount.

Depending on the market, the interest rate paid may be high or low; and the redemption rate could be higher than the purchase price. If the investment is risky, a corporation may have to pay higher rates to attract investors.

Another privilege is **conversion**. This allows a debt investor to convert his debt securities to equity securities. These are called convertible bonds and convertible debentures. The security agreement must state specifically the number of shares, time period, and procedure that the investor and corporation must follow for the conversion. This may be advantageous to an investor if the corporation is prosperous and begins to pay dividends. It may give the investor the best of both worlds. It guarantees interest as a debt security with the ability to convert to equity securities if the corporation grows.

A very rare privilege is voting rights. If debt securities are allowed to vote, the securities will be treated as a separate class of stock. This right must be authorized in the articles of incorporation and by state statute.

Debt and Equity Considerations

How to finance the corporation is a very important decision and should be reviewed carefully. Future financing needs also should be considered. If the corporation does not want debt, several classes of stock should be established. If this is done at the initial incorporation stage, the articles will not have to be amended for later financing. If additional owners (who will have ownership rights) are not wanted, debt security may be the more desirable alternative. Keep in mind that the corporation is obligated to pay interest to creditors but is not obligated to declare or to pay dividends.

Another important consideration is taxes. Debt securities avoid double taxation. The interest a corporation pays on debt is deducted as an expense before the corporation pays taxes. Some corporations issue debt securities instead of equity securities to avoid double taxation. The IRS will scrutinize a corporation if it has more debt than equity. This is known as a **thin corporation**. The IRS may characterize the interest as dividends. If this happens, the corporation will be faced with the double taxation issue. It may be wise to have a mix of debt and equity securities.

Key Terms

Authorized shares

Blue sky laws

Bond

Capital surplus

Circular holdings

Common stock

Consideration

Conversion

Debenture

Debt securities

Diluted shares

Discount stock

Dividends

Earned surplus account

Equity securities

Fractional share

Indenture

Issued and outstanding

Mortgage bonds

Preferred stock

Redemption rights

Scrip

Sinking fund

Stated capital account

Stated value

Thin corporation

Transfer agent

Treasury shares

Watered stock

Quiz

1. List the two types of securities that a corporation issues to generate capital.

2. Define equity securities.

3. Define debt securities.

4. List the entity that regulates securities and the major legislation related to securities.

5. Identify the ownership rights of an equity security holder.

6. Briefly explain "issued and outstanding" as it relates to equity securities.

7. Briefly explain the concept of watered stock.

8. Identify and briefly discuss stock that is repurchased by a corporation.

9. Briefly explain the concepts of stated capital and capital surplus accounts.

10. Explain where on the ledger sheet the profit of the corporation appears.

11. Identify the basic class of stock for a corporation.

12. Briefly explain the term "circular holdings."

13. Briefly describe the rights that common stockholders have in the corporation.

14. Briefly explain why a corporation would issue preferred stock.

15. What types of consideration are allowed for the purchase of stock? Explain briefly.

16. List and describe the various types of debt securities.

17. Explain the interest of the IRS in a thin corporation.

13 Ownership Agreements

Many types of agreements can affect the ownership of shares of stock. Shareholders can enter into voting agreements for a particular purpose. Agreements also can be made in a close corporation to preserve its status by restricting the transfer of shares. These types of agreements are discussed in this chapter.

Share Transfer Restrictions

Most close corporations have shareholder agreements that restrict the transfer of shares. This is to ensure that the close corporation's status is maintained. However, the restriction cannot completely bar the transfer of shares. A **transfer restriction** may be included in the articles of incorporation, in the bylaws, or in a shareholder agreement. The restriction must appear on all stock certificates. The most common restriction is a requirement that the selling shareholder first must offer her shares of stock to the corporation. The corporation and the other shareholders must be given the first option to buy, before the shares are offered to outsiders.

The Model Business Corporation Act (MBCA) authorizes share transfer restrictions to maintain the corporate status if that status depends on the number and identity of the shareholders. Types of corporations subject to this are close corporations, professional corporations, and Subchapter S corporations. Also, restrictions are allowed under the MBCA to preserve federal and state law exemptions. The MBCA has a catch-all authorization for any other reasonable purpose.

The transfer restriction must have a lawful purpose, which should be recited in the agreement to avoid future problems. Restrictions usually are used to ensure that no outsider will be allowed to purchase stock. However, a complete ban on selling stock to anyone at any time is unenforceable and against public policy.

A share transfer restriction is activated when a shareholder receives a **good faith offer** to purchase her shares. A shareholder cannot threaten a corporation with a possible sale; there must be a bona fide offer. A good faith offer to purchase requires that there be an agreement with the purchaser, in writing. The agreement should state the provisions regarding the offer, including the fact that an earnest money deposit has been made, and there should be an escrow for the balance of the purchase. The agreement may disclose the purchaser's identity; however, this is not required.

The restriction may include an **option to purchase** provision. This allows the corporation the right of first refusal to buy the selling shareholder's stock. If the corporation declines, the other shareholders have the option to purchase. When drafting the share transfer restriction, one should decide whether this restriction will be an "all or nothing" restriction. This means that either all shares subject to the option will be purchased by the corporation or none of them can be purchased.

Another event that triggers the restriction is the death of a shareholder. If a shareholder dies, the corporation and surviving shareholders must decide whether they wish to purchase the shares. Some corporations use life insurance to fund this restriction. The corporation buys life insurance for the value of each shareholder's stock. This money is used after the death of a shareholder, to purchase the stock from his or her estate. The agreement will provide that the shareholder's estate must sell to the corporation. (See the *Miller Waste Mills* case for an example.)

Retirement, disability, and termination of employment also may trigger the share transfer restriction. It may be too costly for the corporation or shareholders to raise

---

Miller Waste Mills, Inc. v. Mackay, 520 N.W.2d 490 (Minn. 1994)

The plaintiff is a family-owned corporation. The shareholders approved a share restriction that required corporate approval before transferring shares. It also allowed the corporation the right of first refusal.

The corporation did not invoke this restriction at all times. When two sons of the founders died, the corporation exercised the restriction and notified their estates of its intent to purchase the shares. The two estates entered into a voting agreement. This agreement represented 52 percent of the voting stock.

The parties to the voting agreement contended that the restrictions on transfers were unenforceable. The court held:

> A transfer restriction may be enforced as long as the restriction is not "manifestly unreasonable under the circumstances" and is "noted conspicuously" on the stock certificate. Several types of restrictions are always deemed "not manifestly unreasonable," including any restriction which requires the holder to give the corporation, the other shareholders, or any combination of either or both, a right of first refusal or an option to purchase the shares.

Id. at 494 (citations omitted).

The parties further argued that legal title to the stock was not in the corporation and, therefore, that they could vote the stock. The court held:

> When a corporation exercises a valid contractual repurchase option, like Article XVI, the corporation becomes the equitable owner of the stock; and the shares cannot then be voted contrary to the equitable owner's interests.

Id. at 495. In this case, the corporation, as the equitable owner of the shares of the estates, had the right to enforce the stock redemption provision.

---

the money to buyout the shareholder. Therefore, the initial agreement should provide alternative means, such as installment payments or insurance, to provide the necessary funds.

Mandatory Buyout/Sellout Agreements

Share transfer restrictions discourage the transfer of shares, but mandatory **buyout/sellout agreements** require the transfer of shares under certain circumstances. Requiring the corporation to buy shares protects shareholders when there is no market for their shares. The corporation also has the right to purchase shares from the shareholders.

Death, retirement, disability, termination of employment, or the loss of a shareholder's occupational license could trigger a mandatory buyout. Like share transfer restrictions, life insurance or other insurance may be used to fund the buyout. These provisions should be stated in the agreement. The agreement also should obligate the shareholders to purchase if the corporation does not have the funds or if there are legal restrictions under the state statutes.

The shareholders can agree to force a buyout. This usually occurs when there are only two shareholders and they are equal owners. They may not want to be in business with each other any longer, or one shareholder simply may want out; however, no event triggering a mandatory buyout has happened. The forced buyout provisions will require the other owner to purchase or sell at a fair price.

One procedure is an **auction**. This allows the corporation to purchase shares at the lowest possible price. All shareholders must submit an offer to the corporation to sell their shares. The agreement must establish a penalty for not making an offer to sell, as well as any terms relating to the shares. These terms may include:

1. Not all shares must be offered
2. A covenant not to compete with the corporation for a period of time
3. Resignations from offices and the board
4. Warranties that there are no liens against the shares.

It is anticipated that shareholders who want to stay or get rid of another shareholder will submit high offers. The corporation is required to accept the lowest offer. Another procedure entails one shareholder giving notice to the other that the buyout provisions are being initiated. The notice provides an offer to sell or to buy shares of the corporation at a certain price subject to other terms and conditions. The shareholder receiving the notice must either buy or sell during the period given in the notice. The offer usually is fair, because the shareholder initiating the forced buyout may be the one who is bought out.

All agreements involving the purchase of shares should state the price and payment provisions. Share transfer restrictions and mandatory buyout/sellout agreements must establish a price for the offer or price to be paid. The price can be determined in a variety of ways. The price can be a **firm offer** that will not change. The price can be an **adjusted stated value**; under this valuation, the price will be changed periodically.

The agreement can set out a **multiple earnings formula**. This takes into account the success of the business, the value of the assets, and the market for the shares. The earnings of the corporation are multiplied by a stated figure in the agreement. One can include a provision in the agreement that puts a minimum floor on the value. The price then cannot be less than this amount. Another formula is **book value**. This is determined by dividing net assets by the number of outstanding shares. A person should be designated in the agreement to determine the book value, or the agreement simply can state that it will use the last financial statement of the corporation.

Other formulas include matching the good faith offer or appraisal. The **appraisal** method is very expensive. The agreement must state who will perform the appraisal or must state the method to pick an appraiser. Also, the appraisal method to be used should be specified, as there are many different ways to appraise a business. Different appraisal methods include liquidation value and going-concern value. The going-concern valuation takes into account goodwill, reputation, life of assets, and the liquidity of the company.

Instead of appraisal, the agreement could specify **arbitration**. Independent arbitrators then would conduct any investigation necessary to value the stock. This method also can be expensive. The arbitrators would expect information and reports from each side, which would entail hiring experts.

Whichever method is used, it should be stated very clearly and precisely in the shareholder agreement (see the *BancOhio* case). The terms of payment also may be stated in the agreement. The corporation may fund the agreement through insurance.

Voting Agreements

Shareholders can agree prior to a shareholders' meeting to vote their shares in a block. These are called **voting agreements**. This type of agreement should be in writing and usually is valid and enforceable.

Voting agreements among shareholders can affect ownership interests in the corporation. They are commonly used to protect minority shareholders. Previously, **cumulative voting** was discussed. Cumulative voting is a protection for minority shareholders. Voting agreements are a way to use cumulative voting to its full potential.

The Model Business Corporation Act approves of voting agreements. Common law long has recognized shareholders' ability to predetermine their position by agreement on normal shareholder business, such as electing directors. Most states will not allow voting agreements that conflict with the statutes, such as changing the minimum number required for a quorum, or that affect the power of the board of directors.

Shareholders can make several types of voting agreements. A **voting trust** is an agreement that separates the legal ownership from the beneficial ownership. The legal

---

BancOhio National Bank v. Nursing Center Services, Inc.,
573 N.E.2d 1122 (Ohio 1988)

The three stockholders (Wilson, Murtha, and Radbill) of Nursing Services Inc. (NCSI) entered into a buy-sell agreement. This agreement required a shareholder to first offer shares to the corporation before selling elsewhere. The certificate also contained restrictions against pledging shares without written consent of the other shareholders.

Radbill, without the knowledge of the others, pledged his shares to secure a loan with the plaintiff. Radbill went bankrupt, and the bankruptcy trustee abandoned the shares to the plaintiff. Murtha and Wilson offered to buy the shares, but the plaintiff refused.

Murtha and Wilson then notified the plaintiff that they intended to buy the shares under the buy-sell agreement. Under the agreement, the shares had a negative value. The plaintiff informed the defendant that it intended to sell the shares at a public sale.

Just prior to the sale, Wilson and Murtha formed a new corporation. They exchanged their shares in the defendant for shares in the new corporation. They canceled Radbill's shares and offered him $250. The two corporations then merged.

The plaintiff argued that the cancellation of Radbill's shares in exchange for $250 constituted a fraudulent conveyance. The court found that the cancellation was not a transfer or conveyance. "The shares were canceled pursuant to a plan of merger or reorganization." Id. at 1125.

The court further found:

> BancOhio, as pledgee of the stock, certainly held the same rights as Radbill, the shareholder of record, whose interest was subordinate to the restrictions first in the buy-sell agreement, and subsequently in the stock purchase agreement. ... [A] debtor could give a security interest to the bank in collateral in which he had an interest; he could give only a security interest to the extent that he had an interest.

Id. (citations omitted).

The plaintiff further argued that the stock pledge by Radbill did not trigger the provisions of the buy-sell agreement and the stock purchase agreement. The court found that Murtha and Wilson properly exercised their rights under the agreement. "The stock purchase agreement superseded and replaced the buy-sell agreement." Id. at 1126. In a pledge transaction, the shareholder is required to offer a price not to exceed the formula price contained in the buy-sell agreement. The court held that the pledge did trigger the buy-sell agreement.

---

ownership is transferred to a trustee. The shares are held in trust by the trustee, but only for the purposes of voting. The trustee has physical possession of the stock certificates. The trustee is allowed to vote the shares in accordance with the agreement. The agreement (trust) may be specific on how the trustee can vote the shares, or it may allow the trustee to use discretion.

A voting trust is limited to a period of ten years under the Model Business Corporation Act. Some states allow a longer duration, up to twenty-one years. The trustee becomes the record owner of the shares and receives notice of all shareholder meetings. Voting trust certificates are issued to the shareholders. The certificate states the name of the trustee and the terms of the trust. To be valid, the trust must meet certain requirements:

1. There must be a written agreement stating the terms and conditions of the trust and giving the trustee the authority to vote the shares within the trust,

2. The shares must be transferred to the trustee,

3. A record of all beneficiaries (shareholders) must be kept by the trustee, including names, addresses, and number of shares.

4. The corporation also must have a copy of the voting trust agreement and a list of the beneficiaries.

This type of voting agreement is enforceable. The trustee is allowed to vote all of the shares in the trust pursuant to the agreement.

Another type of voting agreement is a **stock voting agreement**, also known as a **pooling agreement**. This agreement accomplishes the same things as a voting trust, but it is informal and not enforceable. Shareholders agree, prior to the meeting, about voting their shares. However, there is no mechanism to require a shareholder to vote as agreed.

The Model Business Corporation Act recognizes stock voting agreements. Because they are informal, there usually is no duration requirement, and they can last indefinitely. Also, the agreement can be secret, as nothing need be filed with the corporation.

Another type of voting agreement is one to secure director representation. This can be done through a voting trust; stock voting agreements, through cumulative voting; or by shareholder agreement that at least one seat on the board will be elected by the minority shareholders. All shareholders then vote for this minority representative.

Key Terms

Adjusted stated value	Good faith offer
Appraisal	Multiple earnings formula
Arbitration	Option to purchase
Auction	Pooling agreement
Book value	Transfer restriction
Buyout/sellout agreement	Voting agreement
Cumulative voting	Voting trust
Firm offer	

Quiz

1. Describe briefly a share transfer restriction.

2. Explain how the share transfer restriction is triggered.

3. Describe what must be included in a good faith offer to purchase restricted shares.

4. Explain concisely the concept of mandatory buyout/sellout agreements.

5. Explain briefly the term *forced buyout agreement.*

6. Identify and explain the two procedures for buyout.

7. What are voting agreements? Explain briefly.

8. Explain the different types of voting agreements.

14 Corporate Distributions

A **distribution** is a transfer of money or other property from a corporation to or for the benefit of a shareholder. There are several types of distributions. A **dividend** is the distribution of corporate profits. Dividends can be either money or property. At liquidation, there is a one-time **dissolution distribution** when all assets are liquidated. Also, **stock splits** and corporate buyback of shares are distributions.

The board of directors has discretion to declare dividends. If shareholders want dividends, but the board never declares them, the shareholders have the power to change the board. Shareholders' lawsuits to force dividends are not successful unless the board abuses its discretion. A board always can justify not declaring a dividend if the funds are not there or if the funds are needed for expansion of the business.

In deciding to declare distributions, the board must consider whether there are legally available funds to pay the dividend, as well as the tax ramifications of the distribution. The Model Business Corporation Act allows distributions to be paid from any source as long as the corporation remains solvent. As long as the total assets are greater than total liabilities, the Act permits the distribution. Common sources for the funds to pay dividends are either **earned surplus** or retained earnings, which are accumulated profits.

There are five accounts from which funds can be used to pay distributions:

1. *Net assets account:* the amount by which total assets exceed total debt,
2. *Stated capital account:* the par value of issued shares of stock, the stated value of no-par stock allocated to this account, and other money that the corporation has transferred to this account.
3. *Surplus account:* the excess of net assets over **stated capital**,
4. *Earned surplus account:* equal to the balance of profits, income, gains/losses from the date of incorporation after distributions, transfers to stated capital, and capital surplus. It also includes any money allocated in mergers, consolidations, or acquisitions,
5. *Capital surplus account:* the entire **surplus** of the corporation other than earned surplus.

On the corporate balance sheet, these accounts are the equity accounts. Net worth is established by equity. A corporation must be solvent to issue a distribution. A corporation is insolvent if it is unable to pay its liabilities when they are due. The asset portion of the balance sheet must show enough money or other property to offset any distribution from these five accounts. Any change to the equity or liability portion of the balance sheet must have a corresponding change in the asset section. Even if there is an adequate balance in equity to declare a cash dividend, the corporation must have the cash to pay the dividend.

Dividends

The board of directors is vested with the authority to declare dividends to be paid to shareholders. Dividends can be declared using cash, property, or shares of stock. Cash is the most common form of dividend. If a corporation manufactures a product, dividends of that product are possible. Other types of property dividends include assets of the corporation and stock in another corporation. Dividends do not have to be regularly scheduled. Shareholders who want regular dividends will look to publicly traded stock. They can review the track record for dividends. It is not a guarantee, but it helps the investor to decide whether to purchase the stock.

As discussed in Chapter 8, preferred stock may carry automatic dividends or may have a dividend preference. Therefore, if the board declares a dividend for common stock, it may be required to declare a dividend for preferred stock. Sometimes, though, there are only enough funds to give the preferred stock its dividend.

Dividends must be uniform within a class or series of stock. There is no shareholder right to dividends until they are declared by the board. Once the dividend is declared, the shareholders become creditors to the extent that the dividend remains unpaid.

As stated earlier, the Model Business Corporation Act prohibits the payment of a dividend if the corporation is insolvent or if payment of the dividend will make the corporation insolvent. Dividends can be paid only if total assets exceed total liabilities, which includes any amounts payable to preferred stockholders. Some states restrict the payment of dividends to unreserved and unrestricted earned surplus. Earned surplus represents the profits of a corporation. Earned surplus can be restricted by conditions on a bank loan to keep a certain amount in earned surplus or **treasury shares** to be purchased in the future. Some states require that the amount of earned surplus used to purchase a corporation's own shares be restricted until the shares are no longer treasury shares. Many states do not distinguish between surplus or restricted surplus and allow dividends if earned surplus is adequate.

There is a procedure for declaring, paying, and accounting for the dividend. A resolution is passed by the board at a directors' meeting. The resolution sets the record date, amount of dividend, and type of dividend. If the dividend is paid in cash, both the cash account (asset section of the balance sheet) and earned surplus account (equity section of the balance sheet) are reduced. If the dividend is paid in product, the inventory or a particular property account (asset section of the balance sheet) and the earned surplus account are reduced. A value for the property or inventory is established. Book value usually is used.

As discussed in preceding chapters, there are tax consequences associated with declaring a dividend. The corporation is taxed on its profits, and then the shareholder is taxed on the dividend. This is known as double taxation. It is one of the major disadvantages to incorporation. If shareholders are employees, a corporation may wish to give the employee shareholder a bonus or a raise in salary. The salary is deducted as an expense to the corporation and is taxed to the employee as individual income. Hence, no double taxation occurs on the profits of the corporation. However, the IRS will scrutinize this action and may declare that the bonus or higher salary is a dividend. It generally is better to use a hybrid of dividends and salary for employee shareholders.

If property is used for the dividend, the shareholder will be taxed on the fair market value of the property. The corporation reduces its balance sheet by book value, but the shareholder must use fair market value of the property or product on her income tax return.

A corporation must file informational reports to the IRS regarding dividends, just as all businesses must report any payments that are made to anyone.

Liquidation

When a corporation dissolves, there may be a distribution of assets to the shareholders on a pro rata basis, depending on their ownership interests. Creditors are paid first, however. Although shareholders are creditors to the extent of declared but unpaid dividends, outside creditors have first priority; then preferred stockholders who are owed accrued dividends; and then other shareholders who are owed dividends. See the *Parkinson* case for an example.

If any preferred stockholders have liquidation preference, they are entitled to priority after the creditors. Preferred shareholders may receive their preference and also participate in the remaining distribution on a pro rata basis if their preferred shares include participation rights.

Parkinson v. State Bank of Millard County, 35 P.2d 814 (Utah 1934)

The defendant, a banking corporation, became insolvent and was liquidated. The plaintiff alleged that she had a preferred claim against the defendant and that the bank was paying unsecured creditors. A restraining order was issued.

The bank was a trustee of an estate to which the plaintiff was a heir. A check was issued by the defendant to the plaintiff for her portion of the estate. When the check was endorsed by the plaintiff and presented to the bank for payment, the bank was in bankruptcy and funds were not on hand to pay. The plaintiff alleged that those funds never were an asset of the bank in liquidation and were wrongly withheld.

Judgment was entered by the trial court in favor of the plaintiff. The court gave the plaintiff a prior lien on the capital of the bank. The defendant argued that the plaintiff had a lien only against the "capital" of the bank, which was money paid in by the stockholders for the purchase price of their shares and did not include other assets. Therefore, the defendant continued to settle other claims from the assets.

The court held:

I am of the opinion that to give the word or term "capital" a construction as contended by the commissioner, that it means only money or property paid in or contributed by the stockholders to the corporation in payment of shares of stock issued to them, and not assets though acquired by the use of such moneys so paid in or in which they were invested, is, when applied to a bank or other corporation not required to separately keep such moneys, permitted to use them for all corporate purposes and authorized to act as an executor or administrator of an estate without bond, to destroy the efficacy of the admitted lien created by the statute and to render it fruitless.

Id. at 820.

The court found that the plaintiff had a lien on any assets of the bank, and that the plaintiff should be paid before unsecured creditors.

Corporations may declare a partial liquidation. A **partial liquidation** consists of a combination of a distribution of assets (usually cash) and a purchase of the corporation's own shares. A corporation will declare a partial liquidation when a division of the corporation closes and the trade of that division is no longer performed by the corporation. For example, if ABC Inc. closed its restaurant division and no longer operated any restaurants, ABC Inc. might declare a partial liquidation of the assets belonging to that division.

A partial liquidation begins with a resolution by the board of directors. The resolution sets the record date, the assets to be liquidated, and the accounting procedures.

Share Dividends

A corporation may declare a dividend of its own shares. The shareholders keep their same percentage of ownership. There are some legal restrictions before a corporation can distribute its own shares. First, the distribution can come only from treasury shares or authorized but unissued shares of stock. Otherwise, the articles of incorporation must be amended to increase the number of authorized shares before the dividend can be declared. Second, funds must be available in earned surplus.

The changes to the balance sheet will occur in the equity section only. When authorized but unissued shares are used, the balance sheet will show a transfer from surplus to stated capital. If the stock has a par value, the stock must be issued at or greater than the par value. The amount equal to the aggregate par value must be transferred to stated capital. If the stock has no par value, the value stated by the board of directors transfers to stated capital.

To avoid a dilution of a class of stock, there usually is a restriction on the **share dividend** that dividends of one class of stock cannot be paid to another class of stock. If the articles of incorporation provide otherwise, or if the shareholders of the class of stock to be issued consent, a different class of stock can receive the share dividend.

The board of directors declares the share dividend by a resolution setting the record date, the number of shares to be issued, and the authority to transfer the shares. Again, all accounting entries will be in the equity portion of the balance sheet. Transfer is between the surplus account and the stated capital account.

The New York Stock Exchange requires that the fair market value of the shares to be distributed be used. Most generally accepted accounting methods also use the fair market value.

A share dividend does not give the shareholder any immediate advantage, because the shareholder still owns the same percentage of the corporation. The corporation does not increase in value, so the ownership rights remain the same. The advantage is that if the stock later goes up in value, the shareholder realizes more equity.

There are tax ramifications to a share dividend. The dividend itself is not taxed, because no payment is received. Taxes are paid when the shares are sold by the shareholder. Capital gain or loss is paid by the shareholder based on whether she sold the stock at a gain or at a loss from the basis in the stock. The **basis** is the value of the stock at the time of its purchase or receipt. If the fair market value of the stock at the time the share dividend was declared is $10 and if the shareholder later sells the stock for $12, she has a capital gain per share of $2. Taxes are paid on the capital gain.

Stock Splits

A stock split occurs when the ownership interest in a corporation is divided into a greater number of shares of stock. A stock split affects the capital stock structure of the corporation. A corporation reduces the par value on the stock so that stated capital is not affected. A stock split shifts surplus to stated capital, so it looks like an earnings distribution on the balance sheet. A stock split changes the number of outstanding shares but does not change stated capital.

The board of directors has authority to declare a stock split, although the articles of incorporation have to be amended if a stock split is declared. The par value, if any, must be changed, and the authorized number of shares must be increased. Most states require that shareholders vote on all amendments to the articles. The Model Business Corporation Act does not make a distinction between a share dividend and a stock split; therefore, the board has authority to issue the stock without shareholder approval. The Act views the stock split as a dividend; therefore, shareholder approval is not required.

Stock splits are treated as share dividends. Once the board has declared the distribution and the articles have been amended, certificates are issued for the shares representing the split.

Sue owned 100 shares of stock in ABC Inc. The board of directors declared a stock split at one share of stock for every five already owned. Sue would receive certificates for an additional 20 shares of stock.

Corporation's Purchase of Shares

If state statutes permit and if the board of directors authorizes, a corporation may purchase its own shares. Most states require that the corporation have funds in the earned surplus account that are not restricted. Capital surplus can be used if it is authorized in the articles of incorporation. As in all distributions, a corporation cannot purchase its own shares if it is insolvent or if the purchase will make it insolvent.

The purchased shares become treasury shares. The shares are authorized but unissued. The shares can be canceled. A corporation may cancel shares that have been redeemed through a preferred stock offering. There is no longer a need for this class of stock. If the shares are to be canceled, a **statement of cancellation** must be filed with the secretary of state. This, of course, changes the authorized stock in the articles of incorporation.

Key Terms

Basis	Share dividend
Dissolution distribution	Stated capital
Distribution	Statement of cancellation
Dividend	Stock split
Earned surplus	Surplus
Partial liquidation	Treasury shares

Quiz

1. Explain briefly the concept of distribution.

2. Identify the different types of distributions.

3. What are the factors that the board of directors must consider in deciding to declare a distribution? Explain briefly.

4. Describe the way(s) in which dividends can be paid without violating the law.

5. Other than solvency, what requirements must be met before dividends can be paid?

6. Describe the priorities of distribution of corporate assets upon liquidation.

7. Under what circumstances would a corporation declare a partial liquidation? Explain briefly.

8. Describe briefly the legal restrictions that must be met to declare a share dividend.

9. What are the tax ramifications, if any, of a share dividend?

10. Describe briefly the issues that a corporation should consider when it purchases its own shares.

15 Employment Agreements and Compensation

Corporations and other business entities frequently enter into employment contracts with key employees—those who are essential to the success of the business. An *employment agreement* is an agreement between the employer and the employee that sets out the employee's duties and responsibilities, the compensation to be paid to the employee, the length of the agreement, and the termination rights of either the employer or the employee.

Employment Contracts

An employment agreement (see Figure 15-1) protects the employee. It states what is expected from both the employee and the employer. Also, courts will not require an employee to work for a company against his will. An employer may not be able to terminate the employee, but the employee can quit.

FIGURE 15-1 **Employment Contract**

EMPLOYMENT AGREEMENT

THIS AGREEMENT made this _____ day of _____, 19___, between **Critters, Inc.**, a Nebraska corporation (hereinafter referred to as "Employer"), and **Amy Nalistik, D.V.M.** (hereinafter called the "Employee").

WHEREAS, the Employer is engaged primarily in the practice of veterinary medicine; and

WHEREAS, the Employee, a duly licensed Doctor of Veterinary Medicine, desires to practice as an Employee of the Employer;

NOW, THEREFORE, the parties have mutually agreed that:

1. Term. This Agreement shall be for a period of one (1) year, commencing on the effective date hereof; subject, however, to termination during such year, as provided herein. This Agreement shall be renewed automatically for succeeding periods of one (1) year each, on the same terms and conditions as herein contained unless either the Employer or the Employee shall, at least forty-five (45) days prior to the expiration of any period, give written notice of the Employer's or the Employee's intention not to renew this Agreement.

2. Duties and Responsibilities. The Employer employs the Employee, and the Employee accepts such employment, as a Doctor of Veterinary Medicine.

The Employee agrees to devote substantially all of the Employee's time and energy, pursuant to the terms of this Agreement, to practice on behalf of the Employer to the best of such Employee's abilities. During the term era and any renewal, the Employee shall not, without the written consent of the Employer, render professional services to, or for, any person, firm, or corporation or other organization whether for compensation or not, or engage in any activity that competes with the interests of the Employer, whether the Employee is acting alone, as an independent contractor, or as an officer, director, employee, shareholder, partner, or fiduciary.

Any such consent granted to the Employee shall be revocable by the Employer at any time upon ten (10) days notice, and the Employee agrees to cease and desist from such activities after receipt of such notice.

The Employee does not presently engage in any such activities other than those set forth above nor does the Employee contemplate doing so.

Except if agreed otherwise in writing by the Employer, all income generated by the Employee for professional services and related activities such as consulting, lecturing, and writing, shall belong to the Employer regardless of to whom paid. Any check made payable to the Employee which represents income belonging to the Employer shall be endorsed over to the Employer by the Employee.

117

The Employer recognizes that professional regulatory and advisory groups and bodies may from time to time establish ethical standards and requirements with regard to the practice of veterinary medicine by those licensed to practice veterinary medicine. All restrictions contained herein with respect to the duties and obligations of the Employee shall be subject to the standards and requirements of the aforesaid groups and bodies.

The Employee agrees not to become involved in any professional, business, or personal matters that may adversely affect or reflect upon the Employer.

3. Compensation. In consideration of the Employee's continuing employment, the Employer shall compensate the Employee as follows:

(a) by paying the Employee a salary in the amount of $_____ annually, payable in equal, semi-monthly installments during the Employer's fiscal year. So long as the Employee discharges the Employee's duties and responsibilities to the best of the Employee's ability, the Employee's salary shall not be reduced without the Employee's consent. In addition, the Employee shall receive such increases in salary as shall be determined by the Employer from time to time; provided, however, nothing herein shall be construed as creating a right or entitlement to increase in salary. In any event, the Employee's salary shall be reviewed at least annually.

(b) by providing such other bonus plans, medical plans, profit-sharing or pension plans, or other benefit plans as shall be determined by the Employer from time to time. Employee's participation in and benefits under said plan shall be subject to the terms and conditions thereof as in effect from time to time. Nothing herein shall be construed to require adoption or continuation of any such plans by Employer or to restrict Employer's right to modify or terminate such plans.

4. Employer's Authority and Control. The Employee recognizes that the Employer shall have complete authority with regard to acceptance for treatment or refusal to treat any animal, and the Employer shall have complete authority with regard to the establishment of the appropriate fee for professional services.

The Employee shall perform all veterinary medical services as are assigned to the Employee by the Employer. The performance of said services by the Employee on behalf of the Employer shall be performed at such times and at such places as shall be determined by the Employer and in accordance with such rules as the Employer may establish.

All patient records, files, x-ray films, or other records concerning animals treated or clients consulted or interviewed by Employee during this employment shall be the property of Employer and shall remain with the Employer on termination of this employment.

5. Absences. Authorized and paid absence due to sickness, accidents, or personal necessity shall accrue to the Employee at the rate of 1/2 day per month, up to a limit of six (6) days per year; provided, however, the Employee shall not be absent for longer than two (2) consecutive days without a statement from a licensed physician indicating that absence of such duration is justified.

In the event of absence by the Employee which exceeds the aforementioned limits, the Employer may, in its sole discretion, hire a temporary replacement for the Employee and offset the cost of employing the temporary replacement against the total annual compensation to which the Employee otherwise would be entitled and any other amounts due the Employee from the Employer.

6. Professional Liability Insurance. The Employer shall provide and pay all expenses in connection with obtaining and maintaining professional liability insurance covering Employer for the Employee's services on behalf of Employer during the term of this Agreement while working on and at the premises of Critters Cove Animal Clinic. The foregoing notwithstanding, Employer shall not be required to provide individual coverage for Employee during the term of this Agreement or "tail" coverage for Employee following termination of this employment.

7. Expenses. During the term of this Agreement, the Employee will be reimbursed for the Employee's reasonable expenses for the benefit of the Employer in accordance with the general policy of the Employer as adopted by Employer from time to time.

8. Reimbursement. If, as a consequence of an audit of the income tax returns of the Employer, any compensation paid to the Employee, any expenses paid for the Employee, or any reimbursement for expenses paid to the Employee, shall be disallowed as income tax deductions, and if the Employer does not contest such disallowance or if the disallowance becomes final and binding, the Employee agrees to repay to the Employer all amounts of disallowed compensation and expenses. This provision for repayment shall not be waived by the Employer except by written instrument signed by Employer and specifically referring to this paragraph.

9. Cancellation. Nothing in this Agreement shall be construed to prevent the Employer from terminating the Employee's employment at any time because of such Employee's fraud, misappropriation, embezzlement, other conduct by which the Employee deprive the Employer of its property, or other conduct that reflects adversely upon the professional practice of the Employer such as incompetency, intoxication, or insubordination. The Employer shall be responsible to the Employee for no more than thirty (30) days' compensation from a notice of termination of employment for the above-mentioned reasons.

The Employee may terminate this Agreement at any time upon thirty (30) days' notice to the Employer, and the Employer shall be obligated in advance to pay Employee compensation up to the date of termination only.

The Employer may terminate this Agreement at any time upon thirty (30) days' notice to the Employee, and the Employer shall be obligated in that event to pay Employee compensation up to the date of termination only.

In the event of Employee's death during the term of this Agreement, this Agreement shall terminate immediately; and Employee's legal representatives shall be entitled to receive compensation due Employee up to the time of death.

If, during the term of this Agreement, Employee should fail to perform his/her duties hereunder on account of illness or other incapacity, and such illness or other incapacity shall continue for a period of more than one month, the Employer shall be obligated to pay to Employee compensation up to the date of termination. However, if prior to the date specified in such notice, Employee's illness or incapacity shall have terminated and he/she shall have taken up and performed his/her duties hereunder, Employee shall be entitled to resume his/her employment hereunder as though such notice had not been given.

If, during the term of this Agreement, the Employer should discontinue or interrupt the operation of its business for a period of thirty (30) days, this Agreement shall automatically terminate without further liability on the part of either of the parties hereto.

10. Contract Payments. The parties acknowledge that during the term of this Agreement, the Employee will receive the benefits of the goodwill which has been engendered by the Employer during its existence. The Employer will be introducing the Employee to its clients, will make the Employee familiar with its client lists, and will be training the Employee in its methods of treatment and maintenance of good client relations. The professional reputation of the Employee will be created and/or substantially enhanced by the Employee's association with the Employer. Therefore, if the Employee engages in the practice of veterinary medicine or engages, either directly or indirectly, in any manner or capacity as an adviser, principal, agent, partner, officer, director, employee, or otherwise in any business or activity which at the time shall be competitive with the practice of veterinary medicine conducted by the Employer, and if the Employee is engaged in any such business or activity within a radius of five (5) miles of any business location of the Employer within a period of two (2) years after the termination of the employment of the Employee with the Employer for any reason, the Employee agrees to pay to the Employer an amount equal to fifty percent (50%) of the gross receipts from any such business or activity during the first year after the termination of such employment and twenty-five percent (25%) of the gross receipts from any such business for activity during the second year after the termination of such employment. Employee acknowledges that Employer currently has business locations known as Critters Cove Animal Clinic and Doggey Bone Animal Hospital. For purposes of this Agreement, "business locations" shall include these locations or any other locations at which Employer does business as of the date of Employee's termination. "Gross receipts" shall include all amounts received by the Employee as professional fees, including all fees received by a professional or business corporation or other entity in which such Employee is either directly or indirectly the controlling stockholder, partner, or other owner. In other cases, "gross receipts" shall include salary, commissions, bonuses, reimbursement, and all types of nontaxable compensation paid to Employee, including, but not limited to, premiums for group life and medical insurance, contributions to qualified pension or profit-sharing plans, etc. Employee agrees to account to Employer monthly during the two-year period following termination of this employment to allow Employer to enforce its rights hereunder. Employer shall be allowed to set off amounts due to it from Employee hereunder against any amounts owed to Employee pursuant to this Agreement.

11. Benefit. This Agreement shall be binding upon the heirs and personal representatives of the Employee and upon the successors and assigns of the Employer.

12. Governing Law. This Agreement shall be governed by the laws of the State of Nebraska.

13. Waiver. This Agreement shall not be modified or amended except by further written documents signed by the Employee and the Employer. No provision hereof may be waived except by an agreement in writing, signed by the waiving party. A waiver of any term or provision shall not be construed as a waiver of any other term or provision.

WITNESS the hand of the Employee and the execution hereof by the Employer by its duly authorized officer as of the date first above written.

CRITTERS, INC.

Attest:

By_____
Its President

_____
Secretary

_____
Amy Nalistik

There are employer benefits to an agreement as well. There can be bonus incentives that will motivate the employee to work harder. Also, the employer can include noncompetition clauses in the agreement so the employee cannot quit and then compete against the company.

Duties and Responsibilities   This part of the employment contract should be stated specifically, so there are no misunderstandings about what is expected of the employee. Before entering into a contract, the employer should write a job description as part of the contract. The duties and responsibilities section of the contract can be used to measure the employee's performance. Therefore, the employer should be specific about what is expected from the employee.

Employers want language that allows additional duties to be assigned during the life of the contract. The company may expand, downsize, or make other changes that require the key employee to take on more or different duties. Employers do not want to renegotiate employment contracts every time the company changes.

However, employees want to protect themselves from having duties thrust upon them that have nothing to do with their position. Therefore, employees want language in the contract that allows additional duties only of the type that properly belong to the position. These limitations should be specifically defined in the contract.

Compensation   **Compensation** is the salary paid to the employee as well as all other benefits. Compensation can be a set dollar amount paid periodically. It also can be paid in bonuses. **Bonuses** are additional compensation based upon performance. If the employer pays bonuses, the contract should set out specifically how the bonuses are calculated, when they will be calculated, and when they will be paid. Some companies will give year-end bonuses based on the overall performance of the company; others tie them directly to the particular employee's performance. Bonuses can be paid at any time.

Compensation can be paid in the form of incentive programs. An incentive program should be directly related to the performance of the employee and those she supervises. There is no incentive if compensation is tied to performance over which the employee has no control. Incentive programs should be drafted carefully in the contract. There are several items to include in an employment agreement. One is the date for payment. This allows the employee to anticipate income and to plan cash flow. If accounting terms are used, the terms should be defined in the contract. Also, if any expenses or other items are to be deducted from either gross profits or gross sales to determine the compensation, this should be stated clearly in the contract.

The contract should state who will be responsible for determining the compensation to be paid the employee. Some companies hire independent public accountants to audit the records and make the determination. If this is the method, the contract should specify the accountants and should state that generally accepted accounting methods will be used to make the determination.

Some incentive plans allow the employee to make draws against his future income. A **draw** is an advance payment of income. The agreement should state the terms for draws. If the employee draws more than his entitlement, the contract can provide either that the employee must repay the company or that the excess will be applied to the next year.

Finally, the contract should address the issue of the employee's not working the full year, using a percentage formula. Very rarely are employees hired on the first day of the year. There would not be much incentive for an employee if his compensation were based on the entire year, even though he worked for only six months.

Companies that pay compensation in the form of commission must consider these elements of the incentive program. The contract should state specifically how commissions will be calculated, when they will be calculated, who will make the determination, and when the commission will be paid. Some companies pay an employee a base salary plus commission, allowing the employee to take draws against commission.

Other benefits that companies can offer their employees include life, health, and dental insurance and other insurance plans. Also, vacation and sick leave, disability compensation, and the like are benefits that may be available to an employee. The contract should state what these benefits are and who pays any premiums.

Salary and other benefits (including insurance premiums) are expenses to the corporation and are deducted before corporate income taxes are paid. There are tax considerations for benefits. For example, an employee may be taxed if the premiums paid by the employer exceed a certain amount. However, tax laws and regulations are constantly changing and should be reviewed before entering into any employment contract.

Duration of the Contract   The duration of the agreement is important. An employer usually wants it to be short, at least at the beginning. That way, if the employee does not work out, the contract either can be bought out at a reasonable price or it will terminate soon.

Most employment contracts contain renewal provisions. These can be set up in different ways. The option can be granted either to the employer or to the employee, or it can be renewed automatically unless either party objects. Automatic renewals sometimes include salary increases or changes in other benefits.

If there is no renewal provision in the contract, it terminates on the date stated in the contract, which can be a specific date or upon the occurrence of a certain event or condition.

Termination of the Contract   Employment contracts should contain a provision that allows either party to terminate the agreement for specific reasons. The agreement may allow termination with or without cause. Either way, the contract should be very specific about how to terminate and the consequences of termination. As previously stated, courts will not require an employee to work for an employer if she does not wish to do so; however, terminating the contract may carry financial or other penalties. In contrast, if the employer terminates the contract, the employee usually is protected by salary continuation for a period of time, possibly for the remaining term of the contract.

If the employer is allowed to terminate the employment relationship without cause, notice is required. The contract should be very specific concerning the time frame for notice and whether the employee will be paid salary during that time.

> Sue decides to terminate the employment contract of Jill after six months. The contract with Jill calls for a two-month notice to be given. Sue can either have Jill work those two months or pay her two months' salary and have Jill leave immediately.

Depending on the type of work the employee is doing, the company may want the employee to leave immediately. Sales, computer companies, and other customer- or information-sensitive companies generally prefer not to have a terminated employee continue to work.

This is true regardless of whether the employee or the employer gives the termination notice.

Most employment contracts include provisions on termination for cause. The contract should identify as many causes as are appropriate and then should add a catch-all clause that encompasses other circumstances. Specific clauses might include:

- Employee breach of the contract
- Physical or mental disability of the employee for more than a certain length of time
- A change in the ownership of the business because of a sale, merger, consolidation, or dissolution
- Bankruptcy or insolvency of the business
- The employee's incarceration for conviction of a crime.

This, of course, is not an exhaustive list of causes. The nature of the business and its needs should be considered when drafting this portion of the contract.

Many high-level executive contracts provide substantial severance compensation upon termination of the employment contract, particularly if the employer terminates the contract. The term used for this type of severance package is **golden parachute**. Golden parachute contracts either provide continuation of salary for a long period of time or provide for a lump-sum payment, continuation of benefits, and repurchase of the stock owned by the employee. Usually, the price for the stock repurchase is set in the contract. There are as many variations in severance packages as there are executives to negotiate them.

Employee Rights

Most employees do not have written, individual contracts with their employers. Many companies publish **employee handbooks** or manuals that they distribute to their employees. The manuals typically include the organization and structure of the company, to acquaint the employee with the supervisory hierarchy of the company. The company also includes its equal employment opportunity and antiharassment statements, required by federal law.

All employee benefits and other policies should be in the handbook, including vacation, sick leave, funeral leave, holidays, leaves of absence, insurance, retirement, legal services, education reimbursement, direct banking, pension plans, and any other benefit or policy that the company provides. In addition, general policies regarding compensation should be included, such as payday schedule, overtime, bonuses, and wage advances. The handbook also should set out policies regarding promotions, transfers, grievance procedure, personnel reviews, nepotism, and termination.

Hours of work, flex time, dress code, and standards of conduct for employees generally are part of the handbook. The company should include any security or emergency procedures to be followed by employees.

An employee handbook is tailored to meet the needs of the company and should include any items that could arise in an employee dispute. It should be flexible enough to apply to specific disputes. An employer must keep in mind, however, that courts may look at a manual or handbook as a contract with the employee. The benefits listed in the handbook will be enforceable as to the employees. If an employee is terminated in violation of the policies stated in the employee handbook, a breach of contract action may be brought by the employee.

A company can protect itself by reserving its right to amend or cancel any benefit described in the handbook. This reservation must be clear and must be prominently displayed in the handbook. The company may be able to protect itself by including statements that the handbook does not create a contract and that the employment relationship is at will only.

Employment at will is a common law doctrine that means a company may terminate an employee at any time for any reason. The reason cannot be illegal, however, such as a violation of antidiscrimination laws. If an employer discharges an employee in violation of the law, the employee can bring a **wrongful discharge** action.

Some states do not allow employment at will. Many other states recognize public policy exceptions to the employment-at-will doctrine. Under this rule, an employer may not fire a worker for reasons that violate a fundamental public policy of the jurisdiction. For example, an employer would be prevented from firing someone who serves on a jury or someone who refused to perform an illegal act for the employer.

In addition to state laws, federal law regulates employment benefits: the Employment Retirement Income Security Act, known as ERISA. This law is beyond the scope of this text. Be aware, though, that ERISA's influence is pervasive and its requirements complex.

Covenants

Many types of restrictive or proprietary covenants may be included within an employee contract. These have to do with who owns the **employee work product**, covenants not to compete, and trade secrets.

Does the employer have a right to the employee's work product? The employee may have been hired for the express purpose of developing new products or systems. If the product or system has to do with the job, the employer generally owns the work product. This should be stated specifically in the employment contract. If the work product includes an invention that can be patented, the agreement must specify who will own the patent rights and whether the employee will be paid for the rights in addition to her normal compensation. This provision must be drafted very carefully if the company is hiring an employee to create, invent, or develop new products, ideas, or systems.

If the work product is a procedure or process, it may qualify as a **trade secret**. The law protects trade secrets. Trade secrets can include customer or supplier lists, processes or ingredients used to produce a food item, computer programs, or anything the company believes is an integral part of the company's competitive advantage. Confidentiality is an integral part of trade secrets.

The company will want to include a **nondisclosure clause** in the employment agreement. The nondisclosure clause should extend beyond the term of the contract. A company can bind an employee after her employment never to disclose trade secrets. It should also include secrets the employee used, as well as secrets the employee may have learned during her employment from other employees or from observation. Usually, a liquidated damages clause is included. **Liquidated damages** are an agreed amount specified in a contract in the event of a breach; the provision is used when actual damages cannot be measured. It usually is hard to prove actual damages as the result of divulging a trade secret.

A **covenant not to compete** is common in employment contracts. This covenant prevents the employee from using her talents against the employer. If the restriction is too severe, courts will not enforce it. Courts often view these restrictions as restraints of trade, which are prohibited under several federal laws. The restriction cannot prohibit the employee indefinitely from going to work for a competitor. A company cannot take an employee's livelihood away from her.

The covenants not to compete that are enforceable usually include geographical boundaries and limited time periods.

> Jane sold leather goods for Ann's company. During the time she worked for Ann, Jane developed many contacts. Another company offered Jane a better sales job. However, Jane had signed an employment agreement, when she went to work for Ann, that contained a covenant not to compete. The clause stated that Jane could not sell leather goods for five years within a hundred-mile radius of Ann's territory.

This clause might be upheld by some courts. It does not prohibit Jane from competing indefinitely, and it still allows Jane to seek gainful employment somewhere. Depending on the nature of leather goods sales, other courts might find either the radius or the time frame too restrictive. If so, those courts would not enforce the covenant.

The courts consider several factors when determining whether a covenant not to compete is reasonable and therefore enforceable. Besides the burden on the employee, courts consider whether there is a legitimate need of the employer, whether the restriction is excessive, whether the employer's business relies heavily on trade secrets, whether the business is highly competitive, whether the bargaining power between the employer and employee was equal, and whether the employee understood the covenant. In some states, courts also consider whether the contract is an employment-at-will contract. If so, covenants not to compete usually are not enforceable, as the employer can terminate the employee at will. Otherwise, employers could hire and fire employees just so they could not compete in the marketplace. Consider the *Broome* case.

Broome v. Ginsberg, 283 S.E.2d 1 (Ga. Ct. App. 1981)

Dr. Ginsberg, a dentist, formed a professional corporation and hired Dr. Broome, also a dentist. Dr. Broome signed an employment agreement, which contained a provision not to compete for a period of two years in the same county. Dr. Ginsberg died and Dr. Broome opened up his own dentist office. Mrs. Ginsberg sued Dr. Broome for violating the covenant not to compete.

The court held that restrictive covenants will be scrutinized narrowly because they lessen competition and are a partial restraint of trade. "When the contract involves the practice of a profession, it will be held void if it needlessly oppresses one of the parties without affording any corresponding protection to the other." *Id.* at 2. The court found that because this was a professional corporation and the only stockholder had died, it had ceased to be a professional corporation except for liquidation purposes. Therefore, there was no competition from Dr. Broome and the corporation did not need any protection.

Other Employee Benefits

There are many other benefits a corporation can offer its employees. These are no longer reserved for top-level management; they are benefits and incentives that attract and keep good employees. An **incentive compensation plan** is one such benefit. This can be set up for an individual or for a group. Group incentive plans provide compensation to the members of a group that is directly related to the group's performance. A carefully drafted plan will include a recitation of who decides about awarding the compensation, clear definitions of the eligible members of the group, definitions of all terms, and when the compensation will be paid.

Deferred compensation (sometimes called a 401K plan, referring to the section of the tax code) is another benefit. Income the employee is to receive is deferred until retirement or until the employee becomes incapacitated. Thus, when the employee receives the money, she presumably is in a lower tax bracket. This money is invested while it remains in the 401K plan. Taxes are not paid until the money is taken out, usually after the employee reaches 59½ years of age.

A company can match the employee's contribution, up to a certain percentage. Deferred compensation is governed by the IRC and regulations. There is a cap on how much an employee can defer and how much the employer can match. This is ever changing, so one must research the current state of the law. This incentive remains with the company. A period of time (five years, for example) may have to elapse before the employee can take the employer's matching funds if she quits her employment.

Pension and profit-sharing plans can be used as incentives to keep employees. This can be set up as deferred compensation also. Such a plan must qualify under the IRC. A pension plan is used to induce the employee to stay with the company to receive increased retirement benefits. The profit-sharing plan is based on current profits. The contribution to the plan is based on the production by the employees. It usually is a percentage of the annual profits of the company.

A profit-sharing plan can be better than a pension plan from the employer's viewpoint. It is based on annual profits, so there is no fixed amount (or any amount) that must be contributed each year. In contrast, employers must contribute to pension plans on an annual basis to ensure that the retirement funds are there. The contribution to a pension plan is based on age and length of service, not on profits of the company.

To qualify under the IRC for deductibility of employer contributions, a pension or profit-sharing plan must meet certain requirements. The tax code and regulations must be thoroughly analyzed before drafting a plan.

Incentive stock options are another employee benefit. A stock option incentive plan is an option granted to an employee to buy stock that has tax benefits under the tax code. Instead of money, the employee is given an ownership interest in the corporation.

The stock option itself is a written agreement. It gives the employee a right to purchase stock during a given period of time for a specified rate. The employee does not have to purchase the stock. To be a real incentive, the price of the stock usually is below market price. There are tax advantages to stock option incentive plans.

Things to consider when drafting a stock option plan are:

1. The purpose of the plan. Is it to reward past services, an incentive to continue employment, or an inducement to accept employment?
2. Which employees are eligible and what stock is subject to the plan?
3. At what price will the stock option be set, and what is the duration of the option?
4. How to exercise the option, including notice, conditions, the issuance of certificates, and how heirs will be treated.

Other things to consider are how payment will be made, whether there will be any restrictions on the transfer of this stock, whether there is an employment agreement, and the effective date of the option. Shareholder approval usually is required before a stock option can be given. It is a good idea to obtain IRS approval as well; then the company knows that it has a qualified plan and will receive tax advantages. Also, the plan should consider how a merger, consolidation, or reorganization will affect the plan.

The last benefit plan discussed here is the employee **expense reimbursement** plan. Section 89 of the IRC recognizes five expense reimbursement plans that qualify for tax benefits: group term life insurance plans, qualified group legal services plans, educational assistance programs, dependent care assistance programs, and accident or health insurance plans involving reimbursement of medical payments.

These benefits are taxable income to the employee unless a broad-based segment and certain number of employees are part of the plan. In other words, a company cannot offer expense reimbursement plans only to high-level employees and still gain any tax advantages.

The plan should be carefully drafted so that it does not create tax complications to the employees. The plan should state a purpose, an effective date, and how the plan will be administered. Membership in the plan should be defined. New employees may not be eligible until a certain date. The benefits should be stated with a maximum dollar amount that will be paid. Any appropriate definitions should be included, such as defining who qualifies as beneficiaries. How payments will be paid, as well as any documentation required by the employer before payment is made, should be described in the plan. If the plan can be terminated by the employer, those conditions should be stated in the plan as well.

Benefit plans can be complicated to draft and to administer. If not done correctly, plans can result in negative tax consequences to both employer and employee.

Key Terms

Bonuses

Compensation

Covenant not to compete

Deferred compensation

Draw

Employee handbook

Employee work product

Employment at will

Expense reimbursement

Golden parachute

Incentive compensation plans

Incentive stock options

Liquidated damages

Nondisclosure clause

Pension and profit-sharing plans

Trade secret

Wrongful discharge

Quiz

1. What is an employment agreement? Explain briefly.

2. Briefly define the term *key employee.*

3. Why is it important to have the employment duties and responsibilities set out in an agreement? Explain briefly.

4. Define the term *compensation* and describe the forms that it can take.

5. Briefly define the term *draw.*

6. When an employment contract is drafted, what causes for termination should be included by the employer? Describe briefly.

7. Explain briefly the term *golden parachute.*

8. When an employee does not have an employment contract, what typically provides the basis for his or her employment rights?

9. Define and discuss succinctly the following terms as they relate to the employment relationship: (a) *work product;* (b) *covenant not to compete;* and (c) *trade secrets.*

10. Describe briefly the types of benefits that an employer may provide to employees.

16 Foreign Corporations

A **foreign corporation** is a corporation doing business in a state other than the one in which it was incorporated. Early in the process, incorporators choose the jurisdiction in which to incorporate, either because of certain advantages or because that is where the business will operate. The business thereafter may have expanded across state lines, or possibly the corporation was intended to be a multistate business. The corporation then becomes a foreign corporation in the other states. A corporation incorporated in another country is sometimes referred to as an **alien corporation**.

A corporation is created by state law and is, therefore, a citizen of that state, with the rights guaranteed to all citizens of the state. Under the early common law, a corporation was not permitted to do business in any jurisdiction other than the one where it had incorporated. As businesses began to expand and to outgrow the state in which they incorporated, a question arose as to whether a state could prevent businesses from entering the state unless they incorporated or whether a state could place restrictions on a foreign corporation before it could conduct business. The United States Supreme Court answered these questions. The Constitution guarantees persons the right to move freely among the states. The Court found that corporations are persons. Corporations are allowed to do business in other states, but the states can place reasonable restrictions and conditions upon foreign corporations.

Most states require a corporation to file certain information with the secretary of state. Usually, this is information that will subject the corporation to legal process and will give the public information about the corporation.

Before a corporation can do business in another state, it must be legally qualified to do so. The board of directors must pass a resolution that allows the corporation to be a foreign corporation and that directs the officers to take the necessary steps to qualify.

The Model Business Corporation Act prohibits a foreign corporation from **transacting business** within a state without a **certificate of authority** from that state. Many states have adopted this approach. State laws include a procedure for obtaining a certificate of authority and usually have penalties for failing to comply.

A corporation cannot be denied a certificate of authority simply because the state where it incorporated has different laws governing corporations. However, a corporation can be denied authority if it incorporated for purposes that are illegal in the **host state**. For example, a corporation that is incorporated for gambling purposes in states such as Illinois, Nevada, or New Jersey, where gambling is legal, may be denied a certificate of authority in a state where gambling is illegal. Otherwise, a corporation that is legally incorporated in one state may do business in another.

Certificate of Authority

All states have a procedure for qualifying as a foreign corporation to conduct business within the state. Usually, an application must be filed with the secretary of state. This application requires information such as the corporate structure, solvency, and location of property of the corporation. Also, the articles of incorporation from the domestic state, with a seal, may be required to be filed in the foreign state. Many states require only a certificate of good standing.

The Model Business Corporation Act sets out what should be included in the application for a certificate of authority. This includes the name of the corporation, the state or country where the corporation is incorporated, the date of incorporation and period of duration, street address of the principal office, the name and address of the registered agent in the state, and the names and addresses of the current directors and officers.

Other information that a state may require includes:

- A statement of the purpose of the corporation to be pursued in this state
- The aggregate number of shares the corporation has authority to issue
- The number of shares that have been issued, by class and series
- The value of property to be owned by the corporation, within and without the state
- An estimate of the gross amount of business the corporation will do within and without the state.

This is not an exhaustive list of information that may be required by a state in the application for a certificate of authority. Each state's requirements should be researched, as well as how a foreign corporation is treated in the state's legal system. A company may not want to incorporate in a state where foreign corporations are treated unfairly.

A foreign corporation must comply with the statutes regulating corporate names. This text previously discussed choosing a corporate name. The corporation may have to use a different corporate name in a foreign state if a particular name already is taken. If one knows right away that a business will operate in more than one state, one should reserve the name in all states in which the corporation expects to do business. A foreign corporation can use fictitious or assumed names, just as domestic corporations can.

Another universal requirement for foreign corporations is that they must maintain registered offices and agents within the state for legal process. If a registered office cannot be found, usually the secretary of state can be served. The secretary of state then will send the legal process to the corporation's main offices.

Once a corporation is given authority to conduct business within a state, it receives the same rights and privileges as a domestic corporation. Also, the corporation is subject to the same duties and responsibilities. A corporation is subject to income and other taxes in the host state if it has **substantial contacts** within the state. What constitutes substantial contacts has been hotly litigated. It now is established that receiving a certificate of authority is enough to qualify as "substantial contacts".

This is one reason why a corporation may argue that it is not transacting business within the state and therefore does not have to qualify as a foreign corporation. Once the corporation is qualified as a foreign corporation, it is subject to taxes in that state.

Some states also impose franchise fees on foreign corporations. A **franchise fee** is a tax imposed on a corporation for the right to maintain a business in the state. This fee is based on the authorized capital stock of the corporation. Many states also impose a similar tax on domestic corporations (discussed in Chapter 7).

Many states require the filing of annual reports. Annual reports are required of domestic corporations also. The Model Business Corporation Act states what should be included in an annual report. Most of the information relates to the registered agent, current directors and officers, and the nature of the business. Other information is required so that the state can assess taxes. These items relate to the aggregate number of shares authorized and/or issued and the value of property owned by the corporation.

A foreign corporation as well as a domestic corporation must report all structural changes in the corporation. A foreign corporation must file all amendments made to its articles of incorporation. Once a corporation is qualified to do business in a host state, it is treated the same as a domestic corporation. Therefore, any requirements that a domestic corporation must meet also must be met by a foreign corporation. (See the *Advanced Machine Co.* case for an application of this principle.)

A corporation may decide, for whatever reason, that it does not want to do business in the host state any longer. The corporation must file an application for withdrawal of its certificate of authority with the host state. The authority of any agents of the corporation will be revoked, and the state will assess any unpaid taxes and fees.

> ### *Advanced Machine Co. v. Berry*, 378 So.2d 26 (Fla. 1980)
>
> A Missouri corporation, doing business in Florida as a foreign corporation, dissolved in its home state voluntarily. Defendants brought a tort claim against plaintiff. Plaintiff argued that Missouri had a two-year statute of limitations for claims which should apply. Defendants argued that the Florida three-year statute of limitations should apply.
>
> The court found that Florida statutes should apply. A foreign corporation could not diminish the time for filing claims. "If a foreign corporation desired to take the benefits of doing business in Florida, then it should be subject to the same limitations as applicable to a domestic corporation upon dissolution." *Id.* at 27.

A state may revoke a corporation's certificate of authority. This usually occurs if the corporation fails to comply with state law. Things that may trigger a revocation of a certificate of authority include the failure to file annual reports, failure to pay taxes and fees, failure to maintain a registered agent and office, failure to file amendments, misrepresentation in the application, or use of an unauthorized name.

Transacting Business

The traditional test used by most states to determine when a corporation must qualify to do business in that state is whether the corporation is transacting business within the state. There is no precise definition of what constitutes transacting business; therefore, it has created extensive litigation. Foreign corporations, of course, argue that they are not transacting business and thus are not subject to state regulations requiring a certificate of authority.

Section 15.01 of the Model Business Corporation Act lists certain activities in which a corporation may engage without being considered to be transacting business within a state:

1. Maintaining, defending, or settling any proceeding
2. Holding meetings of the board of directors or shareholders or carrying on other activities concerning internal corporate affairs
3. Maintaining bank accounts
4. Maintaining offices or agencies for the transfer, exchange, and registration of the corporation's own securities or maintaining trustees or depositories with respect to those securities
5. Selling through independent contractors
6. Soliciting or obtaining orders, whether by mail or through employees or agents or otherwise, if the orders require acceptance outside the state before they become contracts
7. Creating or acquiring indebtedness, mortgages, and security interests in real or personal property
8. Securing or collecting debts or enforcing mortgages and security interests in property securing the debts
9. Owning, without more, real or personal property
10. Conducting an isolated transaction that is completed within thirty days and that is not one in the course of repeated transactions of a like nature
11. Transacting business in interstate commerce.

Some states follow the Model Business Corporation Act. Other states have established their own list of permissible activities, and still others have no set guidelines at all. The best thing to do is to research the case law regarding foreign corporations. Most states impose penalties for transacting business without a certificate of authority.

There are several sanctions that a state may impose for conducting business without the authority to do so. The corporation may be denied access to the court system (see the *General Accident* case). A corporation may be allowed to defend itself but may be denied access to sue. A corporation will be liable for all fees and taxes that it should have paid. Fines can be assessed against the corporation and directors, which usually are substantial. Contracts can be declared unenforceable. In some states, all acts of the unqualified corporation are deemed void. An injunction could be sought by a state to enjoin a corporation from doing business. Most states will excuse the sanctions once a corporation becomes qualified under its statutes.

General Accident Fire & Life Assurance Corp. v. AllCity Insurance Co., 279 N.Y. S.2d 422 (1967)

Defendant moved for a change of venue because Nassau County was not the principal place of business for plaintiff, a foreign corporation. Defendant alleged that the proper venue was the residence of the foreign corporation. Residence is the location of its office designated in its application for authority to do business in the state.

The court found that a foreign insurance corporation was specifically exempted from designating an office in the application for authority to do business in New York. Therefore, Nassau County was a proper venue.

Key Terms

Alien corporation

Certificate of authority

Foreign corporation

Host state

Substantial contacts

Transacting business

Quiz

1. Briefly define the term *foreign corporation*.

2. What must a corporation do to qualify to do business in another jurisdiction? Explain briefly.

3. Discuss briefly the concept of substantial contacts.

4. Other than taxes, what requirements may the host state impose on the foreign corporation? Explain briefly.

5. Describe briefly what a foreign corporation must do if it no longer wants to do business in a state.

6. Under what circumstances can a state revoke a foreign corporation's certificate of authority?

7. Identify activities in which a foreign corporation may engage without being considered to be transacting business in a state.

8. What sanctions can be imposed for conducting business without the authority to do so in a particular state?

Answer Key for Chapter Quizzes

Chapter 1

1. An agency is a fiduciary relationship in which one party uses another party to manage a business transaction on behalf of the former.

2. Principal and agent.

3. (1) Disclosed principal—existence is known to the third party. (2) Partially disclosed principal—third party knows there is someone other than the agent but not the principal's identity. (3) Undisclosed principal—third party has no knowledge that there is a principal.

4. Duty to cooperate, to comply with the agency contract, to compensate the agent for services performed for the principal, to act in good faith, and not to interfere with the agency.

5. (1) General agent—an agent who performs tasks connected with the principal's business. The agent is controlled by the principal. The most common general agent is an employee. (2) Special agent—an agent who performs a specific task for the principal. (3) Independent contractor—an agent who performs a specific task but is not controlled by the principal. (4) Subagent—an agent of the original agent (agents are liable for their subagents).

6. (1) Actual express authority—the principal gives specific authority to the agent to perform a task. (2) Apparent authority—the principal holds the agent out as having authority. (3) Implied authority—usual custom and practice in business dealings.

7. An agent has a duty to act only as authorized; an implied duty of loyalty, honesty, good faith, and obedience; a duty to disclose information to the principal; a duty to account for all property and money; and a duty not to act on behalf of third parties.

8. Respondeat superior—an employer is responsible for the acts of an employee. Vicarious liability—a principal is liable for the acts of an agent performed in furtherance of the agency.

9. (1) The purpose of the agency is accomplished; (2) the agency was for a specific time, and the time has lapsed; (3) by mutual agreement; (4) by operation of law; and (5) bankruptcy (in some situations).

10. The elements of an agency are offer, acceptance (mutual assent), consideration, and the capacity to enter into a contract. The subject matter of the agency must be legal.

11. An express agency is formed as the result of an oral or written contract. An implied agency exists by inference from facts and circumstances, such as similar dealings between the parties in the past.

Chapter 2

1. A sole proprietorship is a business owned by one individual. The owner can hire employees and others to help with the business, but the sole proprietor controls and manages the business.

2. The advantages of owning a business as a sole proprietor are the ease of formation, flexibility, and complete control by one owner.

3. The disadvantages of owning a business as a sole proprietor are unlimited personal liability/exposure, difficulty in generating capital until the business is proven, and no continuity (proprietorship ends when the owner dies).

4. Revenue is personal income or loss to the sole proprietor and is reported on Schedule C of Form 1040.

5. There are several ways to terminate the sole proprietorship: (1) the owner can decide to terminate the business; (2) death or incapacity of the owner terminates the proprietorship; and (3) bankruptcy.

6. A trade name is a name the business entity uses to do business, such as Denise's Bistro.

7. There is no guarantee. At best, the sole proprietor can will the business assets to someone in the hope that he or she will continue the business as a new sole proprietor or in some other business form.

Chapter 3

1. Two or more partners. If there is only one owner, the business entity is a sole proprietorship.

2. General partnership and limited partnership.

3. Any person or entity can be a general partner. A general partner does not have to be a natural person.

4. A written agreement defines how the partnership will operate, who will run the business on a day-to-day basis, how control will be divided among the partners, the value of each partner's contribution to the partnership, how distribution at termination will be handled, and how disputes will be resolved (such as by majority vote). It also sets out the percentage of profits and losses that each partner will receive.

5. A partnership may be terminated for several reasons, including (1) mutual agreement; (2) the partnership existence was for a specific time, and that time has elapsed; (3) one partner withdraws either voluntarily or by death, incapacity, or bankruptcy; or (4) the partnership declares bankruptcy.

6. A partner may contribute money, goods, or services. The partner's contribution, other than money, will be given a value in the agreement. Profits, losses, and distribution at liquidation will be based on the percentage of each partner's contribution to the whole business.

7. A partner has the right: (1) to share equally in profits; (2) to receive repayment of contributions; (3) to receive indemnification for payments made on behalf of the partnership; (4) to receive interest on advances and capital contributions; (5) to share in the management of the partnership; (6) to have access to the partnership books; and (7) to have a formal accounting of partnership affairs.

   A partner has the duty: (1) to contribute toward losses of the partnership; (2) to work for the partnership without remuneration; (3) to submit to a majority vote when disputes arise; (4) to disclose to other partners any information the partner has regarding partnership matters; (5) to account to the partnership for any profits derived by partnership transactions or by use of

the partnership property; and (6) to act in good faith (the fiduciary duty).

8. Partners have unlimited liability exposure for the business, just as sole proprietors do. Each partner is 100 percent liable for all partnership obligations. Partners may obligate other partners.

9. The income and losses are taxed as personal income on each partner's individual tax return. Each partner is taxed for her ownership percentage without regard to whether the income is distributed. The partnership must file an informational tax return, Form 1065.

10. A partnership may be formed by oral or written agreement between two or more parties. There does not have to be a formal written agreement.

11. The partnership engages in activities separate from the partners; property can be bought and sold in the partnership name; and partners can become paid employees of the business. Licensing requirements are met in the partnership's name, and judgments can be enforced against partnership property.

12. A partnership name will be considered fictitious and must be registered if all surnames of the partners are not used. If Joe Jones, Sally Smith, and Mary Anderson form a partnership and use Jones, Smith & Anderson as the name of the partnership, the name does not need to be registered. However, if they use Jones & Smith, the name will be considered a fictitious name and must be registered.

13. Profits and losses may be shared in a variety of ways. The partnership agreement should address this question. Profits and losses can be shared equally, proportionate to capital contribution, by guarantee of profits to certain partners, or by allocation of profits to the partner who provided the financial backing until that partner is paid in full. Losses caused by willful conduct of a partner can be specified to be borne by that partner.

14. Marshaling of assets means that creditors of the partnership must look to partnership's assets first to satisfy the debt before the creditors may seek payment from individual partners.

Chapter 4

1. A limited partnership is formed by two or more persons; it has one or more general partners and one or more limited partners.

2. A limited partner has no voice in the day-to-day management and no control of the business.

Limited partners simply are investors in the partnership.

3. The agreement defines the duties and responsibilities of the general partners and limited partners; it ensures that the limited partner remains

a limited partner; it shows the investment of the limited partner, and it allows the limited partnership to continue the business without interruption as general partners and limited partners come and go.

4. A limited partnership, as with any business entity, cannot use a name that is similar or deceptively similar to that of an existing business. A limited partner's surname cannot be used unless it is also the surname of a general partner or unless the limited partnership was another entity first. The name must include some form of the term *limited partnership,* such as Ltd., L.P., or Limited Partnership.

5. Limited partners are liable to creditors to the extent of their investment(s).

6. There may be several causes, including (1) the resignation, retirement, bankruptcy, incapacity, withdrawal, or death of a general partner; (2) specific termination clauses in the partnership agreement; or (3) by court decree. Limited partners may come and go without dissolving the partnership, but they can demand the return of their capital contribution.

7. The priority for payment is creditors first, then partners for the distribution set out in the agreement; finally, the partners will receive a return of their investment. The agreement can provide that limited partners have priority over general partners.

8. Limited partnerships are treated the same as general partnerships. Income is considered paid to all partners and taxed on individual tax returns regardless of whether it is actually distributed. An informational tax return is filed by the limited partnership.

9. Limited partnerships are like corporations because the limited partners have limited liability to the extent of their investment, with no day-to-day involvement in the management of the business; but they can vote on matters that affect their investments. Limited partnerships are like partnerships because the general partners have management and control of the partnership and unlimited personal liability.

10. The certificate of limited partnership contains: name; address of the principal place of business; name and address of agent for service of process; name and address of each general partner; and the latest date upon which the limited partnership is to dissolve. The information is required by the RULPA. Each state can require further information. Usually the state requires use of a particular form that incorporates the mandatory information.

Chapter 5

1. A joint venture is an association of two or more persons formed to carry out a single business enterprise for profit.

2. Joint ventures usually are formed for large-scale development, such as industrial areas or power plants.

3. The similarities are that parties to a joint venture can be individuals, corporations, or partnerships; parties have mutual control and management; parties share in the profits and losses equally; a joint venture can hold title to property; parties have a fiduciary duty to the joint venture; the joint venture does not exist as a separate legal entity.

   The differences are that parties can withdraw without causing dissolution of the joint venture; it terminates at the completion of the project; and a party cannot bind the joint venture.

4. A joint venture will terminate upon completion of the project or at the time specified in the agreement.

5. A joint stock company is an unincorporated association of individuals, organized for the purpose of carrying on a business for profit.

6. A joint stock company is similar to a corporation in these ways: the ownership is in the form of stock; there is a perpetual existence; and it is managed by directors and officers.

   A joint stock company is similar to a partnership in these ways: it is formed by agreement rather than by statute; there is personal liability; and it is not a legal entity separate from its members.

Chapter 6

1. (1) Continuity of life; (2) centralization of management; (3) limited liability; and (4) free transferability of interest.

2. A limited liability company may possess only two of the four corporate characteristics.

3. Because the purpose of forming a limited liability company is to have limited liability for the owners, limited liability is the most common. Centralized management ranks second. Most limited liability companies either hire someone to manage the company or appoint certain members to manage.

4. Membership is not restricted to natural persons. Members can be individuals, partnerships or corporations.

5. Limited liability companies take advantage of the limited liability for all members from the corporate form. Because all income is passed through to members, there is no double taxation, and members can participate in management and control of the business, similar to the partnership form.

6. Uniform laws have not yet been enacted by state legislatures to govern limited liability companies from one state to the next; there is no perpetual existence; and there are restrictions on the transferability of interest. These disadvantages, however, are the very things that keep the limited liability company from being viewed as a corporation by the IRS and state regulations.

7. Members have the right to vote on matters affecting their interest, including who will manage the business and whether a member may transfer his, her, or its interest; the right to manage; the right to remove a manager; the right to inspect the books and records of the company; and the right to attend member meetings.

8. Some states require dissolution of the company when a member withdraws, retires, dies, or is expelled from the company.

9. There are one or more managers who are elected for a specific term to manage the business as described in the operating agreement. Managers are agents of the company. Managers are not liable for the company as general partners are in a partnership.

10. It is financed by contributions from the members, such as cash, property, and securities.

11. The operating agreement can set out the duration; by unanimous written agreement of the members; by court decree; by death, retirement, resignation, expulsion, bankruptcy, or dissolution of a member.

12. The IRS views a limited liability company as a partnership for taxation purposes as long as the company has no more than two of the four corporate characteristics. Some states tax a limited liability company as a corporation, without regard to the entity's treatment by the IRS.

13. Articles of organization must be filed with the state and local authority. The articles must include (1) the name, (2) principal place of business, (3) purpose, (4) name and address of registered agent and office, (5) managers' names and business addresses (if managed by managers) or members names and addresses (if managed by members), (6) latest date the company will be dissolved, (7) names and addresses of the organizers, (8) the capital contributions of the members, (9) the right of the company to admit new members, and (10) the right to continue business if a member leaves.

    The next step would be to draft the operating agreement. The operating agreement would be much like a partnership agreement or the bylaws of a corporation.

    A name must be selected for the company. The name must include some form of *limited liability company*, such as L.L.C., L.C., or Limited Liability Company.

14. The operating agreement should state the internal management of the company and would include such things as: (1) how members will share assets and earnings; (2) right to transfer interest; (3) procedure to amend the operating agreement; (4) whether certificates will be issued; (5) right to borrow money; (6) allocation of profits and gains to the mem bers; (7) distribution of assets to members; (8) what constitutes a quorum for member meetings; (9) the time, place, and date of member meetings; (10) qualifications, terms, and the like of managers; (11) and grounds to dissolve the company.

Chapter 7

1. A corporation is a business organization which is a separate entity and has an existence apart from its owners.

2. Corporations typically grant a corporation the power (1) to sue or be sued; (2) to have a corporate seal; (3) to make its own laws for managing the business; (4) to own, transfer, and mortgage personal and real property; (5) to enter into contracts; (6) to lend and invest money; (7) to establish pension plans; (8) to elect directors, appoint officers, and hire employees; (9) to be a partner, member, or manager of a partnership, joint venture, or other entity; (10) to conduct business in the state; (11) to make charitable

donations and other payments or acts that further the business of the corporation.

3. Shareholders have the right: (1) to vote on amendments, extraordinary matters, and directors; (2) to cumulative voting, if allowed by the articles; (3) to receive dividends and distributions at dissolution; (4) to inspect corporate books and records; (5) to preemptive rights if provided in the articles.

4. The courts may allow creditors to pursue shareholders if the corporation fails to follow the formalities of a corporation as a separate entity; if the corporation is unfunded or is undercapitalized; or if the corporation was established to perpetuate a fraud.

5. The MBCA requires that board members must be natural persons.

6. Directors have the right to participate in meetings and to inspect corporate books. They have the duties of fiduciary due care and loyalty, of electing/appointing officers, and of making financial decisions related to the corporation.

7. Officers manage the corporation on a daily basis (their rights and duties are stated in the bylaws).

8. Double taxation is the major disadvantage. The corporation pays taxes on income; if the income is passed to shareholders as dividends, the dividends are taxed to shareholders as personal income.

9. A business can incorporate for any lawful purpose. Some states restrict the ability of professionals to incorporate. The purpose of the corporation is stated in its articles of incorporation. For flexibility, articles should be very general, to allow the corporation to change directions or to add business interests without having to seek shareholder approval for changes to the articles.

10. If the articles of incorporation grant preemptive rights to shareholders, the shareholders are allowed to purchase newly issued stock in amounts that will preserve their same percentage of ownership.

11. The major advantage of a corporation is limited liability. The shareholders have liability only to the extent of their ownership interest. There is no personal liability for shareholders unless the corporate veil is pierced.

Chapter 8

1. The owners of the business need to review all business forms to determine if a corporation is the best form for that business. The owners also need to decide in which jurisdiction to incorporate. If the business will be operated only in one state, that state probably is the best jurisdiction for incorporation. Otherwise, statutes, tax regulations, case law, and the like should be reviewed to determine the best state. Another factor that may influence this decision is where the investors are located.

2. A promoter may do several different things for a business that plans to incorporate. The promoter may seek investors, look for office space, set up the office, enter into contracts that will bind the business, hire and train employees, and carry out any other duties the business may need. A promoter will be personally liable for contracts until the business incorporates and assumes the contracts.

3. After investors are secured and the business is ready to incorporate, the following must be done: (1) draft articles of incorporation and bylaws; (2) select a corporate name and reserve it; (3) file the articles of incorporation with the secretary of state and any local office required by law; (4) hold the incorporator meeting to elect directors; (5) hold the first board of directors meeting to adopt bylaws and other items as necessary or expedient.

4. The Model Business Corporation Act requires the articles of incorporation to include: (1) the name of the corporation; (2) the number of shares authorized to be issued by the corporation; (3) the name and address of the initial registered agent and office; and (4) the names and addresses of the incorporators.

5. A business may have potential shareholders sign preincorporation share subscriptions. These are offers prior to incorporation to purchase shares in a corporation. They are legally binding and enforceable contracts. This is one way to ensure that a corporation has the required capital to commence business.

6. If the articles of incorporation allow cumulative voting, a shareholder may vote the number of shares that she owns times the number of directors to be elected. This allows minority shareholders a chance to elect at least one director to the board.

7. The bylaws govern the internal affairs of the corporation and typically include: (1) location of the principal office; (2) number of directors as well as the procedure for their election and removal; (3) board of directors authority, quorum, salaries, terms, qualifications, duties, and responsibilities; (4) date, time, and place of board meetings; (5) date, time, and place of shareholder meetings; (6) number and type of officers, their qualifications, duties, responsibilities, and procedure for election and removal; (7) fiscal year of the corporation; and (8) proxy voting restrictions.

8. Bylaws are easier to change. The board of directors has authority to change the bylaws. Any changes made to the articles of incorporation require shareholder approval, and the amended articles must be filed again with the proper authorities. The less that is contained in the articles, the more flexibility the corporation has to make changes and to move in different directions.

Chapter 9

1. Accept the articles of incorporation, elect the initial board of directors, adopt the bylaws, accept share subscriptions, authorize payment of any expenses, issue stock, adopt preincorporation agreements, elect officers, adopt the bank resolution, and adopt an assumed name to do business (if applicable).

   The board of directors takes control from the incorporators as soon as the board members are elected.

2. A shareholder meeting for a large corporation must be organized many months before it is actually held. Notices of the meeting must be prepared and mailed to shareholders. The corporation needs a date to determine who the shareholders are for notices and voting. The board sets a date on which all shareholders of record are considered shareholders for the meeting. Even if shares are sold after the record date, the owner is considered a shareholder for purposes of the meeting. Record dates are also used to determine who should receive dividends.

3. (1) Election and removal of a director; (2) mergers, consolidations, and certain exchanges; (3) dissolution of the corporation; (4) changes to the articles of incorporation; (5) any other matters that affect their ownership rights.

4. (1) Notice or waiver of notice of the meeting; (2) articles of incorporation; (3) minutes of the incorporators' meeting; (4) bylaws; (5) all contracts approved by the board; (6) specimen of the share certificate; (7) written stock subscriptions; (8) bills for expenses of organization; (9) bank resolution; (10) Subchapter S election (if applicable).

5. After the record date is set, a voting list is prepared. This is a list of the record owners which is alphabetical, containing the addresses of the stockholders and the number of shares they own. The purpose of the voting list is to allow shareholders to contact each other prior to the meeting.

6. The bylaws establish the date, time, and place of the meeting. A notice of the meeting must be sent to shareholders. This is done after the record date is set and the voting list is prepared. The notice must be sent not less than ten days, nor more than sixty days, prior to the meeting. Corporations with few shareholders often do not set a record date; instead, they often have the shareholders sign a waiver of notice at the beginning of the meeting. This waiver must be kept with the minutes.

   It usually takes more time to organize the meeting for a publicly traded corporation. There often is proxy information to send; voting lists to be sent to other entities, such as the SEC; reservation of a meeting place; and ordering of supplies. After the meeting, postmeeting reports typically must be sent.

Chapter 10

1. A close corporation is owned by a small group of shareholders (fewer than fifty), who often are family members; shares of the corporation are not publicly traded; shareholders manage the corporation; there often are share transfer restrictions to maintain the close corporation designation. States usually allow a close corporation to dispense with some of the corporate formalities. A close corporation should be so designated in its articles of incorporation.

2. Many corporate formalities are dispensed with for a close corporation; the shareholders manage the close corporation rather than the officers and directors (a close corporation does not require officers and directors); a two-thirds vote is required by most state laws for a close corporation to take action (compared to most regular corporations which need only a majority vote).

3. All shareholders and directors must be of the same profession or same license. A professional corporation cannot be a general partner, a promoter, or a joint venturer. It can conduct only the business of the profession, and the name of the professional corporation must include P.C. or P.A.

4. Most states did not want professionals to incorporate and then be able to hide behind the corporation to avoid malpractice liability. Therefore, state laws usually require the professionals to remain accountable for their individual malpractice even though they incorporate.

5. A Subchapter S corporation refers to the section of the Internal Revenue Code that allows this type of corporation to exist. A corporation must make a Subchapter S election soon after incorporation. A Subchapter S corporation is a small corporation with fewer than seventy-five shareholders. The income (or losses) of the corporation are passed through to the shareholders as if they were partners, so there is no double taxation. The corporation must be domestic. All shareholders must be natural persons. The corporation can have only one class of stock.

6. Section 1244 stock refers to the section of the Internal Revenue Code that authorizes this type of stock. It is stock issued by a small corporation.

If the requirements are met and if the stock shows a loss, this capital loss can be offset against ordinary income. To qualify, a corporation must derive more than 50 percent of its income from other than passive income for a period of five years. The IRS will also look at the amount of money raised by the sale of stock and the amount of existing equity.

7. *Subchapter C corporation* refers to the Internal Revenue Code section that allows this type of corporation. If a corporation meets the requirements, shareholders pay only one-half the tax rate on stock if it has been held for five years. To qualify, a corporation must have less than $50 million in aggregate capital, and 80 percent of its assets must be used in an active trade or business.

A professional corporation would not qualify because its principal asset is skill, which is not considered an active trade or business. A Subchapter C corporation is referred to as a *qualified small business.*

Chapter 11

1. Extraordinary matters are those that are outside the normal business activities of a corporation. Shareholders must approve extraordinary corporate matters.

2. (1) Amendments to the articles of incorporation; (2) merger; (3) consolidation; (4) exchanges; (5) disposition of substantially all assets other than in the ordinary course of business.

3. A corporation must put creditors on notice in writing of the bulk transfer, and the purchasers must keep the goods for at least six months.

4. (a) Merger occurs when two corporations are combined in a way that only one of the corporations continues to exist. (b) Consolidation occurs when two corporations are combined to create a new corporation. (c) Exchange occurs when a corporation gives its stock "in exchange" for the stock of another corporation.

5. A small impact merger occurs when the surviving corporation does not need to change its articles of incorporation because the merger does not increase its outstanding stock by more than 20 percent. Also, the shareholders do not vote on this type of merger because it has very little impact on their ownership rights and because they are otherwise unaffected.

A short-form merger occurs between a parent corporation and a subsidiary. When the parent company already owns at least 90 percent of the shares of the subsidiary, the parent company is allowed to merge the subsidiary into the parent without shareholder approval. This is because the parent company would be voting 90 percent of the stock anyway.

6. These terms all are associated with hostile takeovers. (a) *Sharks* are investors who purchase control shares in a company, (b) *Greenmail* is a term used when the investors sell back their controlling shares at a premium, (c) *Poison pill* refers to the situation when a corporation changes it stock structure to ward off sharks, (d) *People pill* is a "suicide pact" in which the managers of a corporation agree that if some of the management is fired, all of the others will quit. This sometimes will deter the new owners from firing some of the management, as they typically do not want to lose all of the management. (e) *Shark repellent* refers to a corporation's seeking statutory help to prevent the takeover, such as not allowing the new owners of controlling shares to vote unless existing shareholders allow it or allowing the corporation to buy back shares at fair market value. (f) *White knight* refers to an investor who will buy the corporation under terms agreeable to the shareholders, which avoids a hostile takeover.

7. A tender offer is the method by which a corporation seeks a controlling interest in another corporation and publicly makes an offer to purchase shares at higher than market value.

8. Shareholders who do not want to merge, consolidate, or exchange are known as dissenting shareholders. Dissenting shareholders have a right of appraisal, which is the right to have shares appraised and purchased by the corporation.

9. The board of directors passes a resolution to dissolve, and shareholders vote at their regular meeting or a special meeting called for this purpose. Shareholders are allowed to vote to dissolve without a board of directors resolution by unanimous, written approval. Outside creditors then must be given notice. The corporation must file an intent to dissolve with the secretary of state. The corporation must file articles of dissolution with the secretary of state. The corporation then liquidates. In liquidation, creditors are paid first, then expenses of the corporation; contracts are terminated and remaining assets are distributed to shareholders.

10. The state can initiate an involuntary dissolution based on violation of state law; creditors or shareholders, through judicial action.

Chapter 12

1. Debt securities and equity securities.

2. Equity securities are the ownership interest in a corporation. They are intangible personal property evidenced by a stock certificate. They can grow in value and pay dividends.

3. When a corporation borrows money, it issues debt securities. They are loans to the corporation. Holders of debt securities are creditors of the corporation. In return, creditors are paid interest along with the principal.

4. The Securities and Exchange Commission (SEC) regulates securities. There are two federal acts that regulate the issuance and sale of securities: the Securities Act of 1933, which contains disclosure requirements for the public sale of shares or bonds; and the Securities Exchange Act of 1934, which protects potential investors by making sure that they are fully informed about the investment.

5. (1) Right to dividends if declared; (2) right to a distribution of corporate assets at dissolution; and (3) the right to vote on corporate matters.

6. The articles of incorporation state the number of shares that are authorized by the corporation for issue. *Issued* means the board has decided to sell shares. Once the shares of stock are sold, they become *outstanding*. Therefore, stock that is issued and outstanding has been sold by the corporation.

7. The articles of incorporation usually state a par value for stock. Stock must be sold for at least the par value. If stock is sold for less than par value, it is watered or discount stock. A stockholder could be liable for the difference between what was paid and par value.

8. Treasury shares. Corporations are authorized to repurchase shares of stock. Once a corporation exercises this right, the shares remain authorized and issued but are no longer outstanding.

9. These two accounts appear on the ledger sheet of a corporation. The stated capital account is where the capital generated from the sale of stock appears. The par-value amount is put into this account. Any excess that is collected over par value goes into the capital surplus account. Most states require that a corporation have money in its capital surplus account before it can buy treasury shares.

10. The corporation's profit appears in the earned surplus account. Any obligations of the corporation are paid from this account. If there is preferred stock that requires periodic dividends, this amount is considered restricted earned surplus.

11. Common stock. If a corporation has only one class of stock, it will be common stock.

12. Circular holdings occur when corporation A owns a majority of the stock in corporation B and corporation B owns a majority of the stock of corporation A. Shares owned as circular holdings cannot be voted, under the rules of the MBCA.

13. Common stockholders have voting rights, which may include cumulative voting; preemptive rights; the right to dividends and other distributions if declared; and liquidation rights.

14. To obtain investors, a corporation sometimes must give them preferential treatment. Holders of preferred stock are granted preferences with respect to normal shareholder's rights. The preferences can be for distributions, participation rights, liquidation preference, redemption rights, or conversion rights. Typically, preferred stock does not have voting rights.

15. Consideration is the thing paid or exchanged for shares of stock. It must be at least equal to par value or the stated value of no-par stock. Money is one type of consideration, and its value is easily ascertained. If services or property are given as consideration, the value must be determined. The MBCA allows the following to be used as consideration: tangible or intangible property, cash, promissory notes, services already performed, contracts for services to be performed, or other securities.

16. Debt securities may be either secured or unsecured. An unsecured loan is a debenture. It is unsecured because only a promissory note is signed by the corporation. A secured loan is a mortgage bond. The corporation will pledge either real estate or personal property as collateral. If personal property is used, the transaction is governed by the UCC.

17. Debt securities avoid double taxation. The interest a corporation pays on debt is deducted as an expense before the corporation pays taxes. Some corporations will issue debt securities instead of equity securities to avoid double taxation. If a corporation has more debt than equity, it is a thin corporation, and the IRS may characterize the interest payments as dividends.

Chapter 13

1. A share transfer restriction is a shareholder agreement that restricts the transfer of stock. It is used by close corporations to protect their status. Most corporations give the corporation and shareholders the first option to purchase stock. The restriction, however, cannot completely bar the sale of stock.

2. A bona fide, good faith offer received by the shareholder to purchase her shares triggers the restriction. Other triggers include death, retirement, or disability of a shareholder or termination of employment of the shareholder.

3. It must be in writing, there must be an earnest money deposit, and the balance of the purchase price must be in escrow.

4. These agreements require the transfer of shares. The agreement must be in writing. Usually, there are two shareholders who are equal partners. Death, retirement, or termination could trigger the agreement, or it may be that one of them simply wants to leave. The agreement requires that one partner must sell and the other must buy.

5. When shareholders do not want to be in business together anymore, this agreement allows a coercive buyout. One owner either must sell or buy out the other at a fair price. Generally, only two shareholders will be involved.

6. One procedure is by auction. All shareholders submit an offer to the corporation to sell their shares. The corporation is required to accept the lowest offer. It is anticipated that the shareholders who want to stay will submit high offers. The other method requires the shareholders to give notice of an offer to sell their shares or buy the others; this initiates the agreement. Shareholders receiving the notice must either buy or sell during the time period stated in the notice.

7. Shareholders agree, before the shareholder meeting, on how to vote their shares. These agreements usually are used by minority shareholders to gain power. These agreements use cumulative voting to its full potential.

8. A voting trust separates legal ownership from beneficial ownership, Legal ownership is transferred to a trustee, Shares are held in trust by the trustee, but only for voting purposes; the agreement sets out how the trustee will vote the shares. This agreement is enforceable. The trustee actually votes the shares but does not have any other ownership rights.

   Stock voting/pooling occurs when shareholders agree to vote a certain way; these agreements are not enforceable.

   Agreements to secure director representation can be accomplished through voting trusts or stock voting agreements. In addition, all shareholders may agree that the minority shareholders can elect one director.

Chapter 14

1. A distribution by a corporation is the transfer of money or other property from the corporation to or for the benefit of the shareholders.

2. (a) Dividends: a distribution of corporate profits, either money or property. (b) Stock splits: ownership interest is divided into a greater number of shares of stock. (c) Dissolution: at liquidation, there is a one-time distribution when all assets are liquidated. (d) A corporation's buy-back of its shares is considered a distribution.

3. The corporation must stay solvent, so there must be legal funds available for the distribution. The MBCA allows the distribution to be paid from any source as long as the corporation stays solvent. The common sources to pay dividends are earned surplus or retained earnings. Another consideration is any tax ramifications for the corporation and the shareholders.

4. Dividends can be paid in cash, property, or shares of stock. Cash is the most common method. If a corporation manufactures a product, dividends of the product are permissible.

5. The board of directors must declare the dividend. If there is preferred stock, it also will receive a dividend. Dividends must be uniform within a class or series of stock.

6. Outside creditors have first priority to be paid, then preferred stockholders who are owed accrued dividends, then other shareholders who are owed dividends. If there are any assets left, shareholders will participate on a pro rata basis depending on their ownership interest. If a preferred stockholder has liquidation preference, he or she is entitled to priority after the creditors.

7. A corporation may declare a partial liquidation when a division of the corporation closes. A partial liquidation consists of a combination of a distribution of assets, usually cash, and a purchase of the corporation's own shares.

8. The shareholders keep their same percentage of ownership. There are only two permissible sources for the distribution. There must be treasury shares or authorized but unissued shares of stock to meet the distribution. To avoid diluting a class of stock, dividends of one class of stock cannot be paid to another class of stock.

9. The dividend itself is not taxed. Instead, taxes are paid when the shares are sold by the shareholder. There will be a capital gain or loss depending on the value of the stock at distribution, which value will be the basis.

10. Most states require that corporations have funds in the earned surplus account that are not restricted. The purchase cannot make the corporation insolvent. The shares can be canceled after the purchase.

Chapter 15

1. An employment agreement is an agreement between the employer and the employee, which sets out the employee's duties and responsibilities, the compensation to be paid to the employee, the length of the agreement, and the termination rights of either party.

2. Key employees are those employees who are essential to the success of a business.

3. The duties and responsibilities can be used to measure performance. Employers want language that will allow them to add duties because of changes in the corporation. Employees do not want duties that have nothing to do with their positions. Putting the terms in writing prevents misunderstandings as the employment relationship evolves.

4. Compensation is usually the dollar amount being paid to the employee plus benefits. Compensation can be a set salary, bonuses, commissions, incentive program, or any combination.

5. Draw is an advance payment of future income.

6. The employer should include: (a) employee breach of the contract; (b) physical or mental disability of the employee for more than a certain length of time; (c) changes in ownership of the business; (d) bankruptcy or insolvency of the business; and (e) employee incarceration or conviction.

7. A golden parachute is a substantial severance package for high-level executives. They may have a continuation of salary for a long period of time or a lump-sum payment, continuation of benefits, and repurchase of stock owned by the employee.

8. Employee handbooks, which should include the organization of the company, all benefits, hours of work, and general policies.

9. (a) Work product: The result of an employee's labors while in the service of his or her employer generally is the property of the employer. If there is an employment contract, this topic should be included as part of it.

    (b) Covenant not to compete: This provision prevents an employee from using her talents against the employer in a competing enterprise. This type of restriction cannot prohibit the employee from gong to work for a competitor indefinitely. Courts often view these types of covenants as restraints of trade if the restriction is too severe, in which event the covenant will not be enforced. They are not enforceable if the contract of employment is an at-will contract.

    (c) Trade secrets: If work product is a procedure, process, or customer list, the law may protect it as a trade secret. A company can include a nondisclosure clause in an employment contract to forbid an employee from divulging trade secrets during or after employment.

10. Besides the basic sick leave, vacation leave, holidays, and health, life, and dental insurance, an employer may provide incentive compensation, deferred compensation, pension and profit-sharing plans, incentive stock options, or an employee expense reimbursement plan. All of these benefits are subject to specific laws and regulations that govern their implementation, participation, and tax consequences.

Chapter 16

1. A foreign corporation is a corporation doing business in a state other than the one in which it incorporated. Contrast this with an alien corporation, which is a corporation that was formed in another country.

2. A corporation must qualify before it can do business in another state. Most states require a corporation to obtain a certificate of authority from the state. An application is filed with the secretary of state and the articles of incorporation are filed. A foreign corporation must comply with the statutes regulating corporate names. A foreign corporation must maintain registered offices and agents within the state.

3. This issue is hotly litigated. It is now established that receiving a certificate of authority is enough to qualify. Substantial contacts subject the foreign corporation to income and other taxes.

4. The host state may impose franchise fees, which are a tax imposed on a corporation for the right to maintain a business in the state. It also may require the filing of annual reports with information regarding the registered agent, current directors and officers, nature of the business, aggregate number of shares authorized and/or issued, and the value of property owned by the corporation.

5. The foreign corporation must file an application for the withdrawal of its certificate of authority.

6. If a foreign corporation fails to comply with the law, including such things as: failure to file annual reports, failure to pay taxes and fees, failure to maintain a registered agent and office, failure to file amendments, misrepresentation in the application, or use of an unauthorized name.

7. Under the MBCA, a foreign corporation can engage in the following activities: holding board of director or shareholder meetings; maintaining bank accounts; maintaining offices for

registration of securities; selling through independent contractors; soliciting or obtaining orders if acceptance is outside the state; owning, without more, real or personal property; transacting business in interstate commerce. Other activities also may be allowed by a particular state.

8. A corporation may be denied access to the court system, and may become liable for taxes and fees that it should have paid. Also, substantial fines may be imposed, contracts may be declared unenforceable, acts of the corporation could be deemed void, and an injunction could be sought to stop the corporation from doing business.

Bibliography

Note: Many college business law texts contain good materials in this area.

Hamilton, *Corporations*, 3d ed. (Black Letter Series), West Publishing Company.
Hamilton, *The Law of Corporations*, 3d ed. (Nutshell), West Publishing Company.
Koerselman, *CLA® Review Manual*, 2d ed., West Publishing Company.
Moye, *The Law of Business Organizations*, 4th ed., West Publishing Company.

Appendix A

The Uniform Partnership Act

PART I Preliminary Provisions

Sec. 1. Name of Act

This act may be cited as Uniform Partnership Act.

Sec. 2. Definition of Terms

In this act, "Court" includes every court and judge having jurisdiction in the case.

"Business" includes every trade, occupation, or profession.

"Person" includes individuals, partnerships, corporations, and other associations.

"Bankrupt" includes bankrupt under the Federal Bankruptcy Act or insolvent under any state insolvent act.

"Conveyance" includes every assignment, lease, mortgage, or encumbrance.

"Real property" includes land and any interest or estate in land.

Sec. 3. Interpretation of Knowledge and Notice

(1) A person has "knowledge" of a fact within the meaning of this act not only when he has actual knowledge thereof, but also when he has knowledge of such other facts as in the circumstances shows bad faith.

(2) A person has "notice" of a fact within the meaning of this act when the person who claims the benefit of the notice:

(a) States the fact to such person, or

(b) Delivers through the mail, or by other means of communication, a written statement of the fact to such person or to a proper person at his place of business or residence.

Sec. 4. Rules of Construction

(1) The rule that statutes in derogation of the common law are to be strictly construed shall have no application to this act.

(2) The law of estoppel shall apply under this act.

(3) The law of agency shall apply under this act.

(4) This act shall be so interpreted and construed as to effect its general purpose to make uniform the law of those states which enact it.

(5) This act shall not be construed so as to impair the obligations of any contract existing when the act goes into effect, nor to affect any action or proceedings begun or right accrued before this act takes effect.

Sec. 5. Rules for Cases Not Provided for in This Act

In any case not provided for in this act the rules of law and equity, including the law merchant, shall govern.

PART II Nature of Partnership
Sec. 6. Partnership Defined

(1) A partnership is an association of two or more persons to carry on as co-owners a business for profit.

(2) But any association formed under any other statute of this state, or any statute adopted by authority, other than the authority of this state, is not a partnership under this act, unless such association would have been a partnership in this state prior to the adoption of this act; but this act shall apply to limited partnerships except in so far as the statutes relating to such partnerships are inconsistent herewith.

Sec. 7. Rules for Determining the Existence of a Partnership

In determining whether a partnership exists, these rules shall apply:

(1) Except as provided by Section 16 persons who are not partners as to each other are not partners as to third persons.

(2) Joint tenancy, tenancy in common, tenancy by the entireties, joint property, common property, or part ownership does not of itself establish a partnership, whether such co-owners do or do not share any profits made by the use of the property.

(3) The sharing of gross returns does not of itself establish a partnership, whether or not the persons sharing them have a joint or common right or interest in any property from which the returns are derived.

(4) The receipt by a person of a share of the profits of a business is prima facie evidence that he is a partner in the business, but no such inference shall be drawn if such profits were received in payment:

(a) As a debt by installments or otherwise,

(b) As wages of an employee or rent to a landlord,

(c) As an annuity to a widow or representative of a deceased partner,

(d) As interest on a loan, though the amount of payment vary with the profits of the business,

(e) As the consideration for the sale of a goodwill of a business or other property by installments or otherwise.

Sec. 8. Partnership Property

(1) All property originally brought into the partnership stock or subsequently acquired by purchase or otherwise, on account of the partnership, is partnership property.

(2) Unless the contrary intention appears, property acquired with partnership funds is partnership property.

(3) Any estate in real property may be acquired in the partnership name. Title so acquired can be conveyed only in the partnership name.

(4) A conveyance to a partnership in the partnership name, though without words of inheritance, passes the entire estate of the grantor unless a contrary intent appears.

PART III Relations of Partners to Persons Dealing with the Partnership
Sec. 9. Partner Agent of Partnership as to Partnership Business

(1) Every partner is an agent of the partnership for the purpose of its business, and the act of every partner, including the execution in the partnership name of any instrument, for apparently carrying on in the usual way the business of the partnership of which

he is a member binds the partnership, unless the partner so acting has in fact no authority to act for the partnership in the particular matter, and the person with whom he is dealing has knowledge of the fact that he has no such authority.

(2) An act of a partner which is not apparently for the carrying on of the business of the partnership in the usual way does not bind the partnership unless authorized by the other partners.

(3) Unless authorized by the other partners or unless they have abandoned the business, one or more but less than all the partners have no authority to:

(a) Assign the partnership property in trust for creditors or on the assignee's promise to pay the debts of the partnership,

(b) Dispose of the good-will of the business,

(c) Do any other act which would make it impossible to carry on the ordinary business of a partnership,

(d) Confess a judgment,

(e) Submit a partnership claim or liability to arbitration or reference.

(4) No act of a partner in contravention of a restriction on authority shall bind the partnership to persons having knowledge of the restriction.

Sec. 10. Conveyance of Peal Property of the Partnership

(1) Where title to real property is in the partnership name, any partner may convey title to such property by a conveyance executed in the partnership name; but the partnership may recover such property unless the partner's act binds the partnership under the provisions of paragraph (1) of section 9, or unless such property has been conveyed by the grantee or a person claiming through such grantee to a holder for value without knowledge that the partner, in making the conveyance, has exceeded his authority.

(2) Where title to real property is in the name of the partnership, a conveyance executed by a partner, in his own name, passes the equitable interest of the partnership, provided the act is one within the authority of the partner under the provisions of paragraph (1) of section 9.

(3) Where title to real property is in the name of one or more but not all the partners, and the record does not disclose the right of the partnership, the partners in whose name the title stands may convey title to such property, but the partnership may recover such property if the partners' act does not bind the partnership under the provisions of paragraph (1) of section 9, unless the purchaser or his assignee, is a holder for value, without knowledge.

(4) Where the title to real property is in the name of one or more or all the partners, or in a third person in trust for the partnership, a conveyance executed by a partner in the partnership name, or in his own name, passes the equitable interest of the partnership, provided the act is one within the authority of the partner under the provisions of paragraph (1) of section 9.

(5) Where the title to real property is in the names of all the partners a conveyance executed by all the partners passes all their rights in such property.

Sec. 11. Partnership Bound by Admission of Partner

An admission or representation made by any partner concerning partnership affairs within the scope of his authority as conferred by this act is evidence against the partnership.

Sec. 12. Partnership Charged with Knowledge of or Notice to Partner

Notice to any partner of any matter relating to partnership affairs, and the knowledge of the partner acting in the particular matter, acquired while a partner or then present to his mind, and the knowledge of any other partner who reasonably could and should have communicated it to the acting partner, operate as notice to or knowledge of the partnership, except in the case of a fraud on the partnership committed by or with the consent of that partner.

Sec. 13. Partnership Bound by Partner's Wrongful Act

Where, by any wrongful act or omission of any partner acting in the ordinary course of the business of the partnership or with the authority of his co-partners, loss or injury is caused to any person, not being a partner in the partnership, or any penalty is incurred, the partnership is liable therefor to the same extent as the partner so acting or omitting to act.

Sec. 14. Partnership Bound by Partner's Breach of Trust

The partnership is bound to make good the loss:

(a) Where one partner acting within the scope of his apparent authority receives money or property of a third person and misapplies it; and

(b) Where the partnership in the course of its business receives money or property of a third person and the money or property so received is misapplied by any partner while it is in the custody of the partnership.

Sec. 15. Nature of Partner's Liability

All partners are liable

(a) Jointly and severally for everything chargeable to the partnership under sections 13 and 14.

(b) Jointly for all other debts and obligations of the partnership; but any partner may enter into a separate obligation to perform a partnership contract.

Sec. 16. Partner by Estoppel

(1) When a person, by words spoken or written or by conduct, represents himself, or consents to another representing him to any one, as a partner in an existing partnership or with one or more persons not actual partners, he is liable to any such person to whom such representation has been made, who has, on the faith of such representation, given credit to the actual or apparent partnership, and if he has made such representation or consented to its being made in a public manner he is liable to such person, whether the representation has or has not been made or communicated to such person so giving credit by or with the knowledge of the apparent partner making the representation or consenting to its being made.

(a) When a partnership liability results, he is liable as though he were an actual member of the partnership.

(b) When no partnership liability results, he is liable jointly with the other persons, if any, so consenting to the contract or representation as to incur liability, otherwise separately.

(2) When a person has been thus represented to be a partner in an existing partnership, or with one or more persons not actual partners, he is an agent of the persons consenting to such representation to bind them to the same extent and in the same manner as though he were a partner in fact, with respect to persons who rely upon the representation. Where all the members of the existing partnership consent to the representation, a partnership act or obligation results; but in all other cases it is the joint act or obligation of the person acting and the persons consenting to the representation.

Sec. 17. Liability of Incoming Partner

A person admitted as a partner into an existing partnership is liable for all the obligations of the partnership arising before his admission as though he had been a partner when such obligations were incurred, except that this liability shall be satisfied only out of partnership property.

PART IV Relations of Partners to One Another

Sec. 18. Rules Determining Rights and Duties of Partners

The rights and duties of the partners in relation to the partnership shall be determined, subject to any agreement between them, by the following rules:

(a) Each partner shall be repaid his contributions, whether by way of capital or advances to the partnership property and share equally in the profits and surplus remaining after all liabilities, including those to partners, are satisfied; and must contribute towards the losses, whether of capital or otherwise, sustained by the partnership according to his share in the profits.

(b) The partnership must indemnify every partner in respect of payments made and personal liabilities reasonably incurred by him in the ordinary and proper conduct of its business, or for the preservation of its business or property.

(c) A partner, who in aid of the partnership makes any payment or advance beyond the amount of capital which he agreed to contribute, shall be paid interest from the date of the payment or advance.

(d) A partner shall receive interest on the capital contributed by him only from the date when repayment should be made.

(e) All partners have equal rights in the management and conduct of the partnership business.

(f) No partner is entitled to remuneration for acting in the partnership business, except that a surviving partner is entitled to reasonable compensation for his services in winding up the partnership affairs.

(g) No person can become a member of a partnership without the consent of all the partners.

(h) Any difference arising as to ordinary matters connected with the partnership business may be decided by a majority of the partners; but no act in contravention of any agreement between the partners may be done rightfully without the consent of all the partners.

Sec. 19. Partnership Books

The partnership books shall be kept, subject to any agreement between the partners, at the principal place of business of the partnership, and every partner shall at all times have access to and may inspect and copy any of them.

Sec. 20. Duty of Partners to Render Information

Partners shall render on demand true and full information of all things affecting the partnership to any partner or the legal representative of any deceased partner or partner under legal disability.

Sec. 21. Partner Accountable as a Fiduciary

(1) Every partner must account to the partnership for any benefit, and hold as trustee for it any profits derived by him without the consent of the other partners from any transaction connected with the formation, conduct, or liquidation of the partnership or from any use by him of its property.

(2) This section applies also to the representatives of a deceased partner engaged in the liquidation of the affairs of the partnership as the personal representatives of the last surviving partner.

Sec. 22. Right to an Account

Any partner shall have the right to a formal account as to partnership affairs:

(a) If he is wrongfully excluded from the partnership business or possession of its property by his co-partners,

(b) If the right exists under the terms of any agreement,

(c) As provided by section 21,

(d) Whenever other circumstances render it just and reasonable.

Sec. 23. Continuation of Partnership beyond Fixed Term

(1) When a partnership for a fixed term or particular undertaking is continued after the termination of such term or particular undertaking without any express agreement, the rights and duties of the partners remain the same as they were at such termination, so far as is consistent with a partnership at will.

(2) A continuation of the business by the partners or such of them as habitually acted therein during the term, without any settlement or liquidation of the partnership affairs, is prima facie evidence of a continuation of the partnership.

PART V Property Rights of a Partner
Sec. 24. Extent of Property Rights of a Partner

The property rights of a partner are

(1) his rights in specific partnership property,

(2) his interest in the partnership, and

(3) his right to participate in the management.

Sec. 25. Nature of a Partner's Right in Specific Partnership Property

(1) A partner is co-owner with his partners of specific partnership property holding as a tenant in partnership.

(2) The incidents of this tenancy are such that:

(a) A partner, subject to the provisions of this act and to any agreement between the partners, has an equal right with his partners to possess specific partnership property for partnership purposes; but he has no right to possess such property for any other purpose without the consent of his partners.

(b) A partner's right in specific partnership property is not assignable except in connection with the assignment of rights of all the partners in the same property.

(c) A partner's right in specific partnership property is not subject to attachment or execution, except on a claim against the partnership. When partnership property is attached for a partnership debt the partners, or any of them, or the representatives of a deceased partner, cannot claim any right under the homestead or exemption laws.

(d) On the death of a partner his right in specific partnership property vests in the surviving partner or partners, except where the deceased was the last surviving partner, when his right in such property vests in his legal representative. Such surviving partner or partners, or the legal representative of the last surviving partner, has no right to possess the partnership property for any but a partnership purpose.

(e) A partner's right in specific partnership property is not subject to dower, courtesy, or allowances to widows, heirs, or next of kin.

Sec. 26. Nature of Partner's Interest in the Partnership

A partner's interest in the partnership is his share of the profits and surplus, and the same is personal property.

Sec. 27. Assignment of Partner's Interest

(1) A conveyance by a partner of his interest in the partnership does not of itself dissolve the partnership, nor, as against the other partners in the absence of agreement, entitle the assignee, during the continuance of the partnership, to interfere in the management or administration of the partnership business or affairs, or to require any information or account of partnership transactions, or to inspect the partnership books; but it merely entitles the assignee to receive in accordance with his contract the profits to which the assigning partner would otherwise be entitled.

(2) In case of a dissolution of the partnership, the assignee is entitled to receive his assignor's interest and may require an account from the date only of the last account agreed to by all the partners.

Sec. 28. Partner's Interest Subject to Charging Order

(1) On due application to a competent court by any judgment creditor of a partner, the court which entered the judgment, order, or decree, or any other court, may charge the interest of the debtor partner with payment of the unsatisfied amount of such judgment debt with interest thereon; and may then or later appoint a receiver of his share of the profits, and of any other money due or to fall due to him in respect of the partnership, and make all other orders, directions, accounts and inquiries which the debtor partner might have made, or which the circumstances of the case may require.

(2) The interest charged may be redeemed at any time before foreclosure, or in case of a sale being directed by the court may be purchased without thereby causing a dissolution:

(a) With separate property, by any one or more of the partners, or

(b) With partnership property, by any one or more of the partners with the consent of all the partners whose interests are not so charged or sold.

(3) Nothing in this act shall be held to deprive a partner of his right, if any, under the exemption laws, as regards his interest in the partnership.

PART VI Dissolution and Winding up
Sec. 29. Dissolution Defined
The dissolution of a partnership is the change in the relation of the partners caused by any partner ceasing to be associated in the carrying on as distinguished from the winding up of the business.

Sec. 30. Partnership not Terminated by Dissolution
On dissolution the partnership is not terminated, but continues until the winding up of partnership affairs is completed.

Sec. 31. Causes of Dissolution
Dissolution is caused:

(1) Without violation of the agreement between the partners,

(a) By the termination of the definite term or particular undertaking specified in the agreement,

(b) By the express will of any partner when no definite term or particular undertaking is specified,

(c) By the express will of all the partners who have not assigned their interests or suffered them to be charged for their separate debts, either before or after the termination of any specified term or particular undertaking,

(d) By the expulsion of any partner from the business bona fide in accordance with such a power conferred by the agreement between the partners;

(2) In contravention of the agreement between the partners, where the circumstances do not permit a dissolution under any other provision of this section, by the express will of any partner at any time;

(3) By any event which makes it unlawful for the business of the partnership to be carried on or for the members to carry it on in partnership;

(4) By the death of any partner;

(5) By the bankruptcy of any partner or the partnership;

(6) By decree of court under section 32.

Sec. 32. Dissolution by Decree of Court
(1) On application by or for a partner the court shall decree a dissolution whenever:

(a) A partner has been declared a lunatic in any judicial proceeding or is shown to be of unsound mind,

(b) A partner becomes in any other way incapable of performing his part of the partnership contract,

(c) A partner has been guilty of such conduct as tends to affect prejudicially the carrying on of the business,

(d) A partner wilfully or persistently commits a breach of the partnership agreement, or otherwise so conducts himself in matters relating to the partnership business that it is not reasonably practicable to carry on the business in partnership with him,

(e) The business of the partnership can only be carried on at a loss,

(f) Other circumstances render a dissolution equitable.

(2) On the application of the purchaser of a partner's interest under sections 28 or 29 [should read 27 or 28];

(a) After the termination of the specified term or particular undertaking,

(b) At any time if the partnership was a partnership at will when the interest was assigned or when the charging order was issued.

Sec. 33. General Effect of Dissolution on Authority of Partner
Except so far as may be necessary to wind up partnership affairs or to complete transactions begun but not then finished, dissolution terminates all authority of any partner to act for the partnership,

(1) With respect to the partners,

(a) When the dissolution is not by the act, bankruptcy or death of a partner; or

(b) When the dissolution is by such act, bankruptcy or death of a partner, in cases where section 34 so requires.

(2) With respect to persons not partners, as declared in section 35.

Sec. 34. Rights of Partner to Contribution from Copartners after Dissolution
Where the dissolution is caused by the act, death or bankruptcy of a partner, each partner is liable to his copartners for his share of any liability created by any partner acting for the partnership as if the partnership had not been dissolved unless

(a) The dissolution being by act of any partner, the partner acting for the partnership had knowledge of the dissolution, or

(b) The dissolution being by the death or bankruptcy of a partner, the partner acting for the partnership had knowledge or notice of the death or bankruptcy.

Sec. 35. Power of Partner to Bind Partnership to Third Persons after Dissolution
(1) After dissolution a partner can bind the partnership except as provided in Paragraph (3).

(a) By any act appropriate for winding up partnership affairs or completing transactions unfinished at dissolution;

(b) By any transaction which would bind the partnership if dissolution had not taken place, provided the other party to the transaction

(I) Had extended credit to the partnership prior to dissolution and had no knowledge or notice of the dissolution; or

(II) Though he had not so extended credit, had nevertheless known of the partnership prior to dissolution, and, having no knowledge or notice of dissolution, the fact of dissolution had not been advertised in a newspaper of general circulation in the place (or in each place if more than one) at which the partnership business was regularly carried on.

(2) The liability of a partner under paragraph (1b) shall be satisfied out of partnership assets alone when such partner had been prior to dissolution

(a) Unknown as a partner to the person with whom the contract is made; and

(b) So far unknown and inactive in partnership affairs that the business reputation of the partnership could not be said to have been in any degree due to his connection with it.

(3) The partnership is in no case bound by any act of a partner after dissolution

(a) Where the partnership is dissolved because it is unlawful to carry on the business, unless the act is appropriate for winding up partnership affairs; or

(b) Where the partner has become bankrupt; or

(c) Where the partner has no authority to wind up partnership affairs; except by a transaction with one who

(I) Had extended credit to the partnership prior to dissolution and had no knowledge or notice of his want of authority; or

(II) Had not extended credit to the partnership prior to dissolution, and, having no knowledge or notice of his want of authority, the fact of his want of authority has not been advertised in the manner provided for advertising the fact of dissolution in paragraph (1bII).

(4) Nothing in this section shall affect the liability under Section 16 of any person who after dissolution represents himself or consents to another representing him as a partner in a partnership engaged in carrying on business.

Sec. 36. Effect of Dissolution on Partner's Existing Liability

(1) The dissolution of the partnership does not of itself discharge the existing liability of any partner.

(2) A partner is discharged from any existing liability upon dissolution of the partnership by an agreement to that effect between himself, the partnership creditor and the person or partnership continuing the business; and such agreement may be inferred from the course of dealing between the creditor having knowledge of the dissolution and the person or partnership continuing the business.

(3) Where a person agrees to assume the existing obligations of a dissolved partnership, the partners whose obligations have been assumed shall be discharged from any liability to any creditor of the partnership who, knowing of the agreement, consents to a material alteration in the nature or time of payment of such obligations.

(4) The individual property of a deceased partner shall be liable for all obligations of the partnership incurred while he was a partner but subject to the prior payment of his separate debts.

Sec. 37. Right to Wind Up

Unless otherwise agreed the partners who have not wrongfully dissolved the partnership or the legal representative of the last surviving partner, not bankrupt, has the right to wind up the partnership affairs; provided, however, that any partner, his legal representative or his assignee, upon cause shown, may obtain winding up by the court.

Sec. 38. Rights of Partners to Application of Partnership Property

(1) When dissolution is caused in any way, except in contravention of the partnership agreement, each partner, as against his co-partners and all persons claiming through them in respect of their interests in the partnership, unless otherwise agreed, may have the partnership property applied to discharge its liabilities, and the surplus applied to pay in cash the net amount owing to the respective partners. But if dissolution is caused by expulsion of a partner, bona fide under the partnership agreement and if the expelled partner is discharged from all partnership liabilities, either by payment or agreement under section 36(2), he shall receive in cash only the net amount due him from the partnership.

(2) When dissolution is caused in contravention of the partnership agreement the rights of the partners shall be as follows:

(a) Each partner who has not caused dissolution wrongfully shall have,

(I) All the rights specified in paragraph (1) of this section, and

(II) The right, as against each partner who has caused the dissolution wrongfully, to damages for breach of the agreement.

(b) The partners who have not caused the dissolution wrongfully, if they all desire to continue the business in the same name, either by themselves or jointly with others, may do so, during the agreed term for the partnership and for that purpose may possess the partnership property, provided they secure the payment by bond approved by the court, or pay to any partner who has caused the dissolution wrongfully, the value of his interest in the partnership at the dissolution, less any damages recoverable under clause (2a II) of the section, and in like manner indemnify him against all present or future partnership liabilities.

(c) A partner who has caused the dissolution wrongfully shall have:

(I) If the business is not continued under the provisions of paragraph (2b) all the rights of a partner under paragraph (1), subject to clause (2a II), of this section,

(II) If the business is continued under paragraph (2b) of this section the right as against his co-partners and all claiming through them in respect of their interests in the partnership, to have the value of his interest in the partnership, less any damages caused to his co-partners by the dissolution, ascertained and paid to him in cash, or the payment secured by bond approved by the court, and to be released from all existing liabilities of the partnership; but in ascertaining the value of the partner's interest the value of the good-will of the business shall not be considered.

Sec. 39. Rights Where Partnership Is Dissolved for Fraud or Misrepresentation

Where a partnership contract is rescinded on the ground of the fraud or misrepresentation of one of the parties thereto, the party entitled to rescind is, without prejudice to any other right, entitled,

(a) To a lien on, or right of retention of, the surplus of the partnership property after satisfying the partnership liabilities to third persons for any sum of money paid by him for the purchase of an interest in the partnership and for any capital or advances contributed by him; and

(b) To stand, after all liabilities to third persons have been satisfied, in the place of the creditors of the partnership for any payments made by him in respect of the partnership liabilities; and

(c) To be indemnified by the person guilty of the fraud or making the representation against all debts and liabilities of the partnership.

Sec. 40. Rules for Distribution

In settling accounts between the partners after dissolution, the following rules shall be observed, subject to any agreement to the contrary:

(a) The assets of the partnership are:

(I) The partnership property,

(II) The contributions of the partners necessary for the payment of all the liabilities specified in clause (b) of this paragraph.

(b) The liabilities of the partnership shall rank in order of payment, as follows:

(I) Those owing to creditors other than partners,

(II) Those owing to partners other than for capital and profits,

(III) Those owing to partners in respect of capital,

(IV) Those owing to partners in respect of profits.

(c) The assets shall be applied in the order of their declaration in clause (a) of this paragraph to the satisfaction of the liabilities.

(d) The partners shall contribute, as provided by section 18(a) the amount necessary to satisfy the liabilities; but if any, but not all, of the partners are insolvent, or, not being subject to process, refuse to contribute, the other partners shall contribute their share of the liabilities, and, in the relative proportions in which they share the profits, the additional amount necessary to pay the liabilities.

(e) An assignee for the benefit of creditors or any person appointed by the court shall have the right to enforce the contributions specified in clause (d) of this paragraph.

(f) Any partner or his legal representative shall have the right to enforce the contributions specified in clause (d) of this paragraph, to the extent of the amount which he has paid in excess of his share of the liability.

(g) The individual property of a deceased partner shall be liable for the contributions specified in clause (d) of this paragraph.

(h) When partnership property and the individual properties of the partners are in possession of a court for distribution, partnership creditors shall have priority on partnership property and separate creditors on individual property, saving the rights of lien or secured creditors as heretofore.

(i) Where a partner has become bankrupt or his estate is insolvent the claims against his separate property shall rank in the following order:

(I) Those owing to separate creditors,

(II) Those owing to partnership creditors,

(III) Those owing to partners by way of contribution.

Sec. 41. Liability of Persons Continuing the Business in Certain Cases

(1) When any new partner is admitted into an existing partnership, or when any partner retires and assigns (or the representative of the deceased partner assigns) his rights in partnership property to two or more of the partners, or to one or more of the partners and one or more third persons, if the business is continued without liquidation of the partnership affairs, creditors of the first or dissolved partnership are also creditors of the partnership so continuing the business.

(2) When all but one partner retire and assign (or the representative of a deceased partner assigns) their rights in partnership property to the remaining partner, who continues the business without liquidation of partnership affairs, either alone or with others, creditors of the dissolved partnership are also creditors of the person or partnership so continuing the business.

(3) When any partner retires or dies and the business of the dissolved partnership is continued as set forth in paragraphs (1) and (2) of this section, with the consent of the retired partners or the representative of the deceased partner, but without any

assignment of his right in partnership property, rights of creditors of the dissolved partnership and of the creditors of the person or partnership continuing the business shall be as if such assignment had been made.

(4) When all the partners or their representatives assign their rights in partnership property to one or more third persons who promise to pay the debts and who continue the business of the dissolved partnership, creditors of the dissolved partnership are also creditors of the person or partnership continuing the business.

(5) When any partner wrongfully causes a dissolution and the remaining partners continue the business under the provisions of section 38(2b), either alone or with others, and without liquidation of the partnership affairs, creditors of the dissolved partnership are also creditors of the person or partnership continuing the business.

(6) When a partner is expelled and the remaining partners continue the business either alone or with others, without liquidation of the partnership affairs, creditors of the dissolved partnership are also creditors of the person or partnership continuing the business.

(7) The liability of a third person becoming a partner in the partnership continuing the business, under this section, to the creditors of the dissolved partnership shall be satisfied out of partnership property only.

(8) When the business of a partnership after dissolution is continued under any conditions set forth in this section the creditors of the dissolved partnership, as against the separate creditors of the retiring or deceased partner or the representative of the deceased partner, have a prior right to any claim of the retired partner or the representative of the deceased partner against the person or partnership continuing the business, on account of the retired or deceased partner's interest in the dissolved partnership or on account of any consideration promised for such interest or for his right in partnership property.

(9) Nothing in this section shall be held to modify any right of creditors to set aside any assignment on the ground of fraud.

(10) The use by the person or partnership continuing the business of the partnership name, or the name of a deceased partner as part thereof, shall not of itself make the individual property of the deceased partner liable for any debts contracted by such person or partnership.

Sec. 42. Rights of Retiring or Estate of Deceased Partner When the Business Is Continued

When any partner retires or dies, and the business is continued under any of the conditions set forth in section 41 (1, 2, 3, 5, 6), or section 38(2b) without any settlement of accounts as between him or his estate and the person or partnership continuing the business, unless otherwise agreed, he or his legal representative as against such persons or partnership may have the value of his interest at the date of dissolution ascertained, and shall receive as an ordinary creditor an amount equal to the value of his interest in the dissolved partnership with interest, or, at his option or at the option of his legal representative, in lieu of interest, the profits attributable to the use of his right in the property of the dissolved partnership; provided that the creditors of the dissolved partnership as against the separate creditors, or the representative of the retired or deceased partner, shall have priority on any claim arising under this section, as provided by section 41(8) of this act.

Sec. 43. Accrual of Actions

The right to an account of his interest shall accrue to any partner, or his legal representative, as against the winding up partners or the surviving partners or the person or partnership continuing the business, at the date of dissolution, in the absence of any agreement to the contrary.

PART VII Miscellaneous Provisions
Sec. 44. When Act Takes Effect

This act shall take effect on the _____ day of _____ one thousand nine hundred and _____.

Sec. 45. Legislation Repealed

All acts or parts of acts inconsistent with this act are hereby repealed.

Appendix B

Revised Uniform Limited Partnership Act

Article 1 GENERAL PROVISIONS

Section 101. Definitions.

As used in this [Act], unless the context otherwise requires:

(1) "Certificate of limited partnership" means the certificate referred to in Section 201, and the certificate as amended or restated.

(2) "Contribution" means any cash, property, services rendered, or a promissory note or other binding obligation to contribute cash or property or to perform services, which a partner contributes to a limited partnership in his capacity as a partner.

(3) "Event of withdrawal of a general partner" means an event that causes a person to cease to be a general partner as provided in Section 402.

(4) "Foreign limited partnership" means a partnership formed under the laws of any state other than this State and having as partners one or more general partners and one or more limited partners.

(5) "General partner" means a person who has been admitted to a limited partnership as a general partner in accordance with the partnership agreement and named in the certificate of limited partnership as a general partner.

(6) "Limited partner" means a person who has been admitted to a limited partnership as a limited partner in accordance with the partnership agreement.

(7) "Limited partnership" and "domestic limited partnership" mean a partnership formed by two or more persons under the laws of this State and having one or more general partners and one or more limited partners.

(8) "Partner" means a limited or general partner.

(9) "Partnership agreement" means any valid agreement, written or oral, of the partners as to the affairs of a limited partnership and the conduct of its business.

(10) "Partnership interest" means a partner's share of the profits and losses of a limited partnership and the right to receive distributions of partnership assets.

(11) "Person" means a natural person, partnership, limited partnership (domestic or foreign), trust, estate, association, or corporation.

(12) "State" means a state, territory, or possession of the United States, the District of Columbia, or the Commonwealth of Puerto Rico.

Section 102. Name.

The name of each limited partnership as set forth in its certificate of limited partnership:

(1) shall contain without abbreviation the words "limited partnership";

(2) may not contain the name of a limited partner unless

(i) it is also the name of a general partner or the corporate name of a corporate general partner, or

(ii) the business of the limited partnership had been carried on under that name before the admission of that limited partner;

(3) may not be the same as, or deceptively similar to, the name of any corporation or limited partnership organized under the laws of this State or licensed or registered as a foreign corporation or limited partnership in this State; and

(4) may not contain the following words [here insert prohibited words].

Section 103. Reservation of Name.

(a) The exclusive right to the use of a name may be reserved by:

(1) any person intending to organize a limited partnership under this [Act] and to adopt that name;

(2) any domestic limited partnership or any foreign limited partnership registered in this State which, in either case, intends to adopt that name;

(3) any foreign limited partnership intending to register in this State and adopt that name; and

(4) any person intending to organize a foreign limited partnership and intending to have it register in this State and adopt that name.

(b) The reservation shall be made by filing with the Secretary of State an application, executed by the applicant, to reserve a specified name. If the Secretary of State finds that the name is available for use by a domestic or foreign limited partnership, he [or she] shall reserve the name for the exclusive use of the applicant for a period of 120 days. Once having so reserved a name, the same applicant may not again reserve the same name until more than 60 days after the expiration of the last 120-day period for which that applicant reserved that name. The right to the exclusive use of a reserved name may be transferred to any other person by filing in the office of the Secretary of State a notice of the transfer, executed by the applicant for whom the name was reserved and specifying the name and address of the transferee.

Section 104. Specified Office and Agent.

Each limited partnership shall continuously maintain in this State:

(1) an office, which may but need not be a place of its business in this State, at which shall be kept the records required by Section 105 to be maintained; and

(2) an agent for service of process on the limited partnership, which agent must be an individual resident of this State, a domestic corporation, or a

foreign corporation authorized to do business in this State.

Section 105. Records to Be Kept.

(a) Each limited partnership shall keep at the office referred to in Section 104(1) the following:

(1) a current list of the full name and last known business address of each partner, separately identifying the general partners (in alphabetical order) and the limited partners (in alphabetical order);

(2) a copy of the certificate of limited partnership and all certificates of amendment thereto, together with executed copies of any powers of attorney pursuant to which any certificate has been executed;

(3) copies of the limited partnership's federal, state and local income tax returns and reports, if any, for the three most recent years;

(4) copies of any then effective written partnership agreements and of any financial statements of the limited partnership for the three most recent years; and

(5) unless contained in a written partnership agreement, a writing setting out:

(i) the amount of cash and a description and statement of the agreed value of the other property or services contributed by each partner and which each partner has agreed to contribute;

(ii) the times at which or events on the happening of which any additional contributions agreed to be made by each partner are to be made;

(iii) any right of a partner to receive, or of a general partner to make, distributions to a partner which include a return of all or any part of the partner's contribution; and

(iv) any events upon the happening of which the limited partnership is to be dissolved and its affairs wound up.

(b) Records kept under this section are subject to inspection and copying at the reasonable request and at the expense of any partner during ordinary business hours.

Section 106. Nature of Business.

A limited partnership may carry on any business that a partnership without limited partners may carry on except [here designate prohibited activities].

Section 107. Business Transactions of Partners with Partnership.

Except as provided in the partnership agreement, a partner may lend money to and transact other business with the limited partnership and, subject to other applicable law, has the same rights and obligations with respect thereto as a person who is not a partner.

Article 2 FORMATION; CERTIFICATE OF LIMITED PARTNERSHIP

Section 201. Certificate of Limited Partnership.

(a) In order to form a limited partnership, a certificate of limited partnership must be executed and filed in the office of the Secretary of State. The certificate shall set forth:

(1) the name of the limited partnership;

(2) the address of the office and the name and address of the agent for service of process required to be maintained by Section 104;

(3) the name and the business address of each general partner;

(4) the latest date upon which the limited partnership is to dissolve; and

(5) any other matters the general partners determine to include therein.

(b) A limited partnership is formed at the time of the filing of the certificate of limited partnership in the office of the Secretary of State or at any later time specified in the certificate of limited partnership if, in either case, there has been substantial compliance with the requirements of this section.

202. Amendment to Certificate.

(a) A certificate of limited partnership is amended by filing a certificate of amendment thereto in the office of the Secretary of State. The certificate shall set forth:

(1) the name of the limited partnership;

(2) the date of filing the certificate; and

(3) the amendment to the certificate.

(b) Within 30 days after the happening of any of the following events, an amendment to a certificate of limited partnership reflecting the occurrence of the event or events shall be filed:

(1) the admission of a new general partner;

(2) the withdrawal of a general partner; or

(3) the continuation of the business under Section 801 after an event of withdrawal of a general partner.

(c) A general partner who becomes aware that any statement in a certificate of limited partnership was false when made or that any arrangements or other facts described have changed, making the certificate inaccurate in any respect, shall promptly amend the certificate.

(d) A certificate of limited partnership may be amended at any time for any other proper purpose the general partners determine.

(e) No person has any liability because an amendment to a certificate of limited partnership has not been filed to reflect the occurrence of any event referred to in subsection (b) of this section if the amendment is filed within the 30-day period specified in subsection (b).

(f) A restated certificate of limited partnership may be executed and filed in the same manner as a certificate of amendment.

Section 203. Cancellation of Certificate.

A certificate of limited partnership shall be canceled upon the dissolution and the commencement of winding up of the partnership or at any other time there are no limited partners. A certificate of cancellation shall be filed in the office of the Secretary of State and set forth:

(1) the name of the limited partnership;

(2) the date of filing of its certificate of limited partnership;

(3) the reason for filing the certificate of cancellation;

(4) the effective date (which shall be a date certain) of cancellation if it is not to be effective upon the filing of the certificate; and

(5) any other information the general partners filing the certificate determine.

Section 204. Execution of Certificates.

(a) Each certificate required by this Article to be filed in the office of the Secretary of State shall be executed in the following manner:

(1) an original certificate of limited partnership must be signed by all general partners;

(2) a certificate of amendment must be signed by at least one general partner and by each other general partner designated in the certificate as a new general partner; and

(3) a certificate of cancellation must be signed by all general partners.

(b) Any person may sign a certificate by an attorney-in-fact, but a power of attorney to sign a certificate relating to the admission of a general partner must specifically describe the admission.

(c) The execution of a certificate by a general partner constitutes an affirmation under the penalties of perjury that the facts stated therein are true.

Section 205. Execution by Judicial Act.

If a person required by Section 204 to execute any certificate fails or refuses to do so, any other person who is adversely affected by the failure or refusal may petition the [designate the appropriate court] to direct the execution of the certificate. If the court finds that it is proper for the certificate to be executed and that any person so designated has failed or refused to execute the certificate, it shall order the Secretary of State to record an appropriate certificate.

Section 206. Filing in Office of Secretary of State.

(a) Two signed copies of the certificate of limited partnership and of any certificates of amendment or cancellation (or of any judicial decree of amendment or cancellation) shall be delivered to the Secretary of State. A person who executes a certificate as an agent or fiduciary need not exhibit evidence of his [or her] authority as a prerequisite to filing. Unless the Secretary of State finds that any certificate does not conform to law, upon receipt of all filing fees required by law he [or she] shall:

(1) endorse on each duplicate original the word "Filed" and the day, month, and year of the filing thereof;

(2) file one duplicate original in his [or her] office; and

(3) return the other duplicate original to the person who filed it or his [or her] representative.

(b) Upon the filing of a certificate of amendment (or judicial decree of amendment) in the office of the Secretary of State, the certificate of limited partnership shall be amended as set forth therein, and upon the effective date of a certificate of cancellation (or a judicial decree thereof), the certificate of limited partnership is canceled.

Section 207. Liability for False Statement in Certificate.

If any certificate of limited partnership or certificate of amendment or cancellation contains a false statement, one who suffers loss by reliance on the statement may recover damages for the loss from:

(1) any person who executes the certificate, or causes another to execute it on his behalf, and knew, and any general partner who knew or should have known, the statement to be false at the time the certificate was executed; and

(2) any general partner who thereafter knows or should have known that any arrangement or other fact described in the certificate has changed, making the statement inaccurate in any respect within a sufficient time before the statement was relied upon reasonably to have enabled that general partner to cancel or amend the certificate, or to file a petition for its cancellation or amendment under Section 205.

Section 208. Scope of Notice.

The fact that a certificate of limited partnership is on file in the office of the Secretary of State is notice that the partnership is a limited partnership and the persons designated therein as general partners are general partners, but it is not notice of any other fact.

Section 209. Delivery of Certificates to Limited Partners.

Upon the return by the Secretary of State pursuant to Section 206 of a certificate marked "Filed," the general partners shall promptly deliver or mail a copy of the certificate of limited partnership and each certificate of amendment or cancellation to each limited partner unless the partnership agreement provides otherwise.

Article 3 LIMITED PARTNERS
Section 301. Admission of Additional Limited Partners.

(a) A person becomes a limited partner on the later of:

(1) the date the original certificate of limited partnership is filed; or

(2) the date stated in the records of the limited partnership as the date that person becomes a limited partner.

(b) After the filing of a limited partnership's original certificate of limited partnership, a person may be admitted as an additional limited partner:

(1) in the case of a person acquiring a partnership interest directly from the limited partnership, upon compliance with the partnership agreement or, if the partnership agreement does not so provide, upon the written consent of all partners; and

(2) in the case of an assignee of a partnership interest of a partner who has the power, as provided in Section 704, to grant the assignee the right to become a limited partner, upon the exercise of that power and compliance with any conditions limiting the grant or exercise of the power.

Section 302. Voting.

Subject to Section 303, the partnership agreement may grant to all or a specified group of the limited partners the right to vote (on a per capita or other basis) upon any matter.

Section 303. Liability to Third Parties.

(a) Except as provided in subsection (d), a limited partner is not liable for the obligations of a limited partnership unless he [or she] is also a general partner or, in addition to the exercise of his [or her] rights and powers as a limited partner, he [or she] participates in the control of the business. However, if the limited partner participates in the control of the business, he [or she] is liable only to persons who transact business with the limited partnership reasonably believing, based upon the limited partner's conduct, that the limited partner is a general partner.

(b) A limited partner does not participate in the control of the business within the meaning of subsection (a) solely by doing one or more of the following:

(1) being a contractor for or an agent or employee of the limited partnership or of a general partner or being an officer, director, or shareholder of a general partner that is a corporation;

(2) consulting with and advising a general partner with respect to the business of the limited partnership;

(3) acting as surety for the limited partnership or guaranteeing or assuming one or more specific obligations of the limited partnership;

(4) taking any action required or permitted by law to bring or pursue a derivative action in the right of the limited partnership;

(5) requesting or attending a meeting of partners;

(6) proposing, approving, or disapproving, by voting or otherwise, one or more of the following matters:

(i) the dissolution and winding up of the limited partnership;

(ii) the sale, exchange, lease, mortgage, pledge, or other transfer of all or substantially all of the assets of the limited partnership;

(iii) the incurrence of indebtedness by the limited partnership other than in the ordinary course of its business;

(iv) a change in the nature of the business;

(v) the admission or removal of a general partner;

(vi) the admission or removal of a limited partner;

(vii) a transaction involving an actual or potential conflict of interest between a general partner and the limited partnership or the limited partners;

(viii) an amendment to the partnership agreement or certificate of limited partnership; or

(ix) matters related to the business of the limited partnership not otherwise enumerated in this subsection (b), which the partnership agreement states in writing may be subject to the approval or disapproval of limited partners;

(7) winding up the limited partnership pursuant to Section 803; or

(8) exercising any right or power permitted to limited partners under this [Act] and not specifically enumerated in this subsection (b).

(c) The enumeration in subsection (b) does not mean that the possession or exercise of any other powers by a limited partner constitutes participation by him [or her] in the business of the limited partnership.

(d) A limited partner who knowingly permits his [or her] name to be used in the name of the limited partnership, except under circumstances permitted by Section 102(2), is liable to creditors who extend credit to the limited partnership without actual knowledge that the limited partner is not a general partner.

Section 304. Person Erroneously Believing Himself [or Herself] Limited Partner.

(a) Except as provided in subsection (b), a person who makes a contribution to a business enterprise and erroneously but in good faith believes that he [or she] has become a limited partner in the enterprise is not a general partner in the enterprise and is not bound by its obligations by reason of making the contribution, receiving distributions from the enterprise, or exercising any rights of a limited partner, if, on ascertaining the mistake, he [or she]:

(1) causes an appropriate certificate of limited partnership or a certificate of amendment to be executed and filed; or

(2) withdraws from future equity participation in the enterprise by executing and filing in the office of the Secretary of State a certificate declaring withdrawal under this section.

(b) A person who makes a contribution of the kind described in subsection (a) is liable as a general partner to any third party who transacts business with the enterprise (i) before the person withdraws and an appropriate certificate is filed to show withdrawal, or (ii) before an appropriate certificate is filed to show that he [or she] is not a general partner, but in either case only if the third party actually believed in good faith that the person was a general partner at the time of the transaction.

Section 305. Information.

Each limited partner has the right to:

(1) inspect and copy any of the partnership records required to be maintained by Section 105; and

(2) obtain from the general partners from time to time upon reasonable demand (i) true and full information regarding the state of the business and financial condition of the limited partnership, (ii) promptly after becoming available, a copy of the limited partnership's federal, state, and local income tax returns for each year, and (iii) other information regarding the affairs of the limited partnership as is just and reasonable.

Article 4 GENERAL PARTNERS

Section 401. Admission of Additional General Partners.

After the filing of a limited partnership's original certificate of limited partnership, additional general partners may be admitted as provided in writing in the partnership agreement or, if the partnership agreement does not provide in writing for the admission of additional general partners, with the written consent of all partners.

Section 402. Events of Withdrawal.

Except as approved by the specific written consent of all partners at the time, a person ceases to be a general partner of a limited partnership upon the happening of any of the following events:

(1) the general partner withdraws from the limited partnership as provided in Section 602;

(2) the general partner ceases to be a member of the limited partnership as provided in Section 702;

(3) the general partner is removed as a general partner in accordance with the partnership agreement;

(4) unless otherwise provided in writing in the partnership agreement, the general partner: (i) makes an assignment for the benefit of creditors; (ii) files a voluntary petition in bankruptcy; (iii) is adjudicated a bankrupt or insolvent; (iv) files a petition or answer seeking for himself [or herself] any reorganization, arrangement, composition, readjustment, liquidation, dissolution, or similar relief under any statute, law, or regulation; (v) files an answer or other pleading admitting or failing to contest the material allegations of a petition filed against him [or her] in any proceeding of this nature; or (vi) seeks, consents to, or acquiesces in the appointment of a trustee, receiver, or liquidator of the general partner or of all or any substantial part of his [or her] properties;

(5) unless otherwise provided in writing in the partnership agreement, [120] days after the commencement of any proceeding against the general partner seeking reorganization, arrangement, composition, readjustment, liquidation, dissolution, or similar relief under any statute, law, or regulation, the proceeding has not been dismissed, or if within [90] days after the appointment without his [or her] consent or acquiescence of a trustee, receiver, or liquidator of the general partner or of all or any substantial part of his [or her] properties, the appointment is not vacated or stayed or within [90] days after the expiration of any such stay, the appointment is not vacated;

(6) in the case of a general partner who is a natural person,

(i) his [or her] death; or

(ii) the entry of an order by a court of competent jurisdiction adjudicating him [or her] incompetent to manage his [or her] person or his [or her] estate;

(7) in the case of a general partner who is acting as a general partner by virtue of being a trustee of a trust, the termination of the trust (but not merely the substitution of a new trustee);

(8) in the case of a general partner that is a separate partnership, the dissolution and commencement of winding up of the separate partnership;

(9) in the case of a general partner that is a corporation, the filing of a certificate of dissolution, or its equivalent, for the corporation or the revocation of its charter; or

(10) in the case of an estate, the distribution by the fiduciary of the estate's entire interest in the partnership.

Section 403. General Powers and Liabilities.

(a) Except as provided in this [Act] or in the partnership agreement, a general partner of a limited partnership has the rights and powers and is subject to the restrictions of a partner in a partnership without limited partners.

(b) Except as provided in this [Act], a general partner of a limited partnership has the liabilities of a partner in a partnership without limited partners to persons other than the partnership and the other partners. Except as provided in this [Act] or in the partnership agreement, a general partner of a limited partnership has the liabilities of a partner in a partnership without limited partners to the partnership and to the other partners.

Section 404. Contributions by General Partner.

A general partner of a limited partnership may make contributions to the partnership and share in the profits and losses of, and in distributions from, the limited partnership as a general partner. A general partner also may make contributions to and share in profits, losses, and distributions as a limited partner. A person who is both a general partner and a limited partner has the rights and powers, and is subject to the restrictions and liabilities, of a general partner and, except as provided in the partnership agreement, also has the powers, and is subject to the restrictions, of a limited partner to the extent of his [or her] participation in the partnership as a limited partner.

Section 405. Voting.

The partnership agreement may grant to all or certain identified general partners the right to vote (on a per capita or any other basis), separately or with all or any class of the limited partners, on any matter.

Article 5 FINANCE
Section 501. Form of Contribution.

The contribution of a partner may be in cash, property, or services rendered, or a promissory note or other obligation to contribute cash or property or to perform services.

Section 502. Liability for Contribution.

(a) A promise by a limited partner to contribute to the limited partnership is not enforceable unless set out in a writing signed by the limited partner.

(b) Except as provided in the partnership agreement, a partner is obligated to the limited partnership to perform any enforceable promise to contribute cash or property or to perform services, even if he [or she] is unable to perform because of death, disability, or any other reason. If a partner does not make the required contribution of property or services, he [or she] is obligated at the option of the limited partnership to contribute cash equal to that portion of the value, as stated in the partnership records required to be kept pursuant to Section 105, of the stated contribution which has not been made.

(c) Unless otherwise provided in the partnership agreement, the obligation of a partner to make a contribution or return money or other property paid or distributed in violation of this [Act] may be compromised only by consent of all partners. Notwithstanding the compromise, a creditor of a limited partnership who extends credit, or, otherwise acts in reliance on that obligation after the partner signs a writing which reflects the obligation and before the amendment or cancellation thereof to reflect the compromise may enforce the original obligation.

Section 503. Sharing of Profits and Losses.

The profits and losses of a limited partnership shall be allocated among the partners, and among classes of partners, in the manner provided in writing in the partnership agreement. If the partnership agreement does not so provide in writing, profits and losses shall be allocated on the basis of the value, as stated in the partnership records required to be kept pursuant to Section 105, of the contributions made by each partner to the extent they have been received by the partnership and have not been returned.

Section 504. Sharing of Distributions.

Distributions of cash or other assets of a limited partnership shall be allocated among the partners and among classes of partners in the manner provided in writing in the partnership agreement. If the partnership agreement does not so provide in writing, distributions shall be made on the basis of the value, as stated in the partnership records required to be kept pursuant to Section 105, of the contributions made by each partner to the extent they have been received by the partnership and have not been returned.

Article 6 DISTRIBUTIONS AND WITHDRAWAL
Section 601. Interim Distributions.

Except as provided in this Article, a partner is entitled to receive distributions from a limited partnership before his [or her] withdrawal from the limited partnership and before the dissolution and winding up thereof to the extent and at the times or upon the happening of the events specified in the partnership agreement.

Section 602. Withdrawal of General Partner.

A general partner may withdraw from a limited partnership at any time by giving written notice to the other partners, but if the withdrawal violates the partnership agreement, the limited partnership may recover from the withdrawing general partner damages for breach of the partnership agreement and offset the damages against the amount otherwise distributable to him [or her].

Section 603. Withdrawal of Limited Partner.

A limited partner may withdraw from a limited partnership at the time or upon the happening of events specified in writing in the partnership agreement. If the agreement does not specify in writing the time or the events upon the happening of which a limited partner may withdraw or a definite time for the dissolution and winding up of the limited partnership, a limited partner may withdraw upon not less than six months' prior written notice to each general partner at his [or her] address on the books of the limited partnership at its office in this State.

Section 604. Distribution Upon Withdrawal.

Except as provided in this Article, upon withdrawal any withdrawing partner is entitled to receive any distribution to which he [or she] is entitled under the partnership agreement and, if not otherwise provided in the agreement, he [or she] is entitled to receive, within a reasonable time after withdrawal, the fair value of his [or her] interest in the limited partnership as of the date of withdrawal based upon his [or her] right to share in distributions from the limited partnership.

Section 605. Distribution in Kind.

Except as provided in writing in the partnership agreement, a partner, regardless of the nature of his [or her] contribution, has no right to demand and receive any distribution from a limited partnership in any form other than cash. Except as provided in writing in the partnership agreement, a partner may not be compelled to accept a distribution of any asset in kind from a limited partnership to the extent that the percentage of the asset distributed to him [or her] exceeds a percentage of that asset which is equal to the percentage in which he [or she] shares in distributions from the limited partnership.

Section 606. Right to Distribution.

At the time a partner becomes entitled to receive a distribution, he [or she] has the status of, and is entitled to all remedies available to, a creditor of the limited partnership with respect to the distribution.

Section 607. Limitations on Distribution.

A partner may not receive a distribution from a limited partnership to the extent that, after giving effect to the distribution, all liabilities of the limited partnership, other than liabilities to partners on account of their partnership interests, exceed the fair value of the partnership assets.

Section 608. Liability Upon Return of Contribution.

(a) If a partner has received the return of any part of his [or her] contribution without violation of the partnership agreement or this [Act], he [or she] is liable to the limited partnership for a period of one year thereafter for the amount of the returned contribution, but only to the extent necessary to discharge the limited partnership's liabilities to creditors who extended credit to the limited partnership during the period the contribution was held by the partnership.

(b) If a partner has received the return of any part of his [or her] contribution in violation of the partnership agreement or this [Act], he [or she] is liable to the limited partnership for a period of six years thereafter for the amount of the contribution wrongfully returned.

(c) A partner receives a return of his [or her] contribution to the extent that a distribution to him [or her] reduces his [or her] share of the fair value of the net assets of the limited partnership below the value, as set forth in the partnership records required to be kept pursuant to Section 105, of his [or her] contribution which has not been distributed to him [or her].

Article 7 ASSIGNMENT OF PARTNERSHIP INTERESTS

Section 701. Nature of Partnership Interest.

A partnership interest is personal property.

Section 702. Assignment of Partnership Interest.

Except as provided in the partnership agreement, a partnership interest is assignable in whole or in part. An assignment of a partnership interest does not dissolve a limited partnership or entitle the assignee to become or to exercise any rights of a partner. An assignment entitles the assignee to receive, to the extent assigned, only the distribution to which the assignor would be entitled. Except as provided in the partnership agreement, a partner ceases to be a partner upon assignment of all his [or her] partnership interest.

Section 703. Rights of Creditor.

On application to a court of competent jurisdiction by any judgment creditor of a partner, the court may charge the partnership interest of the partner with payment of the unsatisfied amount of the judgment with interest. To the extent so charged, the judgment creditor has only the rights of an assignee of the partnership interest. This [Act] does not deprive any partner of the benefit of any exemption laws applicable to his [or her] partnership interest.

Section 704. Right of Assignee to Become Limited Partner.

(a) An assignee of a partnership interest, including an assignee of a general partner, may become a limited partner if and to the extent that (i) the assignor gives the assignee that right in accordance with authority described in the partnership agreement, or (ii) all other partners consent.

(b) An assignee who has become a limited partner has, to the extent assigned, the rights and powers, and is subject to the restrictions and liabilities, of a limited partner under the partnership agreement and this [Act]. An assignee who becomes a limited partner also is liable for the obligations of his [or her] assignor to make and return contributions as provided in Articles 5 and 6. However, the assignee is not obligated for liabilities unknown to the assignee at the time he [or she] became a limited partner.

(c) If an assignee of a partnership interest becomes a limited partner, the assignor is not released from his [or her] liability to the limited partnership under Sections 207 and 502.

Section 705. Power of Estate of Deceased or Incompetent Partner.

If a partner who is an individual dies or a court of competent jurisdiction adjudges him [or her] to be incompetent to manage his [or her] person or his [or her] property, the partner's executor, administrator, guardian, conservator, or other legal representative may exercise all of the partner's rights for the purpose of settling his [or her] estate or administering his [or her] property, including any power the partner had to give an assignee the right to become a limited partner. If a partner is a corporation, trust, or other entity and is dissolved or terminated, the powers of that partner may be exercised by its legal representative or successor.

Article 8 DISSOLUTION

Section 801. Non-judicial Dissolution.

A limited partnership is dissolved and its affairs shall be wound up upon the happening of the first to occur of the following:

(1) at the time specified in the certificate of limited partnership;

(2) upon the happening of events specified in writing in the partnership agreement;

(3) written consent of all partners;

(4) an event of withdrawal of a general partner unless at the time there is at least one other general partner and the written provisions of the partnership agreement permit the business of the limited partnership to be carried on by the remaining general partner and that partner does so, but the limited partnership is not dissolved and is not required to be wound up by reason of any event of withdrawal if, within 90 days after the withdrawal, all partners agree in writing to continue the business of the limited partnership and to the appointment of one or more additional general partners if necessary or desired; or

(5) entry of a decree of judicial dissolution under Section 802.

Section 802. Judicial Dissolution.

On application by or for a partner the [designate the appropriate court] court may decree dissolution of a limited partnership whenever it is not reasonably practicable to carry on the business in conformity with the partnership agreement.

Section 803. Winding Up.

Except as provided in the partnership agreement, the general partners who have not wrongfully dissolved a limited partnership or, if none, the limited partners, may wind up the limited partnership's affairs; but the [designate the appropriate court] court may wind up the limited partnership's affairs upon application of any partner, his [or her] legal representative, or assignee.

Section 804. Distribution of Assets.

Upon the winding up of a limited partnership, the assets shall be distributed as follows:

(1) to creditors, including partners who are creditors, to the extent permitted by law, in satisfaction of liabilities of the limited partnership other than liabilities for distributions to partners under Section 601 or 604;

(2) except as provided in the partnership agreement, to partners and former partners in satisfaction of liabilities for distributions under Section 601 or 604; and

(3) except as provided in the partnership agreement, to partners first for the return of their contributions and secondly respecting their partnership interests, in the proportions in which the partners share in distributions.

Article 9 FOREIGN LIMITED PARTNERSHIPS

Section 901. Law Governing.

Subject to the Constitution of this State, (i) the laws of the state under which a foreign limited partnership is organized govern its organization and internal affairs and the liability of its limited partners, and (ii) a foreign limited partnership may not be denied registration by reason of any difference between those laws and the laws of this State.

Section 902. Registration.

Before transacting business in this State, a foreign limited partnership shall register with the Secretary of State. In order to register, a foreign limited partnership shall submit to the Secretary of State, in duplicate, an application for registration as a foreign limited partnership, signed and sworn to by a general partner and setting forth:

(1) the name of the foreign limited partnership and, if different, the name under which it proposes to register and transact business in this State;

(2) the State and date of its formation;

(3) the name and address of any agent for service of process on the foreign limited partnership whom the foreign limited partnership elects to appoint; the agent must be an individual resident of this State, a domestic corporation, or a foreign corporation having a place of business in, and authorized to do business in, this State;

(4) a statement that the Secretary of State is appointed the agent of the foreign limited partnership for service of process if no agent has been appointed

under paragraph (3) or, if appointed, the agent's authority has been revoked or if the agent cannot be found or served with the exercise of reasonable diligence;

(5) the address of the office required to be maintained in the state of its organization by the laws of that state or, if not so required, of the principal office of the foreign limited partnership;

(6) the name and business address of each general partner; and

(7) the address of the office at which is kept a list of the names and addresses of the limited partners and their capital contributions, together with an undertaking by the foreign limited partnership to keep those records until the foreign limited partnership's registration in this State is canceled or withdrawn.

Section 903. Issuance of Registration.

(a) If the Secretary of State finds that an application for registration conforms to law and all requisite fees have been paid, he [or she] shall:

(1) endorse on the application the word "Filed", and the month, day, and year of the filing thereof;

(2) file in his [or her] office a duplicate original of the application; and

(3) issue a certificate of registration to transact business in this State.

(b) The certificate of registration, together with a duplicate original of the application, shall be returned to the person who filed the application or his [or her] representative.

Section 904. Name.

A foreign limited partnership may register with the Secretary of State under any name, whether or not it is the name under which it is registered in its state of organization, that includes without abbreviation the words "limited partnership" and that could be registered by a domestic limited partnership.

Section 905. Changes and Amendments.

If any statement in the application for registration of a foreign limited partnership was false when made or any arrangements or other facts described have changed, making the application inaccurate in any respect, the foreign limited partnership shall promptly file in the office of the Secretary of State a certificate, signed and sworn to by a general partner, correcting such statement.

Section 906. Cancellation of Registration.

A foreign limited partnership may cancel its registration by filing with the Secretary of State a certificate of cancellation signed and sworn to by a general partner. A cancellation does not terminate the authority of the Secretary of State to accept service of process on the foreign limited partnership with

respect to [claims for relief] [causes of action] arising out of the transactions of business in this State.

Section 907. Transaction of Business Without Registration.

(a) A foreign limited partnership transacting business in this State may not maintain any action, suit, or proceeding in any court of this State until it has registered in this State.

(b) The failure of a foreign limited partnership to register in this State does not impair the validity of any contract or act of the foreign limited partnership or prevent the foreign limited partnership from defending any action, suit, or proceeding in any court of this State.

(c) A limited partner of a foreign limited partnership is not liable as a general partner of the foreign limited partnership solely by reason of having transacted business in this State without registration.

(d) A foreign limited partnership, by transacting business in this State without registration, appoints the Secretary of State as its agent for service of process with respect to [claims for relief] [causes of action] arising out of the transaction of business in this State.

Section 908. Action by [Appropriate Official].

The [designate the appropriate official] may bring an action to restrain a foreign limited partnership from transacting business in this State in violation of this Article.

Article 10 DERIVATIVE ACTIONS
Section 1001. Right of Action.

A limited partner may bring an action in the right of a limited partnership to recover a judgment in its favor if general partners with authority to do so have refused to bring the action or if an effort to cause those general partners to bring the action is not likely to succeed.

Section 1002. Proper Plaintiff.

In a derivative action, the plaintiff must be a partner at the time of bringing the action and (i) must have been a partner at the time of the transaction of which he [or she] complains or (ii) his [or her] status as a partner must have devolved upon him by operation of law or pursuant to the terms of the partnership agreement from a person who was a partner at the time of the transaction.

Section 1003. Pleading.

In a derivative action, the complaint shall set forth with particularity the effort of the plaintiff to secure initiation of the action by a general partner or the reasons for not making the effort.

Section 1004. Expenses.

If a derivative action is successful, in whole or in part, or if anything is received by the plaintiff as a result of a judgment, compromise, or settlement of an action or claim, the court may award the plaintiff reasonable expenses, including reasonable attorney's fees, and shall direct him [or her] to remit to the limited partnership the remainder of those proceeds received by him [or her].

Article 11 MISCELLANEOUS
Section 1101. Construction and Application.

This [Act] shall be so applied and construed to effectuate its general purpose to make uniform the law with respect to the subject of this [Act] among states enacting it.

Section 1102. Short Title.

This [Act] may be cited as the Uniform Limited Partnership Act.

Section 1103. Severability.

If any provision of this [Act] or its application to any person or circumstance is held invalid, the invalidity does not affect other provisions or applications of the [Act] which can be given effect without the invalid provision or application, and to this end the provisions of this [Act] are severable.

Section 1104. Effective Date, Extended Effective Date, and Repeal.

Except as set forth below, the effective date of this [Act] is _____ and the following acts [list existing limited partnership acts] are hereby repealed:

(1) The existing provisions for execution and filing of certificates of limited partnerships and amendments thereunder and cancellations thereof continue in effect until [specify time required to create central filing system], the extended effective date, and Sections 102, 103, 104, 105, 201, 202, 203, 204 and 206 are not effective until the extended effective date.

(2) Section 402, specifying the conditions under which a general partner ceases to be a member of a limited partnership, is not effective until the extended effective date, and the applicable provisions of existing law continue to govern until the extended effective date.

(3) Sections 501, 502 and 608 apply only to contributions and distributions made after the effective date of this [Act].

(4) Section 704 applies only to assignments made after the effective date of this [Act].

(5) Article 9, dealing with registration of foreign limited partnerships, is not effective until the extended effective date.

(6) Unless otherwise agreed by the partners, the applicable provisions of existing law governing allocation of profits and losses (rather than the provisions of Section 503), distributions to a withdrawing partner (rather than the provisions of Section 604), and distributions of assets upon the winding up of a limited partnership (rather than the provisions of Section 804) govern limited partnerships formed before the effective date of this [Act].

Section 1105. Rules for Cases Not Provided For in This [Act].

In any case not provided for in this [Act] the provisions of the Uniform Partnership Act govern.

Section 1106. Savings Clause.

The repeal of any statutory provision by this [Act] does not impair, or otherwise affect, the organization or the continued existence of a limited partnership existing at the effective date of this [Act], nor does the repeal of any existing statutory provision by this [Act] impair any contract or affect any right accrued before the effective date of this [Act].

Appendix C

Revised Model Business Corporation Act (Excerpted)

Chapter 1. GENERAL PROVISIONS

1.01. Short Title.

This Act shall be known and may be cited as the "[name of state] Business Corporation Act."

1.02. Reservation of Power to Amend or Repeal.

The [name of state legislature] has power to amend or repeal all or part of this Act at any time and all domestic and foreign corporations subject to this Act are governed by the amendments or repeal.

. . . .

1.40. Act Definitions.

In this Act:

(1) "Articles of incorporation" include amended and restated articles of incorporation and articles of merger.

(2) "Authorized shares" means the shares of all classes a domestic or foreign corporation is authorized to issue.

(3) "Conspicuous" means so written that a reasonable person against whom the writing is to operate should have noticed it. For example, printing in italics or boldface or contrasting color, or typing in capitals or underlined, is conspicuous.

(4) "Corporation" or "domestic corporation" means a corporation for profit, which is not a foreign corporation, incorporated under or subject to the provisions of this Act.

(5) "Deliver" or "delivery" means any method of delivery used in conventional commercial practice, including delivery by hand, mail, commercial delivery, and electronic transmission.

(6) "Distribution" means a direct or indirect transfer of money or other property (except its own shares) or incurrence of indebtedness by a corporation to or for the benefit of its shareholders in respect of any of its shares. A distribution may be in the form of a declaration or payment of a dividend; a purchase, redemption, or other acquisition of shares; a distribution of indebtedness; or otherwise.

(7) "Effective date of notice" is defined in section 1.41.

(7A) "Electronic transmission" or "electronically transmitted" means any process of communication not directly involving the physical transfer of paper that is suitable for the retention, retrieval, and reproduction of information by the recipient.

(8) "Employee" includes an officer but not a director. A director may accept duties that make him also an employee.

(9) "Entity" includes corporation and foreign corporation; not-for-profit corporation; profit and not-for profit unincorporated association; business trust, estate, partnership, trust, and two or more persons having a joint or common economic interest; and state, United States, and foreign government.

(10) "Foreign corporation" means a corporation for profit incorporated under a law other than the law of this state.

(11) "Governmental subdivision" includes authority, county, district, and municipality.

(12) "Includes" denotes a partial definition.

(13) "Individual" includes the estate of an incompetent or deceased individual.

(14) "Means" denotes an exhaustive definition.

(15) "Notice" is defined in section 1.41.

(16) "Person" includes individual and entity.

(17) "Principal office" means the office (in or out of this state) so designated in the annual report where the principal executive offices of a domestic or foreign corporation are located.

(18) "Proceeding" includes civil suit and criminal, administrative, and investigatory action.

(19) "Record date" means the date established under chapter 6 or 7 on which a corporation determines the identity of its shareholders and their shareholdings for purposes of this Act. The determinations shall be made as of the close of business on the record date unless another time for doing so is specified when the record date is fixed.

(20) "Secretary" means the corporate officer to whom the board of directors has delegated responsibility under Section 8.40(c) for custody of the minutes of the meetings of the board of directors and of the shareholders and for authenticating records of the corporation.

(21) "Shareholder" means the person in whose name shares are registered in the records of a corporation or the beneficial owner of shares to the extent of the rights granted by a nominee certificate on file with a corporation.

(22) "Shares" means the unit into which the proprietary interests in a corporation are divided.

(22A) "Sign" or "signature" includes any manual, facsimile, conformed or electronic signature.

(23) "State," when referring to a part of the United States, includes a state and commonwealth (and their agencies and governmental subdivisions) and a territory and insular possession (and their agencies and governmental subdivisions) of the United States.

(24) "Subscriber" means a person who subscribes for shares in a corporation, whether before or after incorporation.

(25) "United States" includes district, authority, bureau, commission, department, and any other agency of the United States.

(26) "Voting group" means all shares of one or more classes or series that under the articles of incorporation or this Act are entitled to vote and be counted together collectively on a matter at a meeting of shareholders. All shares entitled by the articles of incorporation or this Act to vote generally on the matter are for that purpose a single voting group.

1.41. Notice.

(a) Notice under this Act must be in writing unless oral notice is reasonable under the circumstances. Notice by electronic transmission is written notice.

(b) Notice may be communicated in person; by mail or other method of delivery; or by telephone, voice mail or other electronic means. If these forms of personal notice are impracticable, notice may be communicated by a newspaper of general circulation in the area where published; or by radio, television, or other form of public broadcast communication.

(c) Written notice by a domestic or foreign corporation to its shareholder, if in a comprehensible form, is effective (i) upon deposit in the United States mail, if mailed postpaid and correctly addressed to the shareholder's address shown in the corporation's current record of shareholders, or (ii) when electronically transmitted to the shareholder in a manner authorized by the shareholder.

(d) Written notice to a domestic or foreign corporation (authorized to transact business in this state) may be addressed to its registered agent at its registered office or to the corporation or its secretary at its principal office shown in its most recent annual report or, in the case of a foreign corporation that has not yet delivered an annual report, in its application for a certificate of authority.

(e) Except as provided in subsection (c), written notice, if in a comprehensible form, is effective at the earliest of the following:

(1) when received;

(2) five days after its deposit in the United States Mail, if mailed postpaid and correctly addressed;

(3) on the date shown on the return receipt, if sent by registered or certified mail, return receipt requested, and the receipt is signed by or on behalf of the addressee.

(f) Oral notice is effective when communicated if communicated in a comprehensible manner.

(g) If this Act prescribes notice requirements for particular circumstances, those requirements govern. If articles of incorporation or bylaws prescribe notice requirements, not inconsistent with this section or other provisions of this Act, those requirements govern.

1.42. Number of Shareholders.

(a) For purposes of this Act, the following identified as a shareholder in a corporation's current record of shareholders constitutes one shareholder:

(1) three or fewer co-owners;

(2) a corporation, partnership, trust, estate, or other entity;

(3) the trustees, guardians, custodians, or other fiduciaries of a single trust, estate, or account.

(b) For purposes of this Act, shareholdings registered in substantially similar names constitute one shareholder if it is reasonable to believe that the names represent the same person.

Chapter 2. INCORPORATION

2.01. Incorporators.

One or more persons may act as the incorporator or incorporators of a corporation by delivering articles of incorporation to the secretary of state for filing.

2.02. Articles of Incorporation.

(a) The articles of incorporation must set forth:

(1) a corporate name ... ;

(2) the number of shares the corporation is authorized to issue;

(3) the street address of the corporation's initial registered office and the name of its initial registered agent at that office; and

(4) the name and address of each incorporator.

(b) The articles of incorporation may set forth:

(1) the names and addresses of the individuals who are to serve as the initial directors;

(2) provisions not inconsistent with law regarding:

(i) the purpose or purposes for which the corporation is organized;

(ii) managing the business and regulating the affairs of the corporation;

(iii) defining, limiting, and regulating the powers of the corporation, its board of directors, and shareholders;

(iv) a par value for authorized shares or classes of shares;

(v) the imposition of personal liability on shareholders for the debts of the corporation to a specified extent and upon specified conditions;

(3) any provision that under this Act is required or permitted to be set forth in the bylaws; and

(4) a provision eliminating or limiting the liability of a director to the corporation or its shareholders for money damages for any action taken, or any failure to take any action, as a director, except liability for (A) the amount of a financial benefit received by a director to which he is not entitled; (B) an intentional infliction of harm on the corporation or the shareholders; (C) [unlawful distributions]; or (D) an intentional violation of criminal law. . . .

(c) The articles of incorporation need not set forth any of the corporate powers enumerated in this Act.

2.03. Incorporation.

(a) Unless a delayed effective date is specified, the corporate existence begins when the articles of incorporation are filed.

(b) The secretary of state's filing of the articles of incorporation is conclusive proof that the incorporators satisfied all conditions precedent to incorporation except in a proceeding by the state to cancel or revoke the incorporation or involuntarily dissolve the corporation.

2.04. Liability for Preincorporation Transactions.

All persons purporting to act as or on behalf of a corporation, knowing there was no incorporation under this Act, are jointly and severally liable for all liabilities created while so acting.

2.05. Organization of Corporation.

(a) After incorporation:

(1) if initial directors are named in the articles of incorporation, the initial directors shall hold an organizational meeting, at the call of a majority of the directors, to complete the organization of the corporation by appointing officers, adopting bylaws, and carrying on any other business brought before the meeting;

(2) if initial directors are not named in the articles, the incorporator or incorporators shall hold an organizational meeting at the call of a majority of the incorporators:

(i) to elect directors and complete the organization of the corporation; or

(ii) to elect a board of directors who shall complete the organization of the corporation.

(b) Action required or permitted by this Act to be taken by incorporators at an organizational meeting may be taken without a meeting if the action taken is evidenced by one or more written consents describing the action taken and signed by each incorporator.

(c) An organizational meeting may be held in or out of this state.

. . . .

Chapter 3. PURPOSES AND POWERS
3.01. Purposes.

(a) Every corporation incorporated under this Act has the purpose of engaging in any lawful business unless a more limited purpose is set forth in the articles of incorporation.

(b) A corporation engaging in a business that is subject to regulation under another statute of this state may incorporate under this Act only if permitted by, and subject to all limitations of, the other statute.

3.02. General Powers.

Unless its articles of incorporation provide otherwise, every corporation has perpetual duration and succession in its corporate name and has the same powers as an individual to do all things necessary or convenient to carry out its business and affairs, including without limitation power:

(1) to sue and be sued, complain and defend in its corporate name;

(2) to have a corporate seal, which may be altered at will, and to use it, or a facsimile of it, by impressing or affixing it or in any other manner reproducing it;

(3) to make and amend bylaws, not inconsistent with its articles of incorporation or with the laws of this state, for managing the business and regulating the affairs of the corporation;

(4) to purchase, receive, lease, or otherwise acquire, and own, hold, improve, use, and otherwise deal with, real or personal property, or any legal or equitable interest in property, wherever located;

(5) to sell, convey, mortgage, pledge, lease, exchange, and otherwise dispose of all or any part of its property;

(6) to purchase, receive, subscribe for, or otherwise acquire; own, hold, vote, use, sell, mortgage, lend, pledge, or otherwise dispose of; and deal in and with shares or other interests in, or obligations of, any other entity;

(7) to make contracts and guarantees, incur liabilities, borrow money, issue its notes, bonds, and other obligations (which may be convertible into or include the option to purchase other securities of the corporation), and secure any of its obligations by mortgage or pledge of any of its property, franchises, or income;

(8) to lend money, invest and reinvest its funds, and receive and hold real and personal property as security for repayment;

(9) to be a promoter, partner, member, associate, or manager of any partnership, joint venture, trust, or other entity;

(10) to conduct its business, locate offices, and exercise the powers granted by this Act within or without this state;

(11) to elect directors and appoint officers, employees, and agents of the corporation, define their duties, fix their compensation, and lend them money and credit;

(12) to pay pensions and establish pension plans, pension trusts, profit sharing plans, share bonus plans, share option plans, and benefit or incentive plans for any or all of its current or former directors, officers, employees, and agents;

(13) to make donations for the public welfare or for charitable, scientific, or educational purposes;

(14) to transact any lawful business that will aid governmental policy;

(15) to make payments or donations, or do any other act, not inconsistent with law, that furthers the business and affairs of the corporation.

3.03. Emergency Powers.

(a) In anticipation of or during an emergency defined in subsection (d), the board of directors of a corporation may:

(1) modify lines of succession to accommodate the incapacity of any director, officer, employee, or agent; and

(2) relocate the principal office, designate alternative principal offices or regional offices, or authorize the officers to do so.

(b) During an emergency defined in subsection (d), unless emergency bylaws provide otherwise:

(1) notice of a meeting of the board of directors need be given only to those directors whom it is practicable to reach and may be given in any practicable manner, including by publication and radio; and

(2) one or more officers of the corporation present at a meeting of the board of directors may be deemed to be directors for the meeting, in order of rank and within the same rank in order of seniority, as necessary to achieve a quorum.

(c) Corporate action taken in good faith during an emergency under this section to further the ordinary business affairs of the corporation:

(1) binds the corporation; and

(2) may not be used to impose liability on a corporate director, officer, employee, or agent.

(d) An emergency exists for purposes of this section if a quorum of the corporation's directors cannot readily be assembled because of some catastrophic event.

3.04. Ultra Vires.

(a) Except as provided in subsection (b), the validity of corporate action may not be challenged on the ground that the corporation lacks or lacked power to act.

(b) A corporation's power to act may be challenged:

(1) in a proceeding by a shareholder against the corporation to enjoin the act;

(2) in a proceeding by the corporation, directly, derivatively, or through a receiver, trustee, or other legal representative, against an incumbent or former director, officer, employee, or agent of the corporation; or

(3) in a proceeding by the Attorney General under section 14.30.

(c) In a shareholder's proceeding under subsection (b)(1) to enjoin an unauthorized corporate act, the court may enjoin or set aside the act, if equitable and if all affected persons are parties to the proceeding, and may award damages for loss (other than anticipated profits) suffered by the corporation or another party because of enjoining the unauthorized act.

Chapter 4. NAME
4.01. Corporate Name.

(a) A corporate name:

(1) must contain the word "corporation," "incorporated," "company," or "limited," or the abbreviation "corp.," "inc.," "co.," or "ltd.," or words or abbreviations of like import in another language; and

(2) may not contain language stating or implying that the corporation is organized for a purpose other than that permitted by section 3.01 and its articles of incorporation.

(b) Except as authorized by subsections (c) and (d), a corporate name must be distinguishable upon the records of the secretary of state from:

(1) the corporate name of a corporation incorporated or authorized to transact business in this state;

(2) a corporate name reserved or registered under section 4.02 or 4.03;

(3) the fictitious name adopted by a foreign corporation authorized to transact business in this state because its real name is unavailable; and

(4) the corporate name of a not-for-profit corporation incorporated or authorized to transact business in this state.

(c) A corporation may apply to the secretary of state for authorization to use a name that is not distinguishable upon his records from one or more of the names described in subsection (b). The secretary of state shall authorize use of the name applied for if:

(1) the other corporation consents to the use in writing and submits an undertaking in form satisfactory to the secretary of state to change its name to a name that is distinguishable upon the records of the secretary of state from the name of the applying corporation; or

(2) the applicant delivers to the secretary of state a certified copy of the final judgment of a count of competent jurisdiction establishing the applicant's right to use the name applied for in this state.

(d) A corporation may use the name (including the fictitious name) of another domestic or foreign corporation that is used in this state if the other corporation is incorporated or authorized to transact business in this state and the proposed user corporation:

(1) has merged with the other corporation;

(2) has been formed by reorganization of the other corporation; or

(3) has acquired all or substantially all of the assets, including the corporate name, of the other corporation.

(e) This Act does not control the use of fictitious names.

4.02. Reserved Name.

(a) A person may reserve the exclusive use of a corporate name, including a fictitious name for a foreign corporation whose corporate name is not available, by delivering an application to the secretary of state for filing. The application must set forth the name and address of the applicant and the name proposed to be reserved. If the secretary of state finds that the corporate name applied for is available, he shall reserve the name for the applicant's exclusive use for a nonrenewable 120-day period.

(b) The owner of a reserved corporate name may transfer the reservation to another person by delivering to the secretary of state a signed notice of the transfer that states the name and address of the transferee.

4.03. Registered Name.

(a) A foreign corporation may register its corporate name, or its corporate name with any addition required by section 15.06, if the name is distinguishable upon the records of the secretary of state from the corporate names that are not available under section 4.01(b)(3).

(b) A foreign corporation registers its corporate name, or its corporate name with any addition required by section 15.06, by delivering to the secretary of state for filing an application:

(1) setting forth its corporate name, or its corporate name with any addition required by section 15.06, the state or country and date of its incorporation, and a brief description of the nature of the business in which it is engaged; and

(2) accompanied by a certificate of existence (or a document of similar import) from the state or country of incorporation.

(c) The name is registered for the applicant's exclusive use upon the effective date of the application.

(d) A foreign corporation whose registration is effective may renew it for successive years by delivering to the secretary of state for filing a renewal application, which complies with the requirements of subsection (b), between October 1 and December 31 of the preceding year. The renewal application renews the registration for the following calendar year.

(e) A foreign corporation whose registration is effective may thereafter qualify as a foreign corporation under that name or consent in writing to the use of that name by a corporation thereafter incorporated under this Act or by another foreign corporation thereafter authorized to transact business in this state. The registration terminates when the domestic corporation is incorporated or the foreign corporation qualifies or consents to the qualification of another foreign corporation under the registered name.

Chapter 5. OFFICE AND AGENT

5.01. Registered Office and Registered Agent.

Each corporation must continuously maintain in this state:

(1) a registered office that may be the same as any of its places of business; and

(2) a registered agent, who may be:

(i) an individual who resides in this state and whose business office is identical with the registered office;

(ii) a domestic corporation or not-for-profit domestic corporation whose business office is identical with the registered office; or

(iii) a foreign corporation or not-for-profit foreign corporation authorized to transact business in this state whose business office is identical with the registered office.

5.02. Change of Registered Office or Registered Agent.

(a) A corporation may change its registered office or registered agent by delivering to the secretary of state for filing a statement of change that sets forth:

(1) the name of the corporation;

(2) the street address of its current registered office;

(3) if the current registered office is to be changed, the street address of the new registered office;

(4) the name of its current registered agent;

(5) if the current registered agent is to be changed, the name of the new registered agent and the new agent's written consent (either on the statement or attached to it) to the appointment; and

(6) that after the change or changes are made, the street addresses of its registered office and the business office of its registered agent will be identical.

(b) If a registered agent changes the street address of his business office, he may change the street address of the registered office of any corporation for which he is the registered agent by notifying the corporation in writing of the change and signing (either manually or in facsimile) and delivering to the secretary of state for filing a statement that complies with the requirements of subsection (a) and recites that the corporation has been notified of the change.

5.03. Resignation of Registered Agent.

(a) A registered agent may resign his agency appointment by signing and delivering to the secretary of state for filing the signed original and two exact or conformed copies of a statement of resignation. The statement may include a statement that the registered office is also discontinued.

(b) After filing the statement the secretary of state shall mail one copy to the registered office (if not discontinued) and the other copy to the corporation at its principal office.

(c) The agency appointment is terminated, and the registered office discontinued if so provided, on the 31st day after the date on which the statement was filed.

5.04. Service on Corporation.

(a) A corporation's registered agent is the corporation's agent for service of process, notice, or demand required or permitted by law to be served on the corporation.

(b) If a corporation has no registered agent, or the agent cannot with reasonable diligence be served, the corporation may be served by registered or certified mail, return receipt requested, addressed to the secretary of the corporation at its principal office. Service is perfected under this subsection at the earliest of:

(1) the date the corporation receives the mail;

(2) the date shown on the return receipt, if signed on behalf of the corporation; or

(3) five days after its deposit in the United States Mail, as evidenced by the postmark, if mailed postpaid and correctly addressed.

(c) This section does not prescribe the only means, or necessarily the required means, of serving a corporation.

Chapter 6. SHARES AND DISTRIBUTIONS
6.01. Authorized Shares.

(a) The articles of incorporation must prescribe the classes of shares and the number of shares of each class that the corporation is authorized to issue. If more than one class of shares is authorized, the articles of incorporation must prescribe a distinguishing designation for each class, and, prior to the issuance of shares of a class, the preferences, limitations, and relative rights of that class must be described in the articles of incorporation. All shares of a class must have preferences, limitations, and relative rights identical with those of other shares of the same class except to the extent otherwise permitted by section 6.02.

(b) The articles of incorporation must authorize (1) one or more classes of shares that together have unlimited voting rights, and (2) one or more classes of shares (which may be the same class or classes as those with voting rights) that together are entitled to receive the net assets of the corporation upon dissolution.

(c) The articles of incorporation may authorize one or more classes of shares that:

(1) have special, conditional, or limited voting rights, or no right to vote, except to the extent prohibited by this Act;

(2) are redeemable or convertible as specified in the articles of incorporation (i) at the option of the corporation, the shareholder, or another person or upon the occurrence or a designated event; (ii) for cash, indebtedness, securities, or other property; (iii) in a designated amount or in an amount determined in accordance with a designated formula or by reference to extrinsic data or events;

(3) entitle the holders to distributions calculated in any manner, including dividends that may be cumulative, non-cumulative, or partially cumulative;

(4) have preference over any other class of shares with respect to distributions, including dividends and distributions upon the dissolution of the corporation.

(d) The description of the designations, preferences, limitations, and relative rights of share classes in subsection (c) is not exhaustive.

6.02. Terms of Class or Series Determined by Board of Directors.

(a) If the articles of incorporation so provide, the board of directors may determine, in whole or part, the preferences, limitations, and relative rights (within the limits set forth in section 6.01) of (1) any class of shares before the issuance of any shares of that class or (2) one or more series within a class before the issuance of any shares of that series.

(b) Each series of a class must be given a distinguishing designation.

(c) All shares of a series must have preferences, limitations, and relative rights identical with those of other shares of the same series and, except to the extent otherwise provided in the description of the series, of those of other series of the same class.

(d) Before issuing any shares of a class or series created under this section, the corporation must deliver to the secretary of state for filing articles of amendment, which are effective without shareholder action, that set forth:

(1) the name of the corporation;

(2) the text of the amendment determining the terms of the class or series of shares;

(3) the date it was adopted; and

(4) a statement that the amendment was duly adopted by the board of directors.

6.03. Issued and Outstanding Shares.

(a) A corporation may issue the number of shares of each class or series authorized by the articles of incorporation. Shares that are issued are outstanding shares until they are reacquired, redeemed, converted, or canceled.

(b) The reacquisition, redemption, or conversion of outstanding shares is subject to the limitations of subsection (c) of this section and to section 6.40.

(c) At all times that shares of the corporation are outstanding, one or more shares that together have unlimited voting rights and one or more shares that together are entitled to receive the net assets of the corporation upon dissolution must be outstanding.

6.04. Fractional Shares.

(a) A corporation may:

(1) issue fractions of a share or pay in money the value of fractions of a share;

(2) arrange for disposition of fractional shares by the shareholders;

(3) issue scrip in registered or bearer form entitling the holder to receive a full share upon surrendering enough scrip to equal a full share.

(b) Each certificate representing scrip must be conspicuously labeled "scrip" and must contain the information required by section 6.25(b).

(c) The holder of a fractional share is entitled to exercise the rights of a shareholder, including the right to vote, to receive dividends, and to participate in the assets of the corporation upon liquidation. The holder of scrip is not entitled to any of these rights unless the scrip provides for them.

(d) The board of directors may authorize the issuance of scrip subject to any condition considered desirable, including:

(1) that the scrip will become void if not exchanged for full shares before a specified date; and

(2) that the shares for which the scrip is exchangeable may be sold and the proceeds paid to the scrip holders.

6.20. Subscription for Shares Before Incorporation.

(a) A subscription for shares entered into before incorporation is irrevocable for six months unless the subscription agreement provides a longer or shorter period or all the subscribers agree to revocation.

(b) The board of directors may determine the payment terms of subscriptions for shares that were entered into before incorporation, unless the subscription agreement specifies them. A call for payment by the board of directors must be uniform so far as practicable as to all shares of the same class or series, unless the subscription agreement specifies otherwise.

(c) Shares issued pursuant to subscriptions entered into before incorporation are fully paid and nonassessable when the corporation receives the consideration specified in the subscription agreement.

(d) If a subscriber defaults in payment of money or property under a subscription agreement entered into before incorporation, the corporation may collect the amount owed as any other debt. Alternatively, unless the subscription agreement provides otherwise, the corporation may rescind the agreement and may sell the shares if the debt remains unpaid more than 20 days after the corporation sends written demand for payment to the subscriber.

(e) A subscription agreement entered into after incorporation is a contract between the subscriber and the corporation subject to section 6.21.

6.21. Issuance of Shares.

(a) The powers granted in this section to the board of directors may be reserved to the shareholders by the articles of incorporation.

(b) The board of directors may authorize shares to be issued for consideration consisting of any tangible or intangible property or benefit to the corporation, including cash, promissory notes, services performed, contracts for services to be performed, or other securities of the corporation.

(c) Before the corporation issues shares, the board of directors must determine that the consideration received or to be received for shares to be issued is adequate. That determination by the board of directors is conclusive insofar as the adequacy of consideration for the issuance of shares relates to whether the shares are validly issued, fully paid, and nonassessable.

(d) When the corporation receives the consideration for which the board of directors authorized the issuance of shares, the shares issued therefor are fully paid and nonassessable.

(e) The corporation may place in escrow shares issued for a contract for future services or benefits or a promissory note, or make other arrangements to restrict the transfer of the shares, and may credit distributions in respect of the shares against their purchase price, until the services are performed, the note is paid, or the benefits received. If the services are not performed, the note is not paid, or the benefits are not received, the shares escrowed or restricted and the distributions credited may be canceled in whole or part.

6.22. Liability of Shareholders.

(a) A purchaser from a corporation of its own shares is not liable to the corporation or its creditors with respect to the shares except to pay the consideration for which the shares were authorized to be issued (section 6.21) or specified in the subscription agreement (section 6.20).

(b) Unless otherwise provided in the articles of incorporation, a shareholder of a corporation is not personally liable for the acts or debts of the corporation except that he may become personally liable by reason of his own acts or conduct.

6.23. Share Dividends.

(a) Unless the articles of incorporation provide otherwise, shares may be issued pro rata and without consideration to the corporation's shareholders or to the shareholders of one or more classes or series. An issuance of shares under this subsection is a share dividend.

(b) Shares of one class or series may not be issued as a share dividend in respect of shares of another class or series unless (1) the articles of incorporation so authorize, (2) a majority of the votes entitled to be cast by the class or series to be issued approve the issue, or (3) there are no outstanding shares of the class or series to be issued.

(c) If the board of directors does not fix the record date for determining shareholders entitled to a share dividend, it is the date the board of directors authorizes the share dividend.

6.24. Share Options.

A corporation may issue rights, options, or warrants for the purchase of shares of the corporation. The board of directors shall determine the terms upon which the rights, options, or warrants are issued, their form and content, and the consideration for which the shares are to be issued.

6.25. Form and Content of Certificates.

(a) Shares may but need not be represented by certificates. Unless this Act or another statute expressly provides otherwise, the rights and obligations of shareholders are identical whether or not their shares are represented by certificates.

(b) At a minimum each share certificate must state on its face:

   (1) the name of the issuing corporation and that it is organized under the law of this state;

   (2) the name of the person to whom issued; and

   (3) the number and class of shares and the designation of the series, if any, the certificate represents.

(c) If the issuing corporation is authorized to issue different classes of shares or different series within a class, the designations, relative rights, preferences, and limitations applicable to each class and the variations in rights, preferences, and limitations determined for each series (and the authority of the board of directors to determine variations for future series) must be summarized on the front or back of each certificate. Alternatively, each certificate may state conspicuously on its front or back that the corporation will furnish the shareholder this information on request in writing and without charge.

(d) Each share certificate (1) must be signed (either manually or in facsimile) by two officers designated in the bylaws or by the board of directors and (2) may bear the corporate seal or its facsimile.

(e) If the person who signed (either manually or in facsimile) a share certificate no longer holds office when the certificate is issued, the certificate is nevertheless valid.

6.26. Shares Without Certificates.

(a) Unless the articles of incorporation or bylaws provide otherwise, the board of directors of a corporation may authorize the issue of some or all of the shares of any or all of its classes or series without certificates. The authorization does not affect shares already represented by certificates until they are surrendered to the corporation.

(b) Within a reasonable time after the issue or transfer of shares without certificates, the corporation shall send the shareholder a written statement of the information required on certificates by section 6.25(b) and (c), and, if applicable, section 6.27.

6.27. Restriction on Transfer of Shares and Other Securities.

(a) The articles of incorporation, bylaws, an agreement among shareholders, or an agreement between shareholders and the corporation may impose restrictions on the transfer or registration of transfer of shares of the corporation. A restriction does not affect shares issued before the restriction was adopted unless the holders of the shares are parties to the restriction agreement or voted in favor of the restriction.

(b) A restriction on the transfer or registration of transfer of shares is valid and enforceable against the holder or a transferee of the holder if the restriction is authorized by this section and its existence is noted conspicuously on the front or back of the certificate or is contained in the information statement [sent to the shareholder]. Unless so noted, a restriction is not enforceable against a person without knowledge of the restriction.

(c) A restriction on the transfer or registration of transfer of shares is authorized:

   (1) to maintain the corporation's status when it is dependent on the number or identity of its shareholders;

   (2) to preserve exemptions under federal or state securities law;

   (3) for any other reasonable purpose.

(d) A restriction on the transfer or registration of transfer of shares may:

   (1) obligate the shareholder first to offer the corporation or other persons (separately, consecutively, or simultaneously) an opportunity to acquire the restricted shares;

   (2) obligate the corporate or other persons (separately, consecutively, or simultaneously) to acquire the restricted shares;

   (3) require the corporation, the holders of any class of its shares, or another person to approve the transfer of the restricted shares, if the requirement is not manifestly unreasonable;

   (4) prohibit the transfer of the restricted shares to designated persons or classes of persons, if the prohibition is not manifestly unreasonable.

(e) For purposes of this section, "shares" includes a security convertible into or carrying a right to subscribe for or acquire shares.

6.28. Expense of Issue.

A corporation may pay the expenses of selling or underwriting its shares, and of organizing or reorganizing the corporation, from the consideration received for shares.

6.30. Shareholders' Preemptive Rights.

(a) The shareholders of a corporation do not have a preemptive right to acquire the corporation's unissued shares except to the extent the articles of incorporation so provide.

(b) A statement included in the articles of incorporation that "the corporation elects to have preemptive rights" (or words of similar import) means that the following principles apply except to the extent the articles of incorporation expressly provide otherwise:

(1) The shareholders of the corporation have a preemptive right, granted on uniform terms and conditions prescribed by the board of directors to provide a fair and reasonable opportunity to exercise the right, to acquire proportional amounts of the corporation's unissued shares upon the decision of the board of directors to issue them.

(2) A shareholder may waive his preemptive right. A waiver evidenced by a writing is irrevocable even though it is not supported by consideration.

(3) There is no preemptive right with respect to:

(i) shares issued as compensation to directors, officers, agents, or employees of the corporation, its subsidiaries or affiliates;

(ii) shares issued to satisfy conversion or option rights created to provide compensation to directors, officers, agents, or employees of the corporation, its subsidiaries or affiliates;

(iii) shares authorized in articles of incorporation that are issued within six months from the effective date of incorporation;

(iv) shares sold otherwise than for money.

(4) Holders of shares of any class without general voting rights but with preferential rights to distributions or assets have no preemptive rights with respect to shares of any class.

(5) Holders of shares of any class with general voting rights but without preferential rights to distributions or assets have no preemptive rights with respect to shares of any class with preferential rights to distributions or assets unless the shares with preferential rights are convertible into or carry a right to subscribe for or acquire shares without preferential rights.

(6) Shares subject to preemptive rights that are not acquired by shareholders may be issued to any person for a period of one year after being offered to shareholders at a consideration set by the board of directors that is not lower than the consideration set for the exercise of preemptive rights. An offer at a lower consideration or after the expiration of one year is subject to the shareholders' preemptive rights.

(c) For purposes of this section, "shares" includes a security convertible into or carrying a right to subscribe for or acquire shares.

6.31. Corporation's Acquisition of Its Own Shares.

(a) A corporation may acquire its own shares and shares so acquired constitute authorized but unissued shares.

(b) If the articles of incorporation prohibit the reissue of acquired shares, the number of authorized shares is reduced by the number of shares acquired, effective upon amendment of the articles of incorporation.

(c) The board of directors may adopt articles of amendment under this section without shareholder action, and deliver them to the secretary of state for filing. The articles must set forth:

(1) the name of the corporation;

(2) the reduction in the number of authorized shares, itemized by class and series; and

(3) the total number of authorized shares, itemized by class and series, remaining after reduction of the shares.

6.40. Distributions to Shareholders.

(a) A board of directors may authorize and the corporation may make distributions to its shareholders subject to restriction by the articles of incorporation and the limitation in subsection (c).

(b) If the board of directors does not fix the record date for determining shareholders entitled to a distribution (other than one involving a purchase, redemption, or other acquisition of the corporation's shares), it is the date the board of directors authorizes the distribution.

(c) No distribution may be made if, after giving it effect:

(1) the corporation would not be able to pay its debts as they become due in the usual course of business; or

(2) the corporation's total assets would be less than the sum of its total liabilities plus (unless the articles of incorporation permit otherwise) the amount that would be needed, if the corporation were to be dissolved at the time of the distribution, to satisfy the preferential rights upon dissolution of shareholders whose preferential rights are superior to those receiving the distribution.

(d) The board of directors may base a determination that a distribution is not prohibited under subsection (c) either on financial statements prepared on the basis of accounting practices and principles that are reasonable in the circumstances or on a fair valuation or other method that is reasonable in the circumstances.

(e) Except as provided in subsection (g), the effect of a distribution under subsection (c) is measured:

(1) in the case of distribution by purchase, redemption, or other acquisition of the corporation's shares, as of the earlier of (i) the date money or other property is transferred or debt incurred by the

corporation or (ii) the date the shareholder ceases to be a shareholder with respect to the acquired shares;

(2) in the case of any other distribution of indebtedness, as of the date the indebtedness is distributed; and

(3) in all other cases, as of (i) the date the distribution is authorized if the payment occurs within 120 days after the date of authorization or (ii) the date the payment is made if it occurs more than 120 days after the date of authorization.

(f) A corporation's indebtedness to a shareholder incurred by reason of a distribution made in accordance with this section is at parity with the corporation's indebtedness to its general, unsecured creditors except to the extent subordinated by agreement.

(g) Indebtedness of a corporation, including indebtedness issued as a distribution, is not considered a liability for purposes of determination under subsection (c) if its terms provide that payment of principal and interest are made only if and to the extent that payment of a distribution to shareholders could then be made under this section. If the indebtedness is issued as a distribution, each payment of principal or interest is treated as a distribution, the effect of which is measured on the date the payment is actually made.

Chapter 7. SHAREHOLDERS
7.01. Annual Meeting.

(a) A corporation shall hold a meeting of shareholders annually at a time stated in or fixed in accordance with the bylaws.

(b) Annual shareholders' meetings may be held in or out of this state at the place stated in or fixed in accordance with the bylaws. If no place is stated in or fixed in accordance with the bylaws, annual meetings shall be held at the corporation's principal office.

(c) The failure to hold an annual meeting at the time stated in or fixed in accordance with a corporation's bylaws does not affect the validity of any corporate action.

7.02. Special Meeting.

(a) A corporation shall hold a special meeting of shareholders:

(1) on call of its board of directors or the person or persons authorized to do so by the articles of incorporation or bylaws; or

(2) if the holders of at least 10 percent of all the votes entitled to be cast on any issue proposed to be considered at the proposed special meeting sign, date, and deliver to the corporation's secretary one or more written demands for the meeting describing the purpose or purposes for which it is to be held, provided that the articles of incorporation may fix a lower percentage or a higher percentage not exceeding 25

percent of all the votes entitled to be cast on any issue proposed to be considered. ...

(b) If not otherwise fixed under sections 7.03 or 7.07, the record date for determining shareholders entitled to demand a special meeting is the date the first shareholder signs the demand.

(c) Special shareholders' meetings may be held in or out of this state at the place stated in or fixed in accordance with the bylaws. If no place is stated or fixed in accordance with the bylaws, special meetings shall be held at the corporation's principal office.

(d) Only business within the purpose or purposes described in the meeting notice required by section 7.05(c) may be conducted at a special shareholders' meeting.

7.03. Court-Ordered Meeting.

(a) The [name or describe] court of the county where a corporation's principal office (or, if none in this state, its registered office) is located may summarily order a meeting to be held:

(1) on application of any shareholder of the corporation entitled to participate in an annual meeting if an annual meeting was not held within the earlier of 6 months after the end of the corporation's fiscal year or 15 months after its last annual meeting; or

(2) on application of a shareholder who signed a demand for a special meeting valid under section 7.02 if:

(i) notice of the special meeting was not given within 30 days after the date the demand was delivered to the corporation's secretary; or

(ii) the special meeting was not held in accordance with the notice.

(b) The court may fix the time and place of the meeting, determine the shares entitled to participate in the meeting, specify a record date for determining shareholders entitled to notice of and to vote at the meeting, prescribe the form and content of the meeting notice, fix the quorum required for specific matters to be considered at the meeting (or direct that the votes represented at the meeting constitute a quorum for action on those matters), and enter other orders necessary to accomplish the purpose or purposes of the meeting.

7.04. Action Without Meeting.

(a) Action required or permitted by this Act to be taken at a shareholders' meeting may be taken without a meeting if the action is taken by all the shareholders entitled to vote on the action. The action must be evidenced by one or more written consents bearing the date of signature and describing the action taken, signed by all the shareholders entitled to vote on the action, and delivered to the corporation for inclusion in the minutes or filing with the corporate records.

(b) If not otherwise determined under sections 7.03 or 7.07, the record date for determining shareholders entitled to take action without a meeting is the date the first shareholder signs the consent under subsection (a). ...

(c) A consent signed under this section has the effect of a meeting vote and may be described as such in any document.

(d) If this Act requires that notice of proposed action be given to nonvoting shareholders and the action is to be taken by unanimous consent of the voting shareholders, the corporation must give its nonvoting shareholders written notice of the proposed action at least 10 days before the action is taken. The notice must contain or be accompanied by the same material that, under this Act, would have been required to be sent to nonvoting shareholders in a notice of meeting at which the proposed action would have been submitted to the shareholders for action.

7.05. Notice of Meeting.

(a) A corporation shall notify shareholders of the date, time, and place of each annual and special shareholders' meeting no fewer than 10 nor more than 60 days before the meeting date. Unless this Act or the articles of incorporation require otherwise, the corporation is required to give notice only to shareholders entitled to vote at the meeting.

(b) Unless this Act or the articles of incorporation require otherwise, notice of an annual meeting need not include a description of the purpose or purposes for which the meeting is called.

(c) Notice of a special meeting must include a description of the purpose or purposes for which the meeting is called.

(d) If not otherwise fixed ... , the record date for determining shareholders entitled to notice of and to vote at an annual or special shareholders' meeting is the day before the first notice is delivered to shareholders.

(e) Unless the bylaws require otherwise, if an annual or special shareholders' meeting is adjourned to a different date, time, or place, notice need not be given of the new date, time, or place if the new date, time, or place is announced at the meeting before adjournment ... .

7.06. Waiver of Notice.

(a) A shareholder may waive any notice required by this Act, the articles of incorporation, or bylaws before or after the date and time stated in the notice. The waiver must be in writing, be signed by the shareholder entitled to the notice, and be delivered to the corporation for inclusion in the minutes or filing with the corporate records.

(b) A shareholder's attendance at a meeting:

(1) waives objection to lack of notice or defective notice of the meeting, unless the shareholder at the beginning of the meeting objects to holding the meeting or transacting business at the meeting;

(2) waives objection to consideration of a particular matter at the meeting that is not within the purpose or purposes described in the meeting notice, unless the shareholder objects to considering the matter when it is presented.

7.07. Record Date.

(a) The bylaws may fix or provide the manner of fixing the record date for one or more voting groups in order to determine the shareholders entitled to notice of a shareholders' meeting, to demand a special meeting, to vote, or to take any other action. If the bylaws do not fix or provide for fixing a record date, the board of directors of the corporation may fix a future date as the record date.

(b) A record date fixed under this section may not be more than 70 days before the meeting or action requiring a determination of shareholders.

(c) A determination of shareholders entitled to notice of or to vote at a shareholders' meeting is effective for any adjournment of the meeting unless the board of directors fixes a new record date, which it must do if the meeting is adjourned to a date more than 120 days after the date fixed for the original meeting.

(d) If a court orders a meeting adjourned to a date more than 120 days after the date fixed for the original meeting, it may provide that the original record date continues in effect or it may fix a new record date.

. . . .

7.20. Shareholders' List for Meeting.

(a) After fixing a record date for a meeting, a corporation shall prepare an alphabetical list of the names of all its shareholders who are entitled to notice of a shareholders' meeting. The list must be arranged by voting group (and within each voting group by class or series of shares) and show the address of and number of shares held by each shareholder.

(b) The shareholders' list must be available for inspection by any shareholder, beginning two business days after notice of the meeting is given for which the list was prepared and continuing through the meeting, at the corporation's principal office or at a place identified in the meeting notice in the city where the meeting will be held. A shareholder, his agent, or attorney is entitled on written demand to inspect and, subject to the requirements of section 16.02(c), to copy the list, during regular business hours and at his expense, during the period it is available for inspection.

(c) The corporation shall make the shareholders' list available at the meeting, and any shareholder, his agent, or attorney is entitled to inspect the list at any time during the meeting or any adjournment.

(d) If the corporation refuses to allow a shareholder, his agent, or attorney to inspect the shareholders' list before or at the meeting (or copy the list as permitted by subsection (b)), the [name or describe] court of the county where a corporation's principal office (or, if none in this state, its registered office) is located, on application of the shareholder, may summarily order the inspection or copying at the corporation's expense and may postpone the meeting for which the list was prepared until the inspection or copying is complete.

(e) Refusal or failure to prepare or make available the shareholders' list does not affect the validity of action taken at the meeting.

7.21. Voting Entitlement of Shares.

(a) Except as provided in subsections (b) and (c) or unless the articles of incorporation provide otherwise, each outstanding share, regardless of class, is entitled to one vote on each matter voted on at a shareholders' meeting. Only shares are entitled to vote.

(b) Absent special circumstances, the shares of a corporation are not entitled to vote if they are owned, directly or indirectly, by a second corporation, domestic or foreign, and the first corporation owns, directly or indirectly, a majority of the shares entitled to vote for directors of the second corporation.

(c) Subsection (b) does not limit the power of a corporation to vote any shares, including its own shares, held by it in a fiduciary capacity.

(d) Redeemable shares are not entitled to vote after notice of redemption is mailed to the holders and a sum sufficient to redeem the shares has been deposited with a bank, trust company, or other financial institution under an irrevocable obligation to pay the holders the redemption price on surrender of the shares.

7.22. Proxies.

(a) A shareholder may vote his shares in person or by proxy.

(b) A shareholder or his agent or attorney-in-fact may appoint a proxy to vote or otherwise act for the shareholders by signing an appointment form or by an electronic transmission. An electronic transmission must contain or be accompanied by information from which one can determine that the shareholder, the shareholder's agent, or the shareholder's attorney-in-fact authorized the electronic transmission.

(c) An appointment of a proxy is effective when a signed appointment form or an electronic transmission of the appointment is received by the inspector of election or the officer or agent of the corporation authorized to tabulate votes. An appointment is valid for 11 months unless a longer period is expressly provided in the appointment.

(d) An appointment of a proxy is revocable unless the appointment form or electronic transmission states that it is irrevocable and the appointment is coupled with an interest. Appointments coupled with an interest include the appointment of:

(1) a pledgee;

(2) a person who purchased or agreed to purchase the shares;

(3) a creditor of the corporation who extended it credit under terms requiring the appointment;

(4) an employee of the corporation whose employment contract requires the appointment; or

(5) a party to a voting agreement created under section 7.31.

(e) The death or incapacity of the shareholder appointing a proxy does not affect the right of the corporation to accept the proxy's authority unless notice of the death or incapacity is received by the secretary or other officer or agent authorized to tabulate votes before the proxy exercises his authority under the appointment.

(f) An appointment made irrevocable under subsection (d) is revoked when the interest with which it is coupled is extinguished.

(g) A transferee for value of shares subject to an irrevocable appointment may revoke the appointment if he did not know of its existence when he acquired the shares and the existence of the irrevocable appointment was not noted conspicuously on the certificate representing the shares or on the information statement for shares without certificates.

(h) Subject to section 7.24 and to any express limitation on the proxy's authority stated in the appointment form or electronic transmission, a corporation is entitled to accept the proxy's vote or other action as that of the shareholder making the appointment.

7.23. Shares Held by Nominees.

(a) A corporation may establish a procedure by which the beneficial owner of shares that are registered in the name of a nominee is recognized by the corporation as the shareholder. The extent of this recognition may be determined in the procedure.

(b) The procedure may set forth:

(1) the types of nominees to which it applies;

(2) the rights or privileges that the corporation recognizes in a beneficial owner;

(3) the manner in which the procedure is selected by the nominee;

(4) the information that must be provided when the procedure is selected;

(5) the period for which selection of the procedure is effective; and

(6) other aspects of the rights and duties created.

7.24. Corporation's Acceptance of Votes.

(a) If the name signed on a vote, consent, waiver, or proxy appointment corresponds to the name of a shareholder, the corporation if acting in good faith is entitled to accept the vote, consent, waiver, or proxy appointment and give it effect as the act of the shareholder.

(b) If the name signed on a vote, consent, waiver, or proxy appointment does not correspond to the name of its shareholder, the corporation if acting in good faith is nevertheless entitled to accept the vote, consent, waiver, or proxy appointment and give it effect as the act of the shareholder if:

(1) the shareholder is an entity and the name signed purports to be that of an officer or agent of the entity;

(2) the name signed purports to be that of an administrator, executor, guardian, or conservator representing the shareholder and, if the corporation requests, evidence of fiduciary status acceptable to the corporation has been presented with respect to the vote, consent, waiver, or proxy appointment;

(3) the name signed purports to be that of a receiver or trustee in bankruptcy of the shareholder and, if the corporation requests, evidence of this status acceptable to the corporation has been presented with respect to the vote, consent, waiver, or proxy appointment;

(4) the name signed purports to be that of a pledgee, beneficial owner, or attorney-in-fact of the shareholder and, if the corporation requests, evidence acceptable to the corporation of the signatory's authority to sign for the shareholder has been presented with respect to the vote, consent, waiver, or proxy appointment;

(5) two or more persons are the shareholder as co-tenants or fiduciaries and the name signed purports to be the name of at least one of the co-owners and the person signing appears to be acting on behalf of all the co-owners.

(c) The corporation is entitled to reject a vote, consent, waiver, or proxy appointment if the secretary or other officer or agent authorized to tabulate votes, acting in good faith, has reasonable basis for doubt about the validity of the signature on it or about the signatory's authority to sign for the shareholder.

(d) The corporation and its officer or agent who accepts or rejects a vote, consent, waiver, or proxy appointment in good faith and in accordance with the standards of this section ... are not liable in damages to the shareholder for the consequences of the acceptance or rejection.

(e) Corporate action based on the acceptance or rejection of a vote, consent, waiver, or proxy appointment under this section ... is valid unless a court of competent jurisdiction determines otherwise.

7.25. Quorum and Voting Requirements for Voting Groups.

(a) Shares entitled to vote as a separate voting group may take action on a matter at a meeting only if a quorum of those shares exists with respect to that matter. Unless the articles of incorporation or this Act provide otherwise, a majority of the votes entitled to be cast on the matter by the voting group constitutes a quorum of that voting group for action on that matter.

(b) Once a share is represented for any purpose at a meeting, it is deemed present for quorum purposes for the remainder of the meeting and for any adjournment of that meeting unless a new record date is or must be set for that adjourned meeting.

(c) If a quorum exists, action on a matter (other than the election of directors) by a voting group is approved if the votes cast within the voting group favoring the action exceed the votes cast opposing the action, unless the articles of incorporation or this Act require a greater number of affirmative votes.

(d) An amendment of articles of incorporation adding, changing, or deleting a quorum or voting requirement for a voting group greater than specified in subsection (a) or (c) is governed by section 7.27.

(e) The election of directors is governed by section 7.28.

7.26. Action by Single and Multiple Voting Groups.

(a) If the articles of incorporation or this Act provide for voting by a single voting group on a matter, action on that matter is taken when voted upon by that voting group as provided in section 7.25.

(b) If the articles of incorporation or this Act provide for voting by two or more voting groups on a matter, action on that matter is taken only when voted upon by each of those voting groups counted separately as provided in section 7.25. Action may be taken by one voting group on a matter even though no action is taken by another voting group entitled to vote on the matter.

7.27. Greater Quorum or Voting Requirements.

(a) The articles of incorporation may provide for a greater quorum or voting requirement for shareholders (or voting groups of shareholders) than is provided for by this Act.

(b) An amendment to the articles of incorporation that adds, changes, or deletes a greater quorum or voting requirement must meet the same quorum requirement and be adopted by the same vote and voting groups required to take action under the quorum and voting requirements then in effect or proposed to be adopted, whichever is greater.

7.28. Voting for Directors; Cumulative Voting.

(a) Unless otherwise provided in the articles of incorporation, directors are elected by a plurality of the votes cast by the shares entitled to vote in the election at a meeting at which a quorum is present.

(b) Shareholders do not have a right to cumulate their votes for directors unless the articles of incorporation so provide.

(c) A statement in the articles of incorporation that "[all] [a designated voting group of] shareholders are entitled to cumulate their votes for directors" (or words of similar import) means that the shareholders designated are entitled to multiply the number of votes they are entitled to cast by the number of directors for whom they are entitled to vote and cast the product for a single candidate or distribute the product among two or more candidates.

(d) Shares otherwise entitled to vote cumulatively may not be voted cumulatively at a particular meeting unless:

(1) the meeting notice or proxy statement accompanying the notice states conspicuously that cumulative voting is authorized; or

(2) a shareholder who has the right to cumulate his votes gives notice to the corporation not less than 48 hours before the time set for the meeting of his intent to cumulate his votes during the meeting, and if one shareholder gives this notice all other shareholders in the same voting group participating in the election are entitled to cumulate their votes without giving further notice.

. . . .

7.30. Voting Trusts.

(a) One or more shareholders may create a voting trust, conferring on a trustee the right to vote or otherwise act for them, by signing an agreement setting out the provisions of the trust (which may include anything consistent with its purpose) and transferring their shares to the trustee. When a voting trust agreement is signed, the trustee shall prepare a list of the names and addresses of all owners of beneficial interests in the trust, together with the number and class of shares each transferred to the trust, and deliver copies of the list and agreement to the corporation's principal office.

(b) A voting trust becomes effective on the date the first shares subject to the trust are registered in the trustee's name. A voting trust is valid for not more than 10 years after its effective date unless extended under subsection (c).

(c) All or some of the parties to a voting trust may extend it for additional terms of not more than 10 years each by signing an extension agreement and obtaining the voting trustee's written consent to the extension. An extension is valid for 10 years from the date the first shareholder signs the extension agreement. The voting trustee must deliver copies of the extension agreement and list of beneficial owners to the corporation's principal office. An extension agreement binds only those parties signing it.

7.31. Voting Agreements.

(a) Two or more shareholders may provide for the manner in which they will vote their shares by signing an agreement for that purpose. A voting

agreement created under this section is not subject to the provisions of section 7.30.

(b) A voting agreement created under this section is specifically enforceable.

7.32. Shareholder Agreements.

(a) An agreement among the shareholders of a corporation that complies with this section is effective among the shareholders and the corporation even though it is inconsistent with one or more other provisions of this Act in that it:

(1) eliminates the board of directors or restricts the discretion or powers of the board of directors;

(2) governs the authorization or making of distributions whether or not in proportion to ownership of shares, subject to the limitations in section 6.40;

(3) establishes who shall be directors or officers of the corporation, or their terms of office or manner of selection or removal;

(4) governs, in general or in regard to specific matters, the exercise or division of voting power by or between the shareholders and directors or by or among any of them, including use of weighted voting rights or director proxies;

(5) establishes the terms and conditions of any agreement for the transfer or use of property or the provision of services between the corporation and any shareholder, director, officer or employee of the corporation or among any of them;

(6) transfers to one or more shareholders or other persons all or part of the authority to exercise the corporate powers or to manage the business and affairs of the corporation, including the resolution of any issue about which there exists a deadlock among directors or shareholders;

(7) requires dissolution of the corporation at the request of one or more of the shareholders or upon the occurrence of a specified event or contingency; or

(8) otherwise governs the exercise of the corporate powers or the management of the business and affairs of the corporation or the relationship among the shareholders, the directors and the corporation, or among any of them, and is not contrary to public policy.

(b) An agreement authorized by this section shall be:

(1) set forth (A) in the articles of incorporation or bylaws and approved by all persons who are shareholders at the time of the agreement or (B) in a written agreement that is signed by all persons who are shareholders at the time of the agreement and is made known to the corporation;

(2) subject to amendment only by all persons who are shareholders at the time of the amendment, unless the agreement provides otherwise, and

(3) valid for 10 years, unless the agreement provides otherwise.

(c) The existence of an agreement authorized by this section shall be noted conspicuously on the front or back of each certificate for outstanding shares or on the information statement required by section 6.26(b). If at the time of the agreement the corporation has shares outstanding represented by certificates, the corporation shall recall the outstanding certificates and issue substitute certificates that comply with this subsection. The failure to note the existence of the agreement on the certificate or information statement shall not affect the validity of the agreement or any action taken pursuant to it. Any purchaser of shares who, at the time of purchase, did not have knowledge of the existence of the agreement shall be entitled to rescission of the purchase. A purchaser shall be deemed to have knowledge of the existence of the agreement if its existence is noted on the certificate or information statement for the shares in compliance with this subsection and, if the shares are not represented by a certificate, the information statement is delivered to the purchaser at or prior to the time of purchase of the shares. An action to enforce the right of rescission authorized by this subsection must be commenced within the earlier of 90 days after discovery of the existence of the agreement or two years after the time of purchase of the shares.

(d) An agreement authorized by this section shall cease to be effective when shares of the corporation are listed on a national securities exchange or regularly traded in a market maintained by one or more members of a national or affiliated securities association. If the agreement ceases to be effective for any reason, the board of directors may, if the agreement is contained or referred to in the corporation's articles of incorporation or bylaws, adopt an amendment to the articles of incorporation or bylaws, without shareholder action, to delete the agreement and any references to it.

(e) An agreement authorized by this section that limits the discretion or powers of the board of directors shall relieve the directors of, and impose upon the person or persons in whom such discretion or powers are vested, liability for acts or omissions imposed by law on directors to the extent that the discretion or powers of the directors are limited by the agreement.

(f) The existence or performance of an agreement authorized by this section shall not be a ground for imposing personal liability on any shareholder for the acts or debts of the corporation even if the agreement or its performance treats the corporation as if it were a partnership or results in failure to observe the corporate formalities otherwise applicable to the matters governed by the agreement.

(g) Incorporators or subscribers for shares may act as shareholders with respect to an agreement authorized by this section if no shares have been issued when the agreement is made.

7.40. Subchapter Definitions.

In this subchapter:

(1) "Derivative proceeding" means a civil suit in the right of a domestic corporation or, to the extent provided in section 7.47, in the right of a foreign corporation.

(2) "Shareholder" includes a beneficial owner whose shares are held in a voting trust or held by a nominee on the beneficial owner's behalf.

7.41. Standing.

A shareholder may not commence or maintain a derivative proceeding unless the shareholder:

(1) was a shareholder of the corporation at the time of the act or omission complained of or became a shareholder through transfer by operation of law from one who was a shareholder at that time; and

(2) fairly and adequately represents the interests of the corporation in enforcing the right of the corporation.

7.42. Demand.

No shareholder may commence a derivative proceeding until:

(1) a written demand has been made upon the corporation to take suitable action; and

(2) 90 days have expired from the date the demand was made unless the shareholder has earlier been notified that the demand has been rejected by the corporation or unless irreparable injury to the corporation would result by waiting for the expiration of the 90-day period.

7.43. Stay of Proceedings.

If the corporation commences an inquiry into the allegations made in the demand or complaint, the court may stay any derivative proceeding for such period as the court deems appropriate.

7.44. Dismissal.

(a) A derivative proceeding shall be dismissed by the court on motion by the corporation if one of the groups specified in subsections (b) or (f) has determined in good faith after conducting a reasonable inquiry upon which its conclusions are based that the maintenance of the derivative proceeding is not in the best interests of the corporation.

(b) Unless a panel is appointed pursuant to subsection (f), the determination in subsection (a) shall be made by:

(1) a majority vote of independent directors present at a meeting of the board of directors if the independent directors constitute a quorum; or

(2) a majority vote of a committee consisting of two or more independent directors appointed by majority vote of independent directors present at a meeting of the board of directors, whether or not such independent directors constituted a quorum.

(c) None of the following shall by itself cause a director to be considered not independent for purposes of this section:

(1) the nomination or election of the director by persons who are defendants in the derivative proceeding or against whom action is demanded;

(2) the naming of the director as a defendant in the derivative proceeding or as a person against whom action is demanded; or

(3) the approval by the director of the act being challenged in the derivative proceeding or demand if the act resulted in no personal benefit to the director.

(d) If a derivative proceeding is commenced after a determination has been made rejecting a demand by a shareholder, the complaint shall allege with particularity facts establishing either (1) that a majority of the board of directors did not consist of independent directors at the time the determination was made or (2) that the requirements of subsection (a) have not been met.

(e) If a majority of the board of directors does not consist of independent directors at the time the determination is made, the corporation shall have the burden of proving that the requirements of subsection (a) have been met. If a majority of the board of directors consists of independent directors at the time the determination is made, the plaintiff shall have the burden of proving that the requirements of subsection (a) have not been met.

(f) The court may appoint a panel of one or more independent persons upon motion by the corporation to make a determination whether the maintenance of the derivative proceeding is in the best interests of the corporation. In such case, the plaintiff shall have the burden of proving that the requirements of subsection (a) have not been met.

7.45. Discontinuance or Settlement.

A derivative proceeding may not be discontinued or settled without the court's approval. If the court determines that a proposed discontinuance or settlement will substantially affect the interests of the corporation's shareholders or a class of shareholders, the court shall direct that notice be given to the shareholders affected.

7.46. Payment of Expenses.

On termination of the derivative proceeding the court may:

(1) order the corporation to pay the plaintiff's reasonable expenses (including counsel fees) incurred in the proceeding if it finds that the proceeding has resulted in a substantial benefit to the corporation;

(2) order the plaintiff to pay any defendant's reasonable expenses (including counsel fees) incurred in defending the proceeding if it finds that the proceeding was commenced or maintained without reasonable cause or for an improper purpose; or

(3) order a party to pay an opposing party's reasonable expenses (including counsel fees) incurred because of the filing of a pleading, motion or other paper, if it finds that the pleading, motion or other paper was not well grounded in fact, after reasonable inquiry, or warranted by existing law or a good faith argument for the extension, modification or reversal of existing law and was interposed for an improper purpose, such as to harass or to cause unnecessary delay or needless increase in the cost of litigation.

7.47. Applicability to Foreign Corporations.

In any derivative proceeding in the right of a foreign corporation, the matters covered by this subchapter shall be governed by the laws of the jurisdiction of incorporation of the foreign corporation except for sections 7.43, 7.45 and 7.46.

Chapter 8. DIRECTORS AND OFFICERS

8.01, Requirement for and Duties of Board of Directors.

(a) Except as provided in section 7.32, each corporation must have a board of directors.

(b) All corporate powers shall be exercised by or under the authority of, and the business and affairs of the corporation managed under the direction of, its board of directors, subject to any limitation set forth in the articles of incorporation or in an agreement authorized under section 7.32.

. . . .

8.02. Qualifications of Directors.

The articles of incorporation or bylaws may prescribe qualifications for directors. A director need not be a resident of this state or a shareholder of the corporation unless the articles of incorporation or bylaws so prescribe.

8.03. Number and Election of Directors.

(a) A board of directors must consist of one or more individuals, with the number specified in or fixed in accordance with the articles of incorporation or bylaws.

(b) If a board of directors has power to fix or change the number of directors, the board may increase or decrease by 30 percent or less the number of directors last approved by the shareholders, but only the shareholders may increase or decrease by more than 30 percent the number of directors last approved by the shareholders.

(c) The articles of incorporation or bylaws may establish a variable range for the size of the board of directors by fixing a minimum and maximum number of directors. If a variable range is established, the number of directors may be fixed or changed from time to time, within the minimum and maximum, by the shareholders or the board of directors. After shares are issued, only the shareholders may change the range for the size of the board or change from a fixed to a variable-range size board or vice versa.

(d) Directors are elected at the first annual shareholders' meeting and at each annual meeting thereafter unless their terms are staggered under section 8.06.

8.04. Election of Directors by Certain Classes of Shareholders.

If the articles of incorporation authorize dividing the shares into classes, the articles may also authorize the election of all or a specified number of directors by the holders of one or more authorized classes of shares. Each class (or classes) of shares entitled to elect one or more directors is a separate voting group for purposes of the election of directors.

8.05. Terms of Directors Generally.

(a) The terms of the initial directors of a corporation expire at the first shareholders' meeting at which directors are elected.

(b) The terms of all other directors expire at the next annual shareholders' meeting following their election unless their terms are staggered under section 8.06.

(c) A decrease in the number of directors does not shorten an incumbent director's term.

(d) The term of a director elected to fill a vacancy expires at the next shareholders' meeting at which directors are elected.

(e) Despite the expiration of a director's term, he continues to serve until his successor is elected and qualifies or until there is a decrease in the number of directors.

8.06. Staggered Terms for Directors.

If there are nine or more directors, the articles of incorporation may provide for staggering their terms by dividing the total number of directors into two or three groups, with each group containing one-half or one-third of the total, as near as may be. In that event, the terms of directors in the first group expire at the first annual shareholders' meeting after their election, the terms of the second group expire at the second annual shareholders' meeting after their election, and the terms of the third group, if any, expire at the third annual shareholders' meeting after their election. At each annual shareholders' meeting held thereafter, directors shall be chosen for a term of two years or three years, as the case may be, to succeed those whose terms expire.

8.07. Resignation of Directors.

(a) A director may resign at any time by delivering written notice to the board of directors, its chairman, or to the corporation.

(b) A resignation is effective when the notice is delivered unless the notice specifies a later effective date.

8.08. Removal of Directors by Shareholders.

(a) The shareholders may remove one or more directors with or without cause unless the articles of incorporation provide that directors may be removed only for cause.

(b) If a director is elected by a voting group of shareholders, only the shareholders of that voting group may participate in the vote to remove him.

(c) If cumulative voting is authorized, a director may not be removed if the number of votes sufficient to elect him under cumulative voting is voted against his removal. If cumulative voting is not authorized, a director may be removed only if the number of votes cast to remove him exceeds the number of votes cast not to remove him.

(d) A director may be removed by the shareholders only at a meeting called for the purpose of removing him and the meeting notice must state that the purpose, or one of the purposes, of the meeting is removal of the director.

8.09. Removal of Directors by Judicial Proceeding.

(a) The [name or describe] court of the county where a corporation's principal office (or, if none in this state, its registered office) is located may remove a director of the corporation from office in a proceeding commenced either by the corporation or by its shareholders holding at least 10 percent of the outstanding shares of any class if the court finds that (1) the director engaged in fraudulent or dishonest conduct, or gross abuse of authority or discretion, with respect to the corporation and (2) removal is in the best interest of the corporation.

(b) The court that removes a director may bar the director from reelection for a period prescribed by the court.

(c) If shareholders commence a proceeding under subsection (a), they shall make the corporation a party defendant.

8.10. Vacancy on Board.

(a) Unless the articles of incorporation provide otherwise, if a vacancy occurs on a board of directors, including a vacancy resulting from an increase in the number of directors:

(1) the shareholders may fill the vacancy;

(2) the board of directors may fill the vacancy; or

(3) if the directors remaining in office constitute fewer than a quorum of the board, they may fill the vacancy by the affirmative vote of a majority of all the directors remaining in office.

(b) If the vacant office was held by a director elected by a voting group of shareholders, only the holders of shares of that voting group are entitled to vote to fill the vacancy if it is filled by the shareholders.

(c) A vacancy that will occur at a specific later date (by reason of a resignation effective at a later date under section 8.07(b) or otherwise) may be filled before the vacancy occurs but the new director may not take office until the vacancy occurs.

8.11. Compensation of Directors.

Unless the articles of incorporation or bylaws provide otherwise, the board of directors may fix the compensation of directors.

8.20. Meetings.

(a) The board of directors may hold regular or special meetings in or out of this state.

(b) Unless the articles of incorporation or bylaws provide otherwise, the board of directors may permit any or all directors to participate in a regular or special meeting by, or conduct the meeting through the use of, any means of communication by which all directors participating may simultaneously hear each other during the meeting. A director participating in a meeting by this means is deemed to be present in person at the meeting.

8.21. Action Without Meeting.

(a) Unless the articles of incorporation or bylaws provide otherwise, action required or permitted by this Act to be taken at a board of directors' meeting may be taken without a meeting if the action is taken by all members of the board. The action must be evidenced by one or more written consents describing the action taken, signed by each director, and included in the minutes or filed with the corporate records reflecting the action taken.

(b) Action taken under this section is effective when the last director signs the consent, unless the consent specifies a different effective date.

(c) A consent signed under this section has the effect of a meeting vote and may be described as such in any document.

8.22. Notice of Meeting.

(a) Unless the articles of incorporation or bylaws provide otherwise, regular meetings of the board of directors may be held without notice of the date, time, place, or purpose of the meeting.

(b) Unless the article of incorporation or bylaws provide for a longer or shorter period, special meetings of the board of directors must be preceded by at least two days' notice of the date, time, and place of the meeting. The notice need not describe the purpose of the special meeting unless required by the articles of incorporation or bylaws.

8.23. Waiver of Notice.

(a) A director may waive any notice required by this Act, the articles of incorporation, or bylaws before or after the date and time stated in the notice. Except as provided by subsection (b), the waiver must be in writing, signed by the director entitled to the notice, and filed with the minutes or corporate records.

(b) A director's attendance at or participation in a meeting waives any required notice to him of the meeting unless the director at the beginning of the meeting (or promptly upon his arrival) objects to holding the meeting or transacting business at the meeting and does not thereafter vote for or assent to action taken at the meeting.

8.24. Quorum and Voting.

(a) Unless the articles of incorporation or bylaws require a greater number or unless otherwise specifically provided in this Act, a quorum of a board of directors consists of:

(1) a majority of the fixed number of directors if the corporation has a fixed board size; or

(2) a majority of the number of directors prescribed, or if no number is prescribed the number in office immediately before the meeting begins, if the corporation has a variable-range size board.

(b) The articles of incorporation or bylaws may authorize a quorum of a board of directors to consist of no fewer than one-third of the fixed or prescribed number of directors determined under subsection (a).

(c) If a quorum is present when a vote is taken, the affirmative vote of a majority of directors present is the act of the board of directors unless the articles of incorporation or bylaws require the vote of a greater number of directors.

(d) A director who is present at a meeting of the board of directors or a committee of the board of directors when corporate action is taken is deemed to have assented to the action taken unless: (1) he objects at the beginning of the meeting (or promptly upon his arrival) to holding it or transacting business at the meeting; (2) his dissent or abstention from the action taken is entered in the minutes of the meeting; or (3) he delivers written notice of his dissent or abstention to the presiding officer of the meeting before its adjournment or to the corporation immediately after adjournment of the meeting. The right of dissent or abstention is not available to a director who votes in favor of the action taken.

8.25. Committees.

(a) Unless the articles of incorporation or bylaws provide otherwise, a board of directors may create one or more committees and appoint members of the board of directors to serve on them. Each committee may have two or more members, who serve at the pleasure of the board of directors.

(b) The creation of a committee and appointment of members to it must be approved by the greater of (1) a majority of all the directors in office when the action is taken or (2) the number of directors required by the articles of incorporation or bylaws to take action under section 8.24.

(c) Sections 8.20 through 8.24, which govern meetings, action without meetings, notice and wavier of notice, and quorum and voting requirements of the board of directors, apply to committees and their members as well.

(d) To the extent specified by the board of directors or in the articles of incorporation or bylaws, each committee may exercise the authority of the board of directors under section 8.01.

(e) A committee may not, however:

(1) authorize distributions;

(2) approve or propose to shareholders action that this Act requires be approved by shareholders;

(3) fill vacancies on the board of directors or on any of its committees;

(4) amend articles of incorporation pursuant to section 10.02;

(5) adopt, amend, or repeal bylaws;

(6) approve a plan of merger not requiring shareholder approval;

(7) authorize or approve reacquisition of shares, except according to a formula or method prescribed by the board of directors; or

(8) authorize or approve the issuance or sale or contract for sale of shares, or determine the designation and relative rights, preferences, and limitations of a class or series of shares, except that the board of directors may authorize a committee (or a senior executive officer of the corporation) to do so within limits specifically prescribed by the board of directors.

(f) The creation of, delegation of authority to, or action by a committee does not alone constitute compliance by a director with the standards of conduct described in section 8.30.

8.30. Standards of Conduct for Directors.

(a) Each member of the board of directors, when discharging the duties of a director, shall act: (1) in good faith, and (2) in a manner the director reasonably believes to be in the best interests of the corporation.

(b) The members of the board of directors or a committee of the board, when becoming informed in connection with their decision-making function or devoting attention to their oversight function, shall discharge their duties with the care that a person in a like position would reasonably believe appropriate under similar circumstances.

(c) In discharging board or committee duties a director, who does not have knowledge that makes reliance unwarranted, is entitled to rely on the performance by any of the persons specified in subsection (e)(1) or subsection (e)(3) to whom the board may have delegated, formally or informally by

course of conduct, the authority or duty to perform one or more of the board's functions that are delegable under applicable law.

(d) In discharging board or committee duties a director, who does not have knowledge that makes reliance unwarranted, is entitled to rely on information, opinions, reports or statements, including financial statements and other financial data, prepared or presented by any of the persons specified in subsection (e).

(e) A director is entitled to rely, in accordance with subsection (c) or (d), on:

(1) one or more officers or employees of the corporation whom the director reasonably believes to be reliable and competent in the functions performed or the information, opinions, reports or statements provided;

(2) legal counsel, public accountants, or other persons retained by the corporation as to matters involving skills or expertise the director reasonably believes are matters (i) within the particular person's professional or expert competence or (ii) as to which the particular person merits confidence; or

(3) a committee of the board of directors of which the director is not a member if the director reasonably believes the committee merits confidence.

8.31. Standards of Liability for Directors.

(a) A director shall not be liable to the corporation or its shareholders for any decision to take or not to take action, or any failure to take any action, as a director, unless the party asserting liability in a proceeding establishes that:

(1) any provision in the articles of incorporation authorized by section 2.02(b)(4) or the protection afforded by section 8.61 for action taken in compliance with section 8.62 or 8.63, if interposed as a bar to the proceeding by the director, does not preclude liability; and

(2) the challenged conduct consisted or was the result of:

(i) action not in good faith; or

(ii) a decision

(A) which the director did not reasonably believe to be in the best interests of the corporation, or

(B) as to which the director was not informed to an extent the director reasonably believed appropriate in the circumstances; or

(iii) a lack of objectivity due to the director's familial, financial or business relationship with, or a lack of independence due to the director's domination or control by, another person having a material interest in the challenged conduct

(A) which relationship or which domination or control could reasonably be expected to have affected the director's judgment respecting the challenged conduct in a manner adverse to the corporation; and

      (B) after a reasonable expectation to such effect has been established, the director shall not have established that the challenged conduct was reasonably believed by the director to be in the best interests of the corporation; or

      (iv) a sustained failure of the director to devote attention to ongoing oversight of the business and affairs of the corporation, or a failure to devote timely attention, by making (or causing to be made) appropriate inquiry, when particular facts and circumstances of significant concern materialize that would alert a reasonably attentive director to the need therefor; or

      (v) receipt of a financial benefit to which the director was not entitled or any other breach of the director's duties to deal fairly with the corporation and its shareholders that is actionable under applicable law.

(b) The party seeking to hold the director liable:

      (1) for money damages, shall also have the burden of establishing that:

      (i) harm to the corporation or its shareholders has been suffered, and

      (ii) the harm suffered was proximately caused by the director's challenged conduct; or

      (2) for other money payment under a legal remedy, such as compensation for the unauthorized use of corporate assets, shall also have whatever persuasion burden may be called for to establish that the payment sought is appropriate in the circumstances; or

      (3) for other money payment under an equitable remedy, such as profit recovery by or disgorgement to the corporation, shall also have whatever persuasion burden may be called for to establish that the equitable remedy sought is appropriate in the circumstances.

(c) Nothing contained in this section shall (1) in any instance where fairness is at issue, such as consideration of the fairness of a transaction to the corporation under section 8.61(b)(3), alter the burden of proving the fact or lack of fairness otherwise applicable; (2) alter the fact or lack of liability of a director under another section of this Act, such as the provisions governing the consequences of an unlawful distribution under section 8.33 or a transactional interest under 8.61, or (3) affect any rights to which the corporation or a shareholder may be entitled under another statute of this state or the United States.

8.32. [Reserved].

8.33. Directors' Liability for Unlawful Distributions.

(a) A director who votes for or assents to a distribution in excess of what may be authorized and made pursuant to section 6.40(a) is personally liable to the corporation for the amount of the distribution that exceeds what could have been distributed without violating section 6.40(a) if the party asserting liability establishes that when taking the action the director did not comply with section 8.30.

(b) A director held liable under subsection (a) for an unlawful distribution is entitled to:

      (1) contribution from every other director who could be held liable under subsection (a) for the unlawful distribution; and

      (2) recoupment from each shareholder of the prorata portion of the amount of the unlawful distribution the shareholder accepted, knowing the distribution was made in violation of section 6.40(a).

(c) A proceeding to enforce:

      (1) the liability of a director under subsection (a) is barred unless it is commenced within two years after the date on which the effect of the distribution was measured under section 6.40(e) or (g) or as of which the violation of section 6.40(a) occurred as the consequence of disregard of a restriction in the articles of incorporation; or

      (2) contribution or recoupment under subsection (b) is barred unless it is commenced within one year after the liability of the claimant has been finally adjudicated under subsection (a).

8.40. Required Officers.

(a) A corporation has the officers described in its bylaws or appointed by the board of directors in accordance with the bylaws.

(b) A duly appointed officer may appoint one or more officers or assistant officers if authorized by the bylaws or the board of directors.

(c) The bylaws or the board of directors shall delegate to one of the officers responsibility for preparing minutes of the directors' and shareholders' meetings and for authenticating records of the corporation.

(d) The same individual may simultaneously hold more than one office in a corporation.

8.41. Duties of Officers.

Each officer has the authority and shall perform the duties set forth in the bylaws or, to the extent consistent with the bylaws, the duties prescribed by the board of directors or by direction of an officer authorized by the board of directors to prescribe the duties of other officers.

8.42. Standards of Conduct for Officers.

(a) An officer with discretionary authority shall discharge his duties under that authority:

      (1) in good faith;

      (2) with the care an ordinarily prudent person in a like position would exercise under similar circumstances; and

(3) in a manner he reasonably believes to be in the best interests of the corporation.

(b) In discharging his duties an officer is entitled to rely on information, opinions, reports, or statements, including financial statements and other financial data, if prepared or presented by:

(1) one or more officers or employees of the corporation whom the officer reasonably believes to be reliable and competent in the matters presented; or

(2) legal counsel, public accountants, or other persons as to matters the officer reasonably believes are within the person's professional or expert competence.

(c) An officer is not acting in good faith if he has knowledge concerning the matter in question that makes reliance otherwise permitted by subsection (b) unwarranted.

(d) An officer is not liable for any action taken as an officer, or any failure to take any action, if he performed the duties of his office in compliance with this section.

8.43. Resignation and Removal of Officers.

(a) An officer may resign at any time by delivering notice to the corporation. A resignation is effective when the notice is delivered unless the notice specifies a later effective date. If a resignation is made effective at a later date and the corporation accepts the future effective date, its board of directors may fill the pending vacancy before the effective date if the board of directors provides that the successor does not take office until the effective date.

(b) A board of directors may remove any officer at any time with or without cause.

8.44. Contract Rights of Officers.

(a) The appointment of an officer does not itself create contract rights.

(b) An officer's removal does not affect the officer's contract rights, if any, with the corporation. An officer's resignation does not affect the corporation's contract rights, if any, with the officer.

. . . .

Chapter 11. MERGER AND SHARE EXCHANGE

11.01. Merger.

(a) One or more corporations may merge into another corporation if the board of directors of each corporation adopts and its shareholders (if required ...) approve a plan of merger.

(b) The plan of merger must set forth:

(1) the name of each corporation planning to merge and the name of the surviving corporation into which each other corporation plans to merge;

(2) the terms and conditions of the merger; and

(3) the manner and basis of converting the shares of each corporation into shares, obligations, or other

securities of the surviving or any other corporation or into cash or other property in whole or part.

(c) The plan of merger may set forth:

(1) amendments to the articles of incorporation of the surviving corporation; and

(2) other provisions relating to the merger.

. . . .

11.04. Merger of Subsidiary.

(a) A parent corporation owning at least 90 percent of the outstanding shares of each class of a subsidiary corporation may merge the subsidiary into itself without approval of the shareholders of the parent or subsidiary.

(b) The board of directors of the parent shall adopt a plan of merger that sets forth:

(1) the names of the parent and subsidiary; and

(2) the manner and basis of converting the shares of the subsidiary into shares, obligations, or other securities of the parent or any other corporation or into cash or other property in whole or part.

(c) The parent shall mail a copy or summary of the plan of merger to each shareholder of the subsidiary who does not waive the mailing requirement in writing.

(d) The parent may not deliver articles of merger to the secretary of state for filing until at least 30 days after the date it mailed a copy of the plan of merger to each shareholder of the subsidiary who did not waive the mailing requirement.

(e) Articles of merger under this section may not contain amendments to the articles of incorporation of the parent corporation (except for amendments enumerated in section 10.02).

. . . .

11.06. Effect of Merger or Share Exchange.

(a) When a merger takes effect:

(1) every other corporation party to the merger merges into the surviving corporation and the separate existence of every corporation except the surviving corporation ceases;

(2) the title to all real estate and other property owned by each corporation party to the merger is vested in the surviving corporation without reversion or impairment;

(3) the surviving corporation has all liabilities of each corporation party to the merger;

(4) a proceeding pending against any corporation party to the merger may be continued as if the merger did not occur or the surviving corporation may be substituted in the proceeding for the corporation whose existence ceased;

(5) the articles of incorporation of the surviving corporation are amended to the extent provided in the plan of merger; and

(6) the shares of each corporation party to the merger that are to be converted into shares, obligations, or other securities of the surviving or any other corporation or into cash or other property are converted and the former holders of the shares are entitled only to the rights provided in the articles of merger or to their rights under chapter 13.

(b) When a share exchange takes effect, the shares of each acquired corporation are exchanged as provided in the plan, and the former holders of the shares are entitled only to the exchange rights provided in the articles of share exchange or to their rights under chapter 13.

. . . .

Chapter 13. DISSENTERS' RIGHTS

. . . .

13.02. Right to Dissent.

(a) A shareholder is entitled to dissent from, and obtain payment of the fair value of his shares in the event of, any of the following corporate actions:

(1) consummation of a plan of merger to which the corporation is a party (i) if shareholder approval is required for the merger by [statute] or the articles of incorporation and the shareholder is entitled to vote on the merger or (ii) if the corporation is a subsidiary that is merged with its parent under section 11.04;

(2) consummation of a plan of share exchange to which the corporation is a party as the corporation whose shares will be acquired, if the shareholder is entitled to vote on the plan;

(3) consummation of a sale or exchange of all, or substantially all, of the property of the corporation other than in the usual and regular course of business, if the shareholder is entitled to vote on the sale or exchange, including a sale in dissolution, but not including a sale pursuant to court order or a sale for cash pursuant to a plan by which all or substantially all of the net proceeds of the sale will be distributed to the shareholders within one year after the date of sale;

(4) an amendment of the articles of incorporation that materially and adversely affects rights in respect of a dissenter's shares because it:

(i) alters or abolishes a preferential right of the shares;

(ii) creates, alters, or abolishes a right in respect of redemption, including a provision respecting a sinking fund for the redemption or repurchase, of the shares;

(iii) alters or abolishes a preemptive right of the holder of the shares to acquire shares or other securities;

(iv) excludes or limits the right of the shares to vote on any matter, or to cumulate votes, other than a limitation by dilution through issuance of shares or other securities with similar voting rights; or

(v) reduces the number of shares owned by the shareholder to a fraction of a share if the fractional share so created is to be acquired for cash ... ; or

(5) any corporate action taken pursuant to a shareholder vote to the extent the articles of incorporation, bylaws, or a resolution of the board of directors provides that voting or nonvoting shareholders are entitled to dissent and obtain payment for their shares.

(b) A shareholder entitled to dissent and obtain payment for his shares under this chapter may not challenge the corporate action creating his entitlement unless the action is unlawful or fraudulent with respect to the shareholder or the corporation.

. . . .

13.21. Notice of Intent to Demand Payment.

(a) If proposed corporate action creating dissenters' rights under section 13.02 is submitted to a vote at a shareholders' meeting, a shareholder who wishes to assert dissenters' rights (1) must deliver to the corporation before the vote is taken written notice of his intent to demand payment for his shares if the proposed action is effectuated and (2) must not vote his shares in favor of the proposed action.

(b) A shareholder who does not satisfy the requirements of subsection (a) is not entitled to payment for his shares under this chapter.

. . . .

13.25. Payment.

. . . .

(a) ... [A]s soon as the proposed corporate action is taken, or upon receipt of a payment demand, the corporation shall pay each dissenter ... the amount the corporation estimates to be the fair value of his shares, plus accrued interest.

. . . .

13.28. Procedure if Shareholder Dissatisfied with Payment or Offer.

(a) A dissenter may notify the corporation in writing of his own estimate of the fair value of his shares and amount of interest due, and demand payment of his estimate (less any payment under section 13.25) ... if

(1) the dissenter believes that the amount paid under section 13.25 ... is less than the fair value of his shares or that the interest due is incorrectly calculated;

(2) the corporation fails to make payment under section 13.25 within 60 days after the date set for demanding payment; or

(3) the corporation, having failed to take the proposed action, does not return the deposited

certificates or release the transfer restrictions imposed on uncertificated shares within 60 days after the date set for demanding payment.

(b) A dissenter waives his right to demand payment under this section unless he notifies the corporation of his demand in writing under subsection (a) within 30 days after the corporation made or offered payment for his shares.

. . . .

Chapter 14. DISSOLUTION

. . . .

14.02. Dissolution by Board of Directors and Shareholders.

(a) A corporation's board of directors may propose dissolution for submission to the shareholders.

(b) For a proposal to dissolve to be adopted:

(1) the board of directors must recommend dissolution to the shareholders unless the board of directors determines that because of conflict of interest or other special circumstances it should make no recommendation and communicates the basis for its determination to the shareholders; and

(2) the shareholders entitled to vote must approve the proposal to dissolve as provided in subsection (e).

(c) The board of directors may condition its submission of the proposal for dissolution on any basis.

(d) The corporation shall notify each shareholder, whether or not entitled to vote, of the proposed shareholders' meeting in accordance with section 7.05. The notice must also state that the purpose, or one of the purposes, of the meeting is to consider dissolving the corporation.

(e) Unless the articles of incorporation or the board of directors (acting pursuant to subsection (c)) require a greater vote or a vote by voting groups, the proposal to dissolve to be adopted must be approved by a majority of all the votes entitled to be cast on that proposal.

. . . .

14.05. Effect of Dissolution.

(a) A dissolved corporation continues its corporate existence but may not carry on any business except that appropriate to wind up and liquidate its business and affairs, including:

(1) collecting its assets;

(2) disposing of its properties that will not be distributed in kind to its shareholders;

(3) discharging or making provision for discharging its liabilities;

(4) distributing its remaining property among its shareholders according to their interests; and

(5) doing every other act necessary to wind up and liquidate its business and affairs.

(b) Dissolution of a corporation does not:

(1) transfer title to the corporation's property;

(2) prevent transfer of its shares or securities, although the authorization to dissolve may provide for closing the corporation's share transfer records;

(3) subject its directors or officers to standards of conduct different from those prescribed in chapter 8;

(4) change quorum or voting requirements for its board of directors or shareholders; change provisions for selection, resignation, or removal of its directors or officers or both; or change provisions for amending its bylaws;

(5) prevent commencement of a proceeding by or against the corporation in its corporate name;

(6) abate or suspend a proceeding pending by or against the corporation on the effective date of dissolution; or

(7) terminate the authority of the registered agent of the corporation.

. . . .

14.30. Grounds for Judicial Dissolution.

The [name or describe court or courts] may dissolve a corporation:

(1) in a proceeding by the attorney general if it is established that:

(i) the corporation obtained its articles of incorporation through fraud; or

(ii) the corporation has continued to exceed or abuse the authority conferred upon it by law;

(2) in a proceeding by a shareholder if it is established that:

(i) the directors are deadlocked in the management of the corporate affairs, the shareholders are unable to break the deadlock, and irreparable injury to the corporation is threatened or being suffered, or the business and affairs of the corporation can no longer be conducted to the advantage of the shareholders generally, because of the deadlock;

(ii) the directors or those in control of the corporation have acted, are acting, or will act in a manner that is illegal, oppressive, or fraudulent;

(iii) the shareholders are deadlocked in voting power and have failed, for a period that includes at least two consecutive annual meeting dates, to elect successors to directors whose terms have expired; or

(iv) the corporate assets are being misapplied or wasted;

(3) in a proceeding by a creditor if it is established that:

(i) the creditor's claim has been reduced to judgment, the execution on the judgment returned unsatisfied, and the corporation is insolvent; or

(ii) the corporation has admitted in writing that the creditor's claim is due and owing and the corporation is insolvent; or

(4) in a proceeding by the corporation to have its voluntary dissolution continued under court supervision.

. . . .

Chapter 16. RECORDS AND REPORTS
16.01. Corporate Records.

(a) A corporation shall keep as permanent records minutes of all meetings of its shareholders and board of directors, a record of all actions taken by the shareholders or board of directors without a meeting, and a record of all actions taken by a committee of the board of directors in place of the board of directors on behalf of the corporation.

(b) A corporation shall maintain appropriate accounting records.

(c) A corporation or its agent shall maintain a record of its shareholders, in a form that permits preparation of a list of the names and addresses of all shareholders, in alphabetical order by class of shares showing the number and class of shares held by each.

(d) A corporation shall maintain its records in written form or in another form capable of conversion into written form within a reasonable time.

(e) A corporation shall keep a copy of the following records at its principal office:

(1) its articles or restated articles of incorporation and all amendments to them currently in effect;

(2) its bylaws or restated bylaws and all amendments to them currently in effect;

(3) resolutions adopted by its board of directors creating one or more classes or series of shares, and fixing their relative rights, preferences, and limitations, if shares issued pursuant to those resolutions are outstanding;

(4) the minutes of all shareholders' meetings, and records of all action taken by shareholders without a meeting, for the past three years;

(5) all written communications to shareholders generally within the past three years, including the financial statements furnished for the past three years ... ;

(6) a list of the names and business addresses of its current directors and officers; and

(7) its most recent annual report delivered to the secretary of state ... .

16.02. Inspection of Records by Shareholders.

(a) A shareholder of a corporation is entitled to inspect and copy, during regular business hours at the corporation's principal office, any of the records of the corporation described in section 16.01(e) if he gives the corporation written notice of his demand at least five business days before the date on which he wishes to inspect and copy.

(b) A shareholder of a corporation is entitled to inspect and copy, during regular business hours at a reasonable location specified by the corporation, any of the following records of the corporation if the shareholder meets the requirements of subsection (c) and gives the corporation written notice of his demand at least five business days before the date on which he wishes to inspect and copy:

(1) excerpts from minutes of any meeting of the board of directors, records of any action of a committee of the board of directors while acting in place of the board of directors on behalf of the corporation, minutes of any meeting of the shareholders, and records of action taken by the shareholders or board of directors without a meeting, to the extent not subject to inspection under section 16.02(a);

(2) accounting records of the corporation; and

(3) the record of shareholders.

(c) A shareholder may inspect and copy the records identified in subsection (b) only if:

(1) his demand is made in good faith and for a proper purpose;

(2) he describes with reasonable particularity his purpose and the records he desires to inspect; and

(3) the records are directly connected with his purpose.

(d) The right of inspection granted by this section may not be abolished or limited by a corporation's articles of incorporation or bylaws.

(e) This section does not affect:

(1) the right of a shareholder to inspect records under section 7.20 or, if the shareholder is in litigation with the corporation, to the same extent as any other litigant;

(2) the power of a court, independently of this Act, to compel the production of corporate records for examination.

(f) For purposes of this section, "shareholder" includes a beneficial owner whose shares are held in a voting trust or by a nominee on his behalf.

. . . .

Index